The Superhuman Life of
GESAR OF LING

─────────

ALEXANDRA DAVID-NEEL &
THE LAMA YONGDEN

Foreword by
CHÖGYAM TRUNGPA

Translated with the collaboration of
VIOLET SYDNEY

T0326290

SHAMBHALA
Boston & London
1987

SHAMBHALA PUBLICATIONS, INC.
Horticultural Hall
300 Massachusetts Avenue
Boston, Massachusetts 02115
www.shambhala.com

Printed in the United States of America

Distributed in the United States by Random House, Inc., and in Canada by Random House of Canada Ltd

LIBRARY OF CONGRESS CATALOGING-IN-PUBLICATION DATA

Gesar. English.
    The superhuman life of Gesar of Ling.
    Reprint. Originally published: Boulder: Prajña Press, 1981.
    ISBN 1-57062-622-7 (pbk.)
    I. David-Neel, Alexandra, 1868–1969.   II. Yongden, Albert Arthur.
    III. Sydney, Violet.   IV. Title.
[PL3748.G4E5   1987]   87-9648
895'.41
BVG 01

Preface

SINCE the first publication of *The Superhuman Life of Gesar of Ling* I have revisited China by way of Russia and Siberia and I have made a second sojourn of over ten years in Eastern Tibet, principally in the country of the Khams, Gesar's native land.

I witnessed fresh incidents in the struggle carried on for centuries —which is still being carried on today—by the indigenous Khams and the wild tribes of Tchinghai against the Chinese who are trying to force them to submit to their administration and at the present time to mould them to the pattern of modern civilization.

These struggles are not at all caused by ideological divergencies; they are merely the result of a fierce desire for complete independence, liberty without restraint, including the right to rob travellers along the highways.

Amongst these backward peoples, I have been able to note that the personality of Gesar has preserved all his prestige, which is perhaps explained by the fact that Gesar originally came from the country of the Khams.

Nonetheless this prestige is not confined to the eastern part of Tibet; it covers the whole of the country. Amongst the masses there are, even today, many who hope for the return of this national Messiah like an invincible conqueror who will give to Tibet the domination of the world.

ALEXANDRA DAVID-NEEL.

Contents

CHAPTER 8

CHAPTER 9

CHAPTER 10

CHAPTER 11

CHAPTER 12

CHAPTER 13

CHAPTER 14

Foreword

IN ORDER for us to understand Gesar of Ling, the great warrior king of Tibet, it is necessary first to understand the principle of warriorship itself. This concept has for centuries been the heart of the lineage of Gesar of Ling, whose Tibetan descendants still exist today. Although it has been somewhat influenced by Buddhism, as has virtually all of Tibetan culture, basically the principle of warriorship stands on its own.

By warriorship we are not particularly talking about the skills necessary to wage war in the conventional sense. We are not talking about learning how to handle lethal weapons and crank up our aggression and territoriality so that we can burst forth and conquer all our enemies. Warriorship here refers to realizing the power, dignity and wakefulness that is inherent in all of us as human beings. It is awakening our basic human confidence which allows us to cheer up, develop a sense of vision and succeed in what we are doing.

Because warriorship is innate in human beings, the way to become a warrior—or the warrior's path—is to see who and what we are as human beings and cultivate that. If we look at ourselves directly, without hesitation or embarrassment, we find that we have a lot of strength and a lot of resources available constantly. From that point of view, if we feel we are without resources, if we feel incompetent or as if we were running out of ideas, it is said that we are being attacked by the enemy of warriorship: our own cowardice. The idea of warriorship is that because of our human potential we can go beyond that, step over the enemy of cowardly mind and discover further banks of resources and inspiration within ourselves.

Cowardly mind is based on the fear of death. Ordinarily we try to ward off any reminders that we are going to die. We constantly produce artificial environments to shield ourselves from any harsh edges. We weave ourselves warm cocoons in which we can live and feel comfortable and sleepy all the time. We try to keep every-thing under control so that nothing unexpected will pop up and give us a nasty shock, reminding us of our impermanence, our mortality. By doing this we are trying to defend ourselves from death, which we could say is the opposite of celebrating life. By maintaining our defensive attitude we keep ourselves surrounded by a familiar fog. We wind up breeding depression and general unhappiness. In fact, that unceasing atmosphere of depression is what makes our little created environments feel so familiar and nestlike. But because it is based on struggle, this cowardly approach of ours is very far from the sense of real joy and playfulness that is associated with warriorship.

Becoming a warrior means that we can look directly at our-selves, see the nature of our cowardly mind, and step out of it. We can trade our small-minded struggle for security for a much vaster vision, one of fearlessness, openness and genuine heroism. This doesn't happen all at once but is a gradual process. Our first inkling of that possibility comes when we begin to sense the claustrophobia and stuffiness of our self-imposed cocoon. At that point our safe home begins to feel like a trap and we begin to sense that an alternative is possible. We begin to have tremendous longing for some kind of ventilation, and finally we actually experience a de-lightful breath of fresh air coming into our stale nest.

At this point we realize that it has been our choice all along to live in this restrictive, and by now somewhat revolting, mentality of defensiveness and cowardice. Simultaneously we realize that we could just as easily switch our allegiance. We could break out of our dark, stuffy prison into the fresh air where it is possible for us to stretch our legs, to walk, run, or even dance and play. We realize that we could drop the oppressive struggle it takes to maintain our cowardice, and relax instead in the greater space of confidence.

It is important to understand what we mean by the confidence of the warrior. The warrior is not developing confidence *in* anything. He is not simply learning one skill, such as swordsmanship, in which he feels he could always take refuge. Nor is he falling back on some mentality of choicelessness, a sense that if only he can hold out long enough and keep a stiff upper lip, then he is bound to come out all right. Those conventional ideas of confidence would simply be further cocoons, based once again on yet further styles of de-fensiveness and fundamental aggression.

In this case we say the warrior has self-existing confidence. This means that he remains in a *state* of confidence free from competition and any notion of struggle. The warrior's confidence is unconditional. In other words, because he is undistracted by any cowardly thoughts the warrior can rest in an unwavering and wakeful state of mind, which needs no reference points whatsoever.

On the other hand we do not mean to say that once the warrior has uncovered his innate confidence there is nothing left for him to do. In many ways the path of the warrior is very similar to the Buddhist notion of the bodhisattva path of selfless action. The bodhisattva is a practitioner who isn't satisfied with the possibility of liberating himself from the pain of samsara, but heroically commits himself not to rest until he has helped saved all sentient beings. In the same way the confident warrior does not simply feel proud of having seen the nature of his cocoon and stepped out of it. He cannot rest in any sense of smugness at his achievement, or even in the sense of freedom and relief itself. Rather his understanding and personal experience of the claustrophobia of cowardly mind serve as an inspiration for the warrior to free others as well as himself. He actually cannot ignore the suffering and depression he sees in those around him. So from his unconditional confidence, spontaneous compassion naturally arises.

The warrior's compassion manifests in different qualities, which all arise from the nature of his basic confidence. Because the warrior's confident state of mind is self-existing, unmanufactured by aggression, he is not bloated or arrogant. Instead he is humble, kind and self-contained in relating with others. The warrior is not captured by doubts, therefore he is humorous, uplifted and perky in his dealings. He is not trapped by the pettiness of hope and fear, so his vision becomes vast and he is not afraid of making mistakes. Finally his mind itself becomes as fathomless as space, so he attains complete mastery over the phenomenal world. With all of these qualities the warrior has a tremendous sense of forward vision. In other words, he is not deterred or depressed by obstacles, but with genuine inquisitiveness and cheerfulness he includes all of them as part of his path.

The confident warrior conducts himself with gentleness, fearlessness and intelligence. Gentleness is the warm quality of the human heart. Because of the warmth of his heart the warrior's confidence is not too hard or brittle. Rather it has a vulnerable, open and soft quality. It is our gentleness which allows us to feel warmth and kindness and to fall in love. But at the same time we are not completely tender. We are tough as well as soft. We are fearless as well as gentle. The warrior meets the world with a slight sense of detachment, a sense of distance and precision. This aspect of confidence is the natural instinct of fearlessness which allows the warrior to meet challenges without losing his integrity. Finally our confidence expresses itself as innate intelligence, which raises ordinary gentleness and fearlessness to the level of warriorship. In other words, it is intelligence that prevents gentleness from becoming cheap romanticism without any vision, and fearlessness from becoming purely macho. Intelligence is our sense of wakeful inquisitiveness towards the world. It is what allows us to appreciate and take delight in the vivid qualities of the world around us.

So what does all of this have to do with Gesar of Ling, the powerful warrior king who bore magic weapons, rode a marvelous winged steed and slew numberless demons and other enemies of the sacred teachings? If we apply a more traditional language of warriorship to what we have discussed it will help make the connection.

We have already called cowardice the warrior's enemy. Cowardice is the seductive and distracting quality of our wandering or neurotic minds which prevents us from resting in our natural state, the state of unwavering wakefulness which we have called the warrior's confidence. Cowardice is actually the force of evil which obstructs what we could call our basic goodness, our inherent state of confidence which is by nature devoid of cowardice and aggression, free from evil. From that point of view, the purpose of warriorship is to conquer the enemy, to subjugate the evil of our cowardly minds and uncover our basic goodness, our confidence.

When we talk here about conquering the enemy, it is important to understand that we are not talking about aggression. The genuine warrior does not become resentful or arrogant. Such ambition or arrogance would be simply another aspect of cowardly mind, another enemy of warriorship in itself. So it is absolutely necessary for the warrior to subjugate his own ambition to conquer at the same time that he is subjugating his other more obvious enemies. Thus the idea of warriorship altogether is that by facing all our enemies fearlessly, with gentleness and intelligence, we can develop ourselves and thereby attain self-realization.

With this understanding of warriorship we can go back and look at the history of Gesar of Ling. At this point we can regard the entire story as a display of how the warrior's mind works. Gesar represents the ideal warrior, the principle of all-victorious confidence. As the central force of sanity he conquers all his enemies, the evil forces of the four directions, who turn people's minds away from the true teachings of Buddhism, the teachings that say it is possible to attain ultimate self-realization. These enemies of the four directions represent quite graphically the different manifestations of cowardly mind which the ideal warrior subjugates through the power of his unconquerable confidence.

Gesar's magical weapons and his magnificent winged charger, Kyang Gö Karkar, are also important principles of energy in the warrior's world. Weapons are the symbol of warriorship itself. The warrior does not carry weapons because he is afraid of being attacked, but rather as an expression of who he is. Weapons actually magnetize the qualities of warriorship and inspire the warrior to be brave and very gentle. Gesar's winged horse symbolizes the warrior's confidence. He is the ideal image of something beautiful, romantic, energetic and wild that the warrior can actually capture and ride. Such a horse could be very dangerous and unworkable, but the idea here is that when the warrior has challenged and conquered the enemies of the four directions, then he can ride the great winged horse of confidence and success with dignity and pride.

I was very pleased to be asked to write this foreword, especially because I regard myself as a descendant of Gesar. I am proud to be a member of the tradition of warriorship and hope that clarifying these precious teachings will help others to bring the inspiration of Gesar's example of warriorship into their lives.

Vajracarya the Venerable
Chögyam Trungpa, Rinpoche
May 1979
Boulder, Colorado

Introduction

AMONG the small number of works that have been translated from the Tibetan, very few belong to profane literature proper. Unquestionably, in Tibet, the importance of this type is not to be compared to that of the philosophic and religious literature, which, in addition to canonical Writings translated from the Sanskrit, embraces thousands of original productions that have been written in Tibetan by authors known or anonymous.

However, in the country of the Lamas, as everywhere else, there exist popular works that, although impregnated with religious sentiments—for religious thought dominates everything in Tibet—constitute what may be termed the 'profane literature' of the Tibetans.

This literature includes productions of different kinds: history, legends, poetry, geography, travels, as well as technical books dealing with medicine, astronomical and astrological calculations, etc.

It is to be noticed that works of the purely imaginative kind, namely novels, do not exist in Tibet, or, at least, do not come under that denomination. Fiction as we understand it is repugnant to Tibetans. It is not that their authors do not use their imaginations. On the contrary, they allow this faculty the fullest possible scope, and the fantastic element flourishes in so exuberant and candid a fashion in their writings, that its equal is only to be found in our fairy tales. Nevertheless, all the extravagant wonders that abound in their narratives are held to have happened, the heroes of the tales to have really lived, and the stories themselves to be authentic from beginning to end. 'What is the good of writing about that which is not true,' remarked a Tibetan to whom I was explaining the nature of our novels and the pleasure that many, at home, find in reading them.

Tibetan profane literature includes some very famous works, and the most celebrated of all is the Gesar of Ling Epic, the Tibetan national poem.[1]

There exist several versions of the fabulous history of Gesar. Although very unlike in detail, they nevertheless present sufficient points of resemblance for J. Hackin, who based his opinion upon the only three versions known at the time, to declare that the legends concerning this hero 'have common origins'. The version that I collected in Eastern Tibet (the Kham country), which is much fuller than the three previous ones, confirms this opinion.

Taking into consideration the fact that this last version is the best known in Tibet, that it is looked upon in the light of an authority not only in the Kham country, which is held to be the Hero's native land, but also in Lhasa and in all Tibet proper; it has a certain right to the title of official version. Still, we must be careful not to see in it an absolutely faithful echo of the primitive legend.

Ten or twelve centuries ago the Gesar Saga consisted of, perhaps, two or three songs only. They were chanted by unknown bards who had been inspired by the scattered traditions concerning the exploits of a great warrior king. Carried to many regions, these songs probably served in their turn as a foundation for the developments that constitute the present versions.

The Mongolian version was the first to be brought to the notice of Europeans. In 1839, I. J. Schmidt wrote a summary of it in German.[2] This Mongolian Saga appears to have been worked out in more primitive surroundings than that in which the Kham version was evolved. In fact, the latter version contains numerous and very lengthy digressions on Buddhist philosophic theories. I have had to omit them in order to avoid making the present book a work of

---

[1] There exists another celebrated poem, the one that narrates the adventures of Lönpo Gara and of the Chinese Princess, Gyaza, but it can hardly be classed as an Epic Poem.

[2] *Die Thaten Bogda Gesser Chan's.* This work was reprinted in 1925.

several volumes. These theories can be found in many treatises written by Tibetan lamas.

From its start, the Mongolian version clearly defines Gesar's character. His mission consists in causing order to reign on earth and in suppressing injustice and violence. The Epic sung by the Kham rhapsodists more particularly assigns to him the role of defender of the Religion; but in Tibetan, the word religion (*chōs*) includes the moral law, the practice of equity, and the protection of the weak in its meaning. It is also as Avenger that Gesar is awaited by those who, relying on certain prophecies, hope for his return.

A Moravian missionary, A. H. Francke, has collected two other versions in Ladakh (Western Tibet). One of these[1] offers as regards episodes, a striking analogy to the Kham version. For instance, in it is to be found the murder of the giant of Hor; the charms by which his widow, who is in love with Gesar, keeps him near her; the abduction of Gesar's wife by the King of Hor; the Hero's masquerade as the apprentice smith; and other incidents. Nevertheless, the details are different, the accounts are much shortened, and all the songs breathe quite another spirit than those of the great Kham Saga.

As it is with many other legends, that of Gesar most probably rests upon an historical basis. This deified warrior chief, whose real personality is today hidden in fantastic narratives, has no doubt existed, and lived, perhaps, at a relatively recent date, between the seventh and the eighth century.

Sarat Chandra Dass, the Indian explorer of Southern Tibet, gives Gesar as a king who reigned in China, in the province of Shensi, and also points out that the Khampas and the Mongols dispute the honour of having had him as compatriot.[2]

I, myself, have heard the claims made by certain of the latter; but if we judge their pretensions by Schmidt's translation, the Mongolian version of the Epic gives no support to such opinions. On the contrary, this confirms the Tibetan origin of Gesar. It makes him say: '*With us, Tibetans*' or: '*Our Tibet*', and it also relates how Princess Ronga Goa, having gone to Tibet in order to find a husband worthy of her, there became Gesar's wife.

I had ample occasion for gleaning particulars of the origin of this

---

[1] *A Lower Ladakhi version of the Kesar Saga.*
[2] Under the word *Gesar* in the *Tibetan Sanskrit Dictionary*, by Sarat Chandra Dass.

Hero during my long stay in Eastern Tibet, where I met a chief who is held to be a descendant of his adopted son and who bears the title of 'King of Ling' (*Ling gi gyalpo*), which was Gesar's.

There is one certain fact, the territory called Ling,[1] the geographical position of which A. H. Francke was unaware in 1902,[2] is part of the land of Kham. It is also possible to recognize in the adjoining regions a good many places mentioned and described in the Epic.

For example, a very important part is given in it to the struggles between the people of Ling and those of Hor, and, as a matter of fact, the territory of Hor is not far from Ling. The reader will see its principal town marked in a map of the province of Szechuan (China). It is called Kanze or Hor-Kanze, and is on the caravan route going from Tachienlu to Lhasa, at the extreme limit of the Tibetan territories that still remain under Chinese control.

There are, however, two other regions called Hor. The first, Hor-Nagchukha, lies to the north of the great Tengri lake; the second is in Turkestan.

In the Kham version, Gesar's army, having started at dawn, reaches the Hor frontier the same day;[3] which time corresponds perfectly to the distance that separates Ling from the borders of the territory in which Hor-Kanze is situated. The Ladakh version also describes Ling and Hor as being adjacent to each other.[4]

The other places mentioned can clearly be located either in the north of the Yunnan or in the country bounded by Likiang, Yunning, Shungtien, and Atunze.

The customs described in the poem are also the same as those of the half-shepherd, half-agriculturist natives belonging to the tribes (those of Ling included) that inhabit the eastern border of the great grass wilderness.

It is possible to suppose that two, or even several chiefs of different origin, have borne the name of Gesar. A supposition that would reconcile the Khampas and the Mongols, explain the divergencies existing among the different versions, and the heterogeneous nature of the speeches and acts attributed to the Hero and to those who surround him. For my part, I am provisionally inclined to believe

---

[1] Tibetan spelling *Gling*.
[2] See page 18 of the first part of *A Lower Ladakhi version of the Kesar Saga*.
[3] See last page of Chapter V.
[4] See page 248, paragraph 7 of the third Part of *A Lower Ladakhi version of the Kesar Saga*.

that the 'King Gesar' who reigned in Shensi and who is presented to us in the character of a divine magician in the national epic of the 'Land of Snows', may have been one of the Tibetan generals of olden time, whose troops advanced as far as the actual capital of Shensi: Sinanfu.

The Tibetans, now become an insignificant nation, had their hour of glory towards the seventh century. Their conquering hordes spread over the whole of Western China, Turkestan, and Nepal; and history appears to confirm, at least in part, that which in the Epic we should be tempted to consider as pure fantasy: an expedition against a Persian prince.

Everything tends to the belief that, originally, all the songs glorifying Gesar were only transmitted orally. (This method still continues, for many of the bards are illiterate.) Then, at a period that is difficult to determine exactly, some songs were collected, written down, and grouped according to subject.

In this form manuscripts are to be found, which the devotees of Gesar lend to one another to copy. I have not come across a printed edition, and many qualified Tibetans, among them the present King of Ling, have assured me that not one exists.[1]

Neither does there exist a collection that includes the whole of the Epic. Each manuscript refers to a special part of the Hero's adventures: the conquest of the Kingdom of Satham; that concerning the precious medicines withheld by the Mutegspas, etc.; or else it is devoted to the role played by some important personage, such as Dikchen Shenpa.

Few of the bards know the whole of Gesar's history in detail. The knowledge of the majority of them does not go beyond a more or less considerable number of songs, and they confine their efforts to the repetition of these at every gathering to which they are called. They often care very little as to the way in which the events they relate can connect with incidents that, in other songs not belonging to their special collection, are said to precede or to follow them. They also scorn, at times, such logical sequence in their own narratives; at least, in the subsidiary parts of these. Consequently, if one listens to a bard who has insufficiently studied his subject or has loss of memory, or, what is worse, to an amateur who has presumed too

[1] Sir Charles Bell, late British Political Representative in Tibet, who has had the opportunity of questioning the most competent people in Lhasa on this subject, also states that the Gesar Epic has never been printed and that there exist very few manuscripts of it.

much upon his talent, the story of the divine Gesar, already fantastic in itself, is transformed into a dumbfounding chaos.

The majority of the bards would feel offended if anyone were to say to them that they had learnt the songs of the poem. They set themselves up as being directly inspired by Gesar or by some other divine personage, who dictates to them the words that they must utter.

I also think that many of them, either voluntarily or involuntarily, fall into a state of trance during the course of their recitations.

One of them with whom I had most to do and who possessed a very extensive knowledge of the Epic was a kind of 'seer'. He gave himself out as being a reincarnation of Dikchen Shenpa,[1] one of the principal characters of the poem, and was generally held to be that by those around him. As his brother bards he also affirmed that gods friendly to Gesar and, sometimes, the Hero himself, prompted him the words he sang. Nevertheless, in order to fix his mind, he always asked for a large sheet of white paper, from which he never lifted his eyes during the whole of his recital, claiming that he saw the text of what he was reciting appear on it. A rather strange assertion on his part, considering he did not know how to read.

He even boasted that he visited the deified Hero, whose kinsman and, consecutively, enemy and ally he had been in one of his previous lives, the story of which is recounted in the poem.

Honest visionary or conscious and clever impostor, he certainly astonished me twice by acts that I have never been able to explain to myself. I will return to this subject later.

I must further add that in Tibet, and particularly in Eastern Tibet, the songs of the Gesar Epic are supposed to have a protective virtue. In the desert where the plundering tribes of Gologs camp, I happened to come across some travellers who sang as they rode, and, upon my questioning them, they told me that they were singing fragments from the story of Gesar. It appeared they expected as a result of these songs to be animated by an invincible strength that would permit them to overpower the brigands, should the latter attack them. A few miracles are also related: some pious singers passed invisible among enemies who were lying in wait either to rob or to kill them; others who were being carried away by the current while crossing a river felt themselves seized by a supernatural lasso and hauled to the shore.

---

[1] *Dikchen* is the ordinary pronunciation. The spelling of this noun varies according to the different manuscripts, but the meaning 'sinner' is always retained.

It therefore follows that among the laity of the land of Kham (the Hero's compatriots), his Epic is read, sung, and listened to with a respect equal to that which is shown to the Buddhist Sacred Writings. However, though it is not in any way forbidden to the monks to read in private the legend of Gesar and to possess the manuscripts of it, the monks, themselves, never exercise the function of bard.

There is good reason to believe that the most ancient traditions relating to Gesar appeared among the Bönpos, the followers of the religion existing in Tibet before the introduction of Buddhism, and that subsequently a Buddhist gloss was given to these traditions.

The founder of the Bönpo religion: Guru Shenrabs, is named and invoked with due reverence in the course of many of the songs of the Epic, the whole of which is impregnated with Shamanism. But, as popular Lamaism is itself scarcely other than ancient Bön Shamanism disguised, the bards' songs can be listened to with reverence by so-called Buddhist listeners without their becoming the least bit shocked by the anti-Buddhist sayings that abound in them, although the prologue to the Epic—at any rate in its first part—is of Mahāyāna Buddhist inspiration.

It is extremely probable that this prologue was added to a more ancient cycle of legends at the time when tradition made the divine Hero an envoy of Padma Sambhava, and his adversaries became fantastic demon-Kings, whose origin it was expedient to explain.

The episode with which the Epic opens and in which two women come upon the scene seems either to be completely borrowed from India or to be a Tibetan adaptation of an Indian tale. It will be noted however, that the story of the Bodhisattva who in a new incarnation becomes the Buddha, differs entirely from the classical Buddhist narratives. These made him descend directly from the Tushita paradise, which he had reached owing to the accumulated merits of myriads of lives concentrated to the practice of the highest virtues. Lamaism also keeps to this version. The account that sends the Saint to be reborn in India, immediately after his sacrifice in Tibet, appears only in the Gesar Epic. At least, I have never come across it elsewhere.

Thus a number of legends concerning the Buddha exist in Tibet at the margin of official Lamaism. I will give the one that claims to relate the prelude to the long series of virtuous lives that ended in that of the 'Perfect One' as Preacher of the 'Good Law' in India.

A rich man possessed many horses, which he treated so cruelly that many of them succumbed under the violence of his blows. This man died and was reborn in one of the purgatories[1] in the form of a horse. As such, he was harnessed to a cart with two companions of his kind. A demon was coachman, and the cart, which was very heavy, had to be dragged up a steep slope. The three animals were unable to make the wheels move and the demon-coachman unmercifully beat them with an iron rod.

This torture lasted for a period of time that our human measures cannot gauge. Then, in the one who had tortured his own horses in the past there awoke a feeling of profound pity for the victims that suffered at his side, and, animated by this sentiment, he rid himself of all egoism. Turning his head towards the demon who held the reins, he said to him:

'Cease to belabour these poor beasts. Unharness them and only keep me. I will force myself to draw the cart to the top of the mountain.'

'What,' roared the demon furiously, 'the three of you cannot do it, yet you propose to attempt it alone! Take this, impudent wretch!' And he struck him a violent blow on the head with his iron whip.

The horse fell dead. Such was the deliverance that his charitable thought procured him; not at all by way of 'recompense', as is believed by the uninstructed, but because the feeling that had prompted this thought had transmuted the cruel nature of the former tormentor of horses. His affinity with cruelty, which had led him into this purgatory, no longer existed, therefore he could not remain there; his nature's new tendencies drew him elsewhere. He regained consciousness in another world, and, from that day, did not cease to give himself to the most arduous works of charity.

The stories that tell of the extraordinary effects of wishes expressed with powerful concentration of thought, especially, but not necessarily, at the time of death, are numerous in all countries where the belief in the plurality of lives prevails. Dozens of them might be cited, of which a few are really curious and interesting.

With reference to this subject, I will relate a fact well known in Japan. The great national hero Masashige, who was conquered after a heroic resistance against troops very superior in number to his own, wished to be reborn seven times in order that in each of these lives he might fight the enemies of the Mikado. Having expressed this desire, he committed suicide together with his lieutenants.

[1] The *nyalwas* are purgatories rather than hells, because those who are born there on account of their bad actions do not remain in them for ever, but die there and are reborn in other worlds. The idea of eternal damnation has no place in the Buddhist doctrine.

On the occasion of the funeral service celebrated in November 1905, in memory of the officers and soldiers who had died on the battlefield during the Russo-Japanese war, the Reverend Soyen Shaku, an eminent Japanese monk, recalled the wish of Masashige and the similar one of Commandant Hirose. While giving these wishes an interpretation that is also familiar to Tibetan mystics, he said:

'. . . It is not only seven times that these heroes have been reborn, but thousands of times; it will be times without number so long as humanity lasts. All those who in the past and during this last war have given their lives to ensure the glory of Japan were born of their wishes. They are Masashige himself. . . .'

In speaking thus, the Reverend Soyen Shaku alluded to the transmission of example, of teaching, and of another more mysterious creative force, which is recognized in the East: concentration of thought.

The prologue to the Gesar Epic, therefore, does not present any fact outside the comprehension of those who hear it recited, and the events that follow it appear to them as a logical sequel.

*   *   *

In the second part of the prologue there comes upon the scene the most celebrated personage in Tibet: Guru Rinpoche Ugyen Pema Jungnes (the Precious Spiritual Master issued from a lotus in the land of Ugyen), after his original Sanskrit name, Padma Sambhava. It is he who rules from on high the action of the poem and directs the acts of his hero, for Gesar incarnated on earth solely in order to carry out Guru Padma's plans.

Who was Padma Sambhava? It is difficult to assert anything positive on the subject. His actual existence towards the eighth century is sufficiently proved, the details of which, however, are shrouded in numerous extravagant legends. The most important of these is the miraculous birth of the future magician, who did not come into the world by the aid of human parents, but issued from the heart of an extraordinary lotus that appeared in the middle of a lake in the gardens of King Indrabhuti.

It is to this circumstance that he owes his name of Padma Sambhava, 'issued from a lotus', which the Tibetans have accurately translated into their language. However, by abbreviation, they call him Guru Rinpoche (the Precious Spiritual Master), or Guru Padma, which they pronounce *Pema* (Spiritual Master Lotus).

In the translation of the Epic, I will often keep to his Sanskrit name of Padma Sambhava, as better known in the West, and also use the expressions 'Precious Guru' and the 'Guru Padma' in order to follow the Tibetan text,

The country of Ugyen, Padma Sambhava's native land, is thought to have been situated in the region of Kabul (modern Afghanistan). At the time of his birth, the inhabitants of Ugyen professed a kind of degenerate Buddhism—such as at present exists in Nepal—that combined certain fundamental teachings of the Buddhist doctrine with the mystical conceptions and practices of the Hindu Tantric-Sivaite sects, and that gave, above all, a large place to magic.

Apparently the attempts that were made before the eighth century to spread Buddhism in Tibet met with but small success. The various traditions are in agreement on this subject and relate how a Buddhist monk named Santarakshita, discouraged by the barbarous customs of the Tibetans, counselled King Ti-song De-tsen (*Khri srong lde bsten*) to appeal to Padma Sambhava, assuring the sovereign that only this Master, in his capacity of magician, could subdue the demons in the service of the Shamanist Böns and bring about the successful conversion of his subjects.

Padma Sambhava did succeed; not, however, in converting the Tibetans to the original Buddhist doctrine, but in making them adopt a heterogeneous mixture of theories and practices more in conformity with their tastes, in which he had cleverly incorporated a number of rites belonging to their ancient religion.

Just as he appeared miraculously, so Padma Sambhava, according to legend, did not die. His mission concluded, he left Tibet riding through the clouds on a winged horse. In this manner he went to Lanka (former name of the island of Ceylon) to convert the *rakshasas* (cannibal demons) or, at least, to prevent them from overrunning the world and devouring men.

The conversion of these monsters would seem still more difficult of accomplishment than was that of the Tibetan Shamanists. Even if the great apostle could think, after dwelling for some years among them, that he had finished his task, nothing, according to his contemporary disciples, forecasts his near departure from the island of 'Cannibals', although he has resided there for a dozen centuries.

Therefore at the indefinite period when the Gesar Epic began to take its present form, Padma Sambhava was said to dwell at Lanka on the 'Noble copper-coloured mountain', *Zang dog dpal ri* (usually pronounced *Zangdo Peri*).

Numerous descriptions exist of this imaginary mountain, and Tibetan painters frequently choose it as subject for their pictures and frescoes. If hearsay is to be believed, the stay of Padma Sambhava among the hideous *rakshasas* is not so painful for him as might be thought. The celebrated magician is not reduced to their company alone. In his Zandog Palri palace he is surrounded by several thousand *dakīnīs* (fairies) some of them very beautiful, others very learned, and some uniting both these qualities.

It would be a great mistake to deduce from the presence of these fairies in Zandog Palri that the inhabitants of this happy abode abandon themselves to sexual pleasures. Such a thing is out of the question.

The beauty of these fair ladies is the outcome of an aesthetic quite other than our own. Some have blue skin, with eyelashes and hair colour of gold. Others are flame red, slender, and serpentine. Others again, black as night and of gigantic stature, have their dark faces lighted up by disturbing green eyes.

All the *dakīnīs* do not inhabit Zandog Palri. They are to be found in many places. Usually called 'mothers', they are sought after in their quality of holders of secret doctrines by the Tibetan occultists who dream of esoteric initiations.

It is said that sometimes magicians or 'diamond-hearted' hermits succeed in drawing one of these strange creatures near them and forcing her to abandon herself to them. I cannot enlarge on these curious loves of which sensuality is not the object, and which often end in an unexpected and tragic fashion for the intrepid lover. Such tales have no connexion with my present subject.

Together with the *dakīnīs*, Zandog Palri is inhabited by thousands of Padma Sambhava's disciples, and by genii, who act as servants. This mythical domain is represented as a veritable paradise, which offers to the sight entrancing landscapes made beautiful with marvellous flowers and graceful tame animals.

Meanwhile, at the foot of this enchanted mountain the *rakshasas* endure a strange torment. Continuing to display his talents as a magician, Padma Sambhava appears every morning at his court in the guise of a young child, at midday he becomes an adult, and at twilight he is seen as an old man.[1]

When this moment comes, the demons of both sexes are exultant. They think that their stern jailor is near his end, that he will soon die and that, then, they will be able to escape from their island prison, overrun the earth, and feast on the flesh of its inhabitants. Alas! they are doomed to disappointment, for at the next dawn their master and conqueror reappears in the form of an infant.

Nevertheless, evening after evening, the same hope revives in their sad hearts. It is, in fact, a kind of infernal torment. There are many learned lamas in Tibet who take it to be an allegory that contains a philosophic meaning.

* * *

I will now give a few essential details concerning the personality of Todong, the supposed uncle of Gesar. He plays a curious part in the Epic.

As it will be seen in the second part of the prologue, Tubpa Gawa (the future Gesar) imposes certain conditions before consenting to undertake the mission with which Padma Sambhava wishes to entrust him. He demands different things, among them a valiant uncle who is a good strategist, and Padma Sambhava promises such a one to him.

Now, the poem, with no pretence at logic, provides him with an uncle who is cowardly, miserly, dissolute, greedy and treacherous. This farcical character brings a comic note into the Hero's story, though often through acts directed against the latter. At the very beginning of the tale this 'uncle' threatens to destroy Padma Sambhava's plan by trying to murder the future Gesar at the time of his birth. The uncle, however, is not a real 'uncle'. Gesar is miraculously born of a virgin; the part of the god Kenzo, who is designated as his father, uniquely consists in making the future mother drink the contents of a chalice of consecrated water in which Tubpa Gawa, who is incarnating as Gesar, has looked at himself.

The fictitious relationship comes from the fact that Todong is the brother of Singlen, with whom Gesar's mother lives as a servant. Singlen, indeed, has some idea of taking her as a second wife, but

---

[1] Some orientalists will perhaps see a solar myth portrayed in these changes. However, the Tibetans give to these symbolic transformations a meaning that has no connexion whatever with the rising and setting of the sun.

24

he does not carry it into effect. When, however, she becomes a mother, the people of Ling consider her master Singlen to be the father of her son. These shepherds, as those in the Bible, saw nothing reprehensible in this fact. It is thus that, according to appearances, Todong is Gesar's uncle.

The antecedents of the personage chosen by Padma Sambhava to produce this 'uncle' by means of an avatar are as disreputable as they are extravagant, but since he occupies an important place in the popular Lamaist pantheon, I will rapidly sketch his character.

The god of demoniacal origin whom the Tibetans call Tamdrin is the Hindu god Hayagriva, but, as it is with all his trans-Himalayan congeners, he has been invested with a new individuality on being adopted in Tibet.

The Hindu Hayagriva is an aspect of the god Vishnu, while the Tibetan Tamdrin is a monster born of the love of an adulterous woman with non-human beings. His history can be summed up as follows:

Guru Tampatogsken was an adept in the esoteric doctrines of the 'Short Path'.[1] He trained his disciples in the dangerous spiritual drill that includes the experience of the passions, for the purpose of dominating these passions through the analysis that is made of them and thus rendering them psychically useful.

Among the young men who, under his direction, practised this dangerous discipline were two friends: Tharpa Nagpo, who was a prince, and Thaiphag. Thaiphag grasped the real meaning of the teaching given by Guru Tampatogsken and advanced along the right path, while his aristocratic friend understood that it was allowable to give way to his passions and to satisfy them in all ways and under all circumstances.

Thaiphag pointed out to the latter the error of his ways, but Tharpa insisted that his conduct was in strict conformity with their master's precepts. As Thaiphag refused to admit such an interpretation, the two disciples referred it to Tampatogsken, who condemned the manner in which Tharpa Nagpo was travestying his teaching.

The prince replied that, if he had entered a wrong path, the fault lay with the ambiguity of the Master's explanations, which had misled him. For his part, he had obeyed, in all sincerity, what he had thought to be the orders of his spiritual guide, and he refused to alter his behaviour.

[1] See *Magic and Mystery in Tibet*, p. 243.

He then left Tampatogsken and led the worst kind of life. However, just before death, Tharpa Nagpo realized that the result of his countless criminal acts would entail his rebirth in the most terrible of purgatories, so he expressed a wish: 'As it is true,' he said, 'that in living as I have done, I really thought to conform to the precepts of my Master, may I, after I have expiated my bad actions, enjoy the fruits of my sincerity. I desire to be reborn in the form of a being with three heads and six hands and to become the master of the whole world.'

During thousands and thousands of years, Tharpa Nagpo sojourned in different purgatories, dying in one to be reborn in another.

When 'the substance of the demerits' that he had woven with his bad actions became worn out, a witch was living in a seaport town. Although she was married, she gave herself to non-human beings. In the morning, she received a flame-coloured spirit; at midday, a malevolent dark-faced demon visited her; and she passed part of the night with a blue-tinted serpent demi-god.

She became pregnant; and one night, while a cyclone was raging, she gave birth to a monster with three heads, six arms and four legs. This horrible abnormality was the reincarnation of Tharpa Nagpo. His mother expired at the moment of his birth. Immediately all sorts of disasters fell upon the country; rivers overflowed their banks and inundated the fields; fires spontaneously lighted themselves; sudden epidemics broke out in all directions.

The inhabitants of the town in which the monster was born were soon aware of the extraordinary event and thronged to see him. They decided to rid themselves of this bringer of ill-fortune, so they attached him to his mother's body and threw them both into the cemetery.[1]

The young demon at first tried to suckle, but the breasts of the dead woman were dry. Then, in order to satisfy his hunger and because he was born with all his teeth, he started to devour the corpse.

In a day he grew as much as an ordinary child grows in a month. Soon he became full-grown and took the name of Matamrudra.[2] He began by subduing the inhabitants of the country where he found himself, then, in turn, he conquered all the nations of the earth, compelling them to worship him.

[1] Without burying them, leaving their bodies to be devoured by beasts of prey.
[2] A name that reveals the Hindu and Sivaite origin of this personage. The Rudras are eleven gods, avatars or emanations of Shiva, who himself bears the name of Rudra. The name signifies 'terrible', 'formidable'.

Still his ambition was not satisfied. He undertook the conquest of the world of gods. These could not withstand him. As soon as he blew his poison-breath in their faces, they were suffocated and fell, lifeless, from their celestial abodes.[1]

Meanwhile, the monster had become the lover of the Queen of the cannibal *rakshasas* of Lanka, and, at the head of them, threatened to destroy humanity. In face of this peril the Gyalwas[2] held counsel. Among them were the then incarnations of Tampatogsken and of Thaiphag, the guru and co-disciple respectively of Matamrudra, when he was Tharpa Nagpo. These two were selected as being the only ones capable of destroying the monster, and for this purpose they had reincarnated on earth.

The queen began to grow tired of her monstrous lover. With relief she welcomed Tampatogsken, who possessed a more pleasing appearance.

A son was born of the Sovereign's clandestine love. Physically he exactly resembled Matamrudra, his supposed father, but it was the spirit of Tampatogsken that animated him. In the beginning, the demon did not question the origin of the child and regarded him as his own, but when the latter had grown up and the monster perceived that his so-called son was trying to dethrone him, he suspected the truth.

A terrible struggle ensued between Matamrudra and the incarnation of Tampatogsken. All the Gyalwas rushed to the aid of their champion and sat on the monster's shoulders and arms so as to paralyse his movements. Incapable of supporting their weight, Matamrudra fell to the ground; then, by his magic power, he immediately enlarged his body to formidable proportions.

In order to have done with him, his former master transformed himself into a horse, entered his body by the orifice of the rectum, and, passing through its whole length, came out at the top of the skull. At the same time, Thaiphag turned himself into a boar, passed through the monster in the opposite direction, entering at the top of the head and issuing by the rectum.

Such treatment was more than Matamrudra was capable of enduring; his body burst and broke into many pieces.

Several versions of this legend exist; one of them relates how, giving way under the torture that was imposed on him, the demon

---

[1] A remote precedent of the use of poison-gas as a war weapon.
[2] The 'Conquerors'; mythical Buddhas.

became converted and swore to become a protector of the Buddhist faith and its adepts.

This version explains the position he holds in the Lamaist pantheon. His statues and his images give him a monstrous red form, while from the crown of his head rises a small head of a horse: discreet allusion to the operation to which the Master of Esoteric Science, Tampatogsken, subjected him, and, perhaps, a veiled threat, one that is designed to keep the ex-demon, now raised to the rank of venerable protector, in the path of duty.

Thus does the personage of whom Todong was an avatar appear to the good people of Tibet.

* * *

There only remains for me to say a few words concerning the *demons*, who play so important a part in the Epic.

The Tibetans' idea of a demon differs completely from the one that is current in the West. For them, demons are not the inhabitants of a hell from which these sometimes escape in order to lead human beings into temptation or cause them harm. That which characterizes the demon, that which makes a being a demon, is, so think the Tibetans, his thoroughly evil nature. The demon is essentially malevolent, cruel; he finds pleasure in bringing about suffering. This baleful individual can exist as a man, an animal, a spirit, a fairy, a faun, a demi-god, or in no matter what other form, and can live no matter where, except, however, in the Paradises from where his bad instincts exclude him, for these could never find satisfaction there.

* * *

I have already said that the Tibetans do not accept the 'novel', as such, but take for real fact all that is presented to them either in books or by oral tradition. Therefore it goes without saying that, with them, the Gesar Epic is not an object of critical examination, except on the part of some rare thinkers, who keep on this subject, as on many others, a prudent silence. As for the majority of the ordinary listeners, the flagrant improbability of the adventures and the contradictions in the Hero's speeches and acts are not apparent to them. It would be ungracious to judge them severely. An absence of the critical faculty is peculiar to the faithful in all countries of the world; as soon as criticism appears, faith disappears.

Nevertheless, the acceptation, without outrage to common sense, of the ultra fantastic element that predominates in the legendary poems of the type under discussion does not depend entirely on a foolish credulity. It results from another cause, which I must point out, for it remains hidden in the poem, and, as it is one that is entirely new to Westerners, it would easily escape the attention of those readers who are not familiar with the philosophical concepts of the Vedanta and of the idealistic School of Mahāyāna Buddhism.

We find this idea clearly expressed by the Indian poet Tulsidas, author of a Rāmayāna. The Rāmayāna is, as is well known, the celebrated poem that extols the heroic acts of Rāma, an avatar of Vishnu. This poem holds a place in India similar to the one that the Gesar Epic occupies in Tibet and, in some points, resembles the latter. The subject of the Rāmayāna has inspired many writers. Besides the work of Valmiki, which through translations has become known throughout the West, there is the Rāmayāna of Tulsidas, which is posterior to that of Valmiki, and which is more popular in the north of India than the latter's. This second version of the amazing adventures of Rāma differs from the preceding one in that, whereas Valmiki recounts the exploits of his heroes as being the real acts of men equally real, Tulsidas, imbued with the theories of the Vedanta on the unreality of the world, makes it understood that the deeds he is describing are the play of shadows without consistency, a phase of the eternal sport (*lila*) that beginningless ignorance (*anadi avidya*) and illusion (*māya*) superimpose on the immobility of the Absolute.

A third version of the Rāmayāna: the Adhyatma Rāmayāna (the esoteric Rāmayāna), of which the author is unknown and which is considered to be of later date than the fourteenth century, reflects the same philosophic tendencies.

Now, Tulsidas makes Rāma, the avatar of Vishnu, say:

'I will play the amusing part of a man.'

Such an explicit declaration is not made by Gesar, but it is understood, or, at least, the hearers or the readers of the Epic who have knowledge of the Lamaist philosophic doctrines instinctively consider the strange events described in it from this point of view.

'As forms created by a mirage or by clouds in the sky, as images seen in a dream, thus must all things be regarded.'

This quotation from the Prajñā Pāramitā rises constantly to the lips of all Tibetans. Although the majority of them do but imperfectly grasp its meaning, yet they are nevertheless influenced by the spirit that emanates from it. The world in which the inhabitants of the high 'Land of Snows' believe is less materially solid than the one that is imagined by the Westerners, consequently the incoherency on the part of the actors in the Epic and the phantasmagoric character of the play itself are more easily accepted by them.

It must be added that many of the personages figuring in the poem are *tulkus* of deities. A *tulku*, according to the Tibetans, is a magic form projected by a being gifted with supernormal psychic force. The creator of a *tulku* is not necessarily a saint or a sage; malevolent beings, demons, can possess this power.

In fact, the *tulku*, though made of flesh and bones and born in the ordinary way (as is the case with all the lamas called 'living Buddhas' by foreigners), is only an instrument animated by the will of the one who has produced it: a sort of puppet whose strings are pulled by an occult power. Sometimes when this 'instrument' is only to be used for a very short time (as is often the case in the Gesar Epic) a *tulpa* is created instead of a *tulku*. The former, a mere phantom, will appear to be material to those with whom it associates, but, its function ended, it will vanish as a mirage.[1]

The fact that the greater number of the characters staged in the poem are magic creations renders still easier the acceptance of their fantastic acts.

*   *   *

It was in Pekin. On a bright, frosty winter's day, Ledzema, a lady of Tibetan origin, took me in her carriage to visit a Lamasery in a remote neighbourhood.

After a long drive, the coachman stopped in front of the entrance to the temple, which appeared insignificant to me. Why had the pretty Ledzema put herself to the trouble of bringing me here, knowing that I could contemplate at leisure other buildings infinitely more magnificent at the Yong Ho Kung monastery, of which Peling-sse,[2] where I was staying, touched the walls. I did not put the question to her, not only out of politeness, but chiefly because I had noticed with astonishment that her pleasing face had taken on

[1] On the subject of *tulkus* see the more complete explanations that are given in *Magic and Mystery in Tibet*, p. 113 and the following.
[2] Yong Ho Kung is the great Lamaist monastery in Pekin; Peling-sse is a Chinese monastery established in an ancient imperial palace.

a strange expression of fervour, one that I had never seen on it before.

'Come,' said the young woman with suppressed emotion, and I followed her, wondering. What was she going to show me in this Pagoda?

The little sanctuary into which we entered did not differ in any respect from a great many others in Pekin.

It was a sombre room, with walls blackened by the smoke of the countless incense sticks that generations of devotees had lighted there.

On the altar, surrounded by carved panels that showed signs of having been gilded in days long past, a curtain of faded silk veiled the little throne, which, according to custom, was occupied by a statue of the one to whom the chapel was dedicated.

Here and there, each carefully put in its place, stood the articles of ritual common to all Chinese cults: vases, drums, bells. All these things and the temple itself gave out the breath of old age. From them emanated a kind of patient serenity, a tranquil assurance, as well as a calm contempt of the world outside, the agitation and noise of which beat against the walls of the adjoining courts. The spirit of the place seemed to await its hour.

The lama sacristan's outward appearance matched the scene in which he moved. He was a bent old man of small, slow gestures. With a trembling hand he drew back the altar curtain, and, in the shadow, I perceived a statue similar to that of a Tao-tse deity.

My companion prostrated herself three times, in the Tibetan fashion, and on getting up murmured in my ear:

'It is King Gesar.'

Before I could ask her for a more ample explanation, the old lama handed us some lighted incense sticks to put, as offerings, in the ash-filled vases that stood on the altar for this purpose.

I never refuse to the gods whom I visit this common act of courtesy. Moreover, I began to remember that Gesar was a historic hero. My first professor of Tibetan, Dawasandup, had never tired of humming the ballads extolling this hero's warrior exploits, and I knew, too, from others, of the fame that this valiant chief of Ling enjoyed in Tibet. Nevertheless, absorbed in my studies, I had neglected to obtain further information on the subject, and I did not know that Gesar was worshipped.

31

I therefore bowed politely, placed my bundles of perfumed sticks before the statue, and, when Madame Ledzema had finished her devotions, went out with her.

In the carriage, I waited until the meditative attitude of my companion had passed away, then I questioned her.

'King Gesar was a chief in the land of Kham, was he not?'

'He is a god, a great god (*lha chenpo*),' answered Ledzema with intense fervour. 'I am of his country. He will certainly hear my prayer.'

Heroes who have been deified are not rare in the East. The apotheosis of Gesar did not astonish me, but I was curious to know what his compatriot expected of him.

I asked her.

'A child,' she said, 'a son, and that he may have strength and courage wherewith to serve the King in the great war.'

Madame Ledzema had been married five years and had not yet become a mother. As she grieved over her misfortune, there was nothing surprising in the object of her prayer. But how could this son, still to be born, become the soldier of a general already dead for many centuries; and in what world beyond the earth were the battles of which she spoke to be fought?

'The King will return here,' she announced, answering my questions. 'His armies will overrun Tibet, China, and the land of the Foreigners; all who resist him will be annihilated. . . . Ah! may my son be among Gesar's lieutenants and distinguish himself before him!'

The future mother's strange ambition amused me; but the return of the Hero from the Land of Shadows in order to make war in our world, interested me much more. What legend was in question?

Ledzema could not tell me; she simply had faith in a popular tradition, of which she neither knew the origin nor the details.

*　　*　　*

'Do you know who King Gesar is?' I asked, a few days later, a lamaist monk who lived in a small house belonging to the Yong Ho Kung.

'Naturally I know,' he answered. 'He is a warrior hero of my country.'

'Of your country? . . . You are a Khampa? . . .'

'Of course not, you know very well that I am a Mongol.'

'What, Gesar was a Mongol?'

'Undoubtedly.'

'But the Tibetans claim him as one of theirs, and Ling, they say, is situated in the country of Kham.'

'I do not know where Ling is, but Gesar certainly is a Mongol, and it is from Mongolia that he will come again with his army.'

'What, you also say that he will return?'

'I say it, and many others say it too. The thing is certain.'

'And why should he return?'

'To exterminate all those who oppose the reign of justice.'

My neighbour came close to me, and continued in a confidential tone:

'Suddenly he will rise in all the greatness of his power and terrify the men of wicked heart who are prone to malicious activity. His numberless horsemen will follow him at lightning speed, the earth will shake with the hammering of their chargers' hoofs, and the thunder of their gallop will resound above the clouds.

'We have slept long, while he, the Invincible, was resting; but we shall waken for his return. To the conquest of the world, he will lead the millions of Asiatics who, today, are drowsing. On the one hand, we shall throw back into the sea those insolent Whites whom the Chinese have so weakly allowed to establish themselves with them as masters; on the other hand, we shall invade their countries in the West, and everywhere the cleansing army will have passed nothing will remain, no, not even a blade of grass!'

Where was I? Who was speaking to me? A moment before I had thought to question a merchant's secretary-accountant, a rather well-educated *trapa*[1] who had stayed at the Depung monastery at Lhasa. Now, in front of this apocalyptic prophet, who announced—and with what passion—another Gengis Khan, I remained open-mouthed.

In the meantime, the speaker resumed his habitual expression, the kind, smiling face of the Mongol.

'Come and have supper with me,' I said, 'Lama Yongden will be pleased to see you.'

'Thank you,' answered the secretary-monk. 'My master expects

[1] A lamaist monk who, not being an ecclesiastical dignitary, has no right to the title of lama.

a Chinese merchant with whom he hopes to do business, my presence is therefore necessary at his house.'

* * *

Several years went by. I found myself in the Kham region.

I had just crossed the interesting and singularly beautiful country that stretches between the high solitudes of the Chang Thangs and the western extremity of the Chinese province of Szechuan, a region almost entirely covered with forests and inhabited by independent tribes. This journey, which lasted seven months, was not inferior either in picturesqueness or in diversity of adventure to the one I was to undertake two years later on my way to Lhasa. I had not yet experienced the joys of a mendicant pilgrim, but I had just known those of being a fairy.

Yes, really a fairy: *Kahdoma* as the Tibetans say. The fairies that they imagine are not little fantastic people, eternally young and beautiful, as those in our tales; but grave and learned ladies, who sometimes incarnate on our earth for very serious reasons.

I had not deliberately invested myself with this curious personality. It was seen in me by some good people who had interpreted, in their own way, certain words uttered by a lama who was venerated as a 'seer'. Finding the part an agreeable one, and one that ensured my own as well as my servants' safety, I had rapidly adapted myself to it.

How many people I blessed, how many houses and fields! How much advice I gave, and how many predictions I uttered! Simple souls are exacting in all countries; there is no end to their demands. They asked for miracles . . . I really think I performed a few. It is difficult to avoid doing so in the presence of such living faith. In order not to allow the Tibetans to bear the burden of an unmerited reputation for exceptional credulity, I must disclose the fact that since my return to Europe I have been solicited, both by letter and by word of mouth, to work more strange wonders than those dreamed of by the native herdsmen of the grass desert.

There is no question of my describing, here, that part of my travels in Tibetan territory. I will simply mention that on my way from Kanze to Bhatang across a region that had been recently taken possession of by the government troops of Lhasa, I had the route barred to me by the Tibetan authorities, who intended that I should retrace my steps.[1] After having decided upon another route, which, this time, I resolutely refused to alter, I proceeded towards Jakyendo, a Chinese outpost situated beyond the conquered zone.

I was travelling by easy stages through this now forbidden country when one morning two men, who seemed to be on the look-out at the side of the road, advanced and seized my horse by the bridle.

Thieves, I immediately thought, for highwaymen swarmed in this part of the country. But one of the two individuals, forestalling any questions on my part, said politely, in a low voice:

'The King of Ling desires to speak to you; he awaits you. . . .' And he pointed to a castle perched on an isolated hill in front of us, on the other side of the river.

The King of Ling! Instantly the name awoke in me the memory of the hero that I had almost forgotten. I remembered the ballads sung by Dawasandup, the image of Gesar that I had bowed to at Pekin, and the messianic predictions of my Mongolian neighbour concerning this warrior of doubtful nationality.

'*Ling gi gyalpo*? (the King of Ling),' I repeated in a tone of interrogation.

'Yes, our Chief,' answered the Tibetan. 'The descendant of Gesar of Ling.'

Gesar had descendants, and one of them invited me to pay him a visit! My involuntary change of route had brought me, without my knowing it, by the castle of the inheritor of his title; and he wished to speak to me! It was a surprising adventure: I was delighted. I let the men lead me.

At the end of the path that wound round the hill, a massive door opened in the fortress's thick wall. Immediately on entering, I found myself in a labyrinth of courts, small gardens, dwellings, barns, cattle-sheds, and stables. A veritable village had been built on the little table-land that formed the summit of the hill. Dominating the other buildings, the castle roofs and those of a temple rose, crowned with gilded *gyaltsen*, emblems of rank and power, the use of which is strictly controlled in Tibet.

Some members of the family came to meet me and offered me scarves of welcome, as is the Tibetan custom; they then showed me into a pretty room where I was served with a hearty meal.

Still the King did not appear. I was told that he was in religious

[1] See the details of this episode in the introduction to *My Journey to Lhasa*.

seclusion and that for the duration of the retreat he must neither leave his private apartment nor receive anyone there. However, as my passage was an exceptional circumstance, I would be admitted to his presence.

In fact, when the meal was ended, his wife asked me to follow her, and she led me to the isolated pavilion, where her husband was engaged in his devotions.

The King of Ling was a man of medium height, about fifty years of age. He had a distinguished air, a fine face, and the high forehead of the thinker. His movements expressed a grave dignity, altogether in keeping with the personality attributed to him. Whether or not he was the great-grandson of Gesar, one nevertheless felt that in his veins ran the blood of a race of chiefs.

That about which he spoke has no connexion with the subject of this book, therefore I will not relate our conversation. However, at the end of it, I discreetly made some inquiries concerning the ancestry of my host; for was he not better able to enlighten me on the subject than anyone else?

He was the descendant of the Hero only by adoption. Gesar, an incarnated god, had left no issue, but had been succeeded by a young man, his adoptive son, who had become chief of Ling when the former, leaving Tibet in a miraculous way, had returned to the paradise whence he had come. It was from this adoptive son that the 'King of Ling' with whom I found myself was descended, and, according to the Chinese customs prevalent in his country, he had every right to style himself Gesar's descendant.

I did not argue the subject with him, but continued to listen. I learned that bards, many of whom passed as being inspired by Gesar himself, wandered over the country singing of the Hero's achievements, and that there existed manuscript copies of some of the songs. The present 'King of Ling' possessed a few of them, which he showed me; some were prettily illuminated, although unfortunately very faded.

My host would willingly have offered me hospitality for some weeks and even for a few months, in order to give me time to study the manuscripts at leisure; but, travelling in a forbidden area against the will of those in authority, it was not possible for me to stop long in the house of a local chief without attracting towards him the suspicion of his new suzerains.

Before leaving him, I risked asking some guarded questions

36

touching the messianic return of Gesar; however the 'King of Ling', who up to that moment had been very frank, became suddenly reticent, and I understood that I was not to insist.

*   *   *

I arrived at Jakyendo at the beginning of September, without having made any plans for the future and very much astounded at having been led by circumstances to a place where I had never dreamed of going and where nothing seemed to call me.

Jakyendo, which the natives call Kyirku,[1] is a market town situated south-east of the immense grass solitudes (Chang Thangs) that occupy all the northern part of Tibet. The importance of the town is due to its position on the track travelled by the caravans that start from Tachienlu, in China, to carry tea to Lhasa: a three months' journey across the grass desert. And if, instead of turning south at Nagchukha, the caravaneers continued their way towards the west, they could, by journeying for another three or four months, reach the vicinity of Ladakh, or Kashmir, or the region of Pamir without coming across either a house or a tree along the route.

To the south of Kyirku, almost uninhabited tracts of land interspersed with woods extend as far as the banks of the Salwen. Proceeding to the north-west one can, after crossing the desert, reach the encampments of the Mongolian shepherds of Tsaidam, and, farther on, the sands of the Gobi in Chinese Turkestan. Or, in striking almost due north it is possible, by crossing the Yellow River near its source and travelling over unoccupied land inset with the marvellous lakes Kyara, Nora, Tossun, Kara, the immense Koko Nor (blue lake) and many others, to arrive at Sining in the Province of Kansu, where operates a great Chino-Tibetan market.

It was in the middle of these solitudes that I found myself stranded, without plans, without an object in view; knowing only that I had no possibility of escape by the route I had followed in coming.

However, for the time being, I left all thought of finding an issue from such a position. A seven months' journey on horseback through mountainous country, without having tired me too much, had given

---

[1] Often spelled *Cherku* on the maps. It is said that really it should be called *lche rku*, 'stolen tongue', a name originating from a local legend. Jakyendo is the name generally used by the Chinese.

me the wish to enjoy a little rest. This remote village with its pretty surroundings, situated in a healthy region at some ten thousand feet above sea-level, did not lack charm. I lingered there.

One day, while strolling through the village, a sudden uproar broke out round me. A kind of giant, with a sword in his hand, rushed from a house and darted down the street followed by about twenty men. Women hastened from the same house, some wailing, others laughing, but all excited and shouting at the top of their voices.

I approached one of them.

'What is happening?' I asked. 'Has someone been killed or wounded? The man who is running away is he mad or drunk?'

'Nothing of the sort,' answered the good woman. 'He is Dikchen Shenpa.'

'*Dikchen*' in Tibetan signifies 'great sinner'. The maniac of whom I had caught a glimpse certainly did not have the appearance that is usually attributed to saints, but what special thing could he have done to be branded as an exceptional sinner?

His second name: Shenpa,[1] that is to say 'butcher', inclined me to think that he exercised such a profession, one that is held to be criminal by the Tibetans, although very few of them abstain from eating meat.

'Oh!' I said, 'then the man I saw escaping is a butcher. Why does he run away with a sword in his hand?'

'He is not a butcher,' exclaimed all the women in chorus. 'He has been Dikchen Shenpa, Gesar's minister. He was singing an account of the Hor war, and as Kurkar, Gesar's enemy, has reincarnated here as a boy, when the memory of his former battles came back to his mind, he drew his sword with the desire to go and kill the King's enemy.'

[1] The manuscripts of the Epic and in particular the one that relates to the installing of Dikchen Shenpa as King of Hor after Kurkar's death, write the hero's name as Shenpa, which is one of the ways of writing the Tibetan term that literally means a butcher, or in the figurative, a cruel man. The more correct spelling is *bshenpa* (the *b* not being pronounced). The current tradition is that Dikchen Shenpa had not really been a butcher, which would have been impossible on account of his adoption, from birth, by a King, but had given proof, in his youth, of great cruelty by killing animals for the sake of killing. Hence his name *sdig* (pronounced *dik*) *chen shenpa*, the great cruel (as a butcher) sinner.

However it is possible that time has brought confusion and that *shenpa* or *bshenpa* was originally *gshenpa*: the name of a very ancient Tibetan family to which belonged, according to tradition, the one whom the Böns consider as the great exponent and preacher of their religion—the Master Shenrabs (written *Gshenrabs*, meaning of '*gshen* ancestry').

'This sort of thing happens to him from time to time when he has had a little too much to drink,' added one of them who was smiling. 'Have no fear our men will overtake him; he will not touch the child.'

Whereupon, they all began to shout together such explanations as they thought proper to give me concerning the reincarnated King of Hor. Their chatter was too confused for me to gather anything from it save that there existed, in Kyirku itself, a little boy that public rumour pointed to as having been in one of his previous lives Gesar's enemy; and, in addition to this, that a minstrel capable of reciting the Hero of Ling epic was in the neighbourhood.

Once again, Gesar was brought to my notice, and, this time, under particularly favourable circumstances. The studies that I had begun with some learned lamas who were staying at the local monastery did not engross me to the extent of my not being able to find the necessary time in which to listen to the story of the great Chief who had been presented to me as a future Messiah.

The bard was giving recitals at the house from which I had seen him escape. The very day after his existence had been revealed to me in the picturesque fashion that I have described, I slipped in among the women who were assembled there to listen to him.

These, seated on some cushions and bits of carpet that lay on a floor of beaten earth, occupied about half the room. Likewise on the ground and tightly pressed one against the other, the men sat facing them. In the centre of this audience, the infuriated madman of the day before was singing, gesturing now and then, but more often fixing his eyes upon a sheet of paper that had been placed on a low table in front of him.

Now that I could look at him at my leisure, I found him to be a very fine man, according to the canon of beauty in vogue in the Kham country, which demands the stature of a giant and the figure of an athlete. The bard not only came up to the required standard, but he was also very handsome. His proud bold features, and his big luminous brown eyes that at times flashed fiercely and imperiously and at other times seemed to reflect a whole world of marvellous visions, gave him a remarkable expression.

His melodic passages were interrupted by a series of onoma-topœia, which he sung with emphasis and used in place of a flourish of trumpets when announcing the entrance upon the scene of the principal personages of the Epic.

Lu ta la la! Alla la la! Ta la la! . . .

Then, in the manner of the heroes of the Iliad, the character would present himself, pompously giving his titles and mentioning his achievements.

'If you do not know me, learn that I am the illustrious one whose sword is more rapid than lightning in cutting off the heads of millions of enemies,' or other declarations equally grandiloquent.

Unfortunately for me, the bard sang his poem in the Kham dialect.[1]

This fact made it difficult for me to follow a chanted recitation, full of elisions, or of vowels added for no other reason than that of lengthening the lines. Moreover the listeners interrupted the tale many times by pious exclamations and interludes of *Oṁ mani padme hūṁ!*, in this way causing me to lose the thread of it.

These recitals did not lack in interest, the intensity of their local colouring enchanted me; but, I understood that if really I wished to study the legend of Gesar I would have to take other measures. First of all, now that my lucky star had brought a bard within my reach, I must get him to recite the poem to me at my house; further I must get some manuscripts of this story procured for me; and then, later on, try to discover other bards and listen to them in their turn.

As a beginning, I sent my son the lama with a beautiful scarf and a substantial present to 'Dikchen Shenpa' to express to him my desire to hear him in private in consideration of suitable remuneration.

I will omit an account of the various interviews, which were difficult, because the bard wished to make certain that he would be listened to with reverence and that I would not offend Gesar in any way.

At last the sittings began. Hypnotized, as it seemed, before a sheet of white paper, the pseudo-Dikchen recited and sang with inexhaustible fervour, while my son and I hastily noted down the poem. In this manner, daily auditions continued for more than six weeks.

The bard was not an ordinary man. His life, socially very humble, had some mysterious sides to it. The village people declared that occasionally he disappeared for a period more or less long, without anyone ever being able to discover where he went. Kyirku is surrounded by immense solitudes in which it would be easy to elude inquiries; but why should the bard disappear in this manner? I put the question to him. At first he was very reticent, then ended by saying that he went to see some genii or some gods. Did he deliberately lie? I have never thought so. Rather was I inclined to think that,

---

[1] I was able to verify later that the manuscripts are often written in this dialect.

while in a state of hallucination, he walked, going who knows where, dreaming, perhaps, of adventures that he remembered when he came to: a phenomenon that happens pretty frequently in certain parts of Tibet.

Or, maybe, he simply paid a visit to a hermit hidden in the mountains, far from Kyirku, and in his imagination raised the saintly man to the rank of deity. Many conjectures could be made. The great Chang Thangs are a land of mystery.

Nevertheless, as I have said in the beginning of the present introduction, this bard puzzled me twice by inexplicable manifestations. I have already given an account of them elsewhere,[1] therefore I will confine myself to a brief repetition.

One day I offered him one of those paper flowers, of Chinese make, that open out into different shapes. Many Tibetans like to decorate their family altar with them, and I thought to give him pleasure. Indeed he seemed pleased, but surprised me by saying in a serious tone:

'In your name I will offer this flower to the King.'

The 'King' signified Gesar. Knowing that the bard boasted of frequenting his Court in mysterious realms, I put such a statement down to a desire to make himself appear important in my eyes, and I paid no more attention to the matter.

Some days later, the self-styled familiar of Gesar brought me a blue flower, saying gravely:

'The King sends you this in order to thank you for your offerings.'

It was a fresh flower, and we were in the middle of winter. The thermometer registered 20 to 25 degrees C. of frost in the valleys surrounding Kyirku. The ground was frozen deep down, the mountains were covered with snow, and the Yang-tse which flows close by under the name of Dichu, was covered with a layer of ice six feet thick. The blue flower belonged to a species that blooms in marshy places in July, and is not to be found, even at that season, in the neighbourhood of Kyirku. Where had he got it from? Some Tibetans who had been told by my servants that the divine Gesar had sent me a flower came to see and venerate it. Its origin has always remained a mystery to me.

The following is the second case.

At the time when, having concluded the recital of Gesar's adventures, the bard was enumerating some of the predictions

[1] In *My Journey to Lhasa*.

concerning the Hero's return to our world, he mentioned that the Tashi Lama would leave his time-honoured residence at Shigatze and go to live in the north, outside Tibet. He even stated precisely that this event, which at that date seemed outside the range of all possibility, would take place in about two and a half years' time. This astonishing prediction became actual fact, in all its details, within the given period. I learnt in Tibet while on my way to Lhasa that the Tashi Lama had escaped by way of the northern deserts,[1] and had taken refuge in Chinese territory. He has, since then, stayed in Mongolia and in Pekin.

Having been warned that the former Dikchen became furious when he thought of the boy whom public opinion designated as the reincarnated enemy of Gesar, I took care not to speak to him about the lad, but I did not fail to see the latter and obtain information concerning his antecedents.

The child was then about ten years old. His mother, servant to a merchant of Tao who had a branch house at Kyirku, had had him by this master. A circumstance that, as I have already stated, did not bring—according to the customs of the country as according to those of Biblical times—any dishonour either to the mother or to the child her son.

Tao is situated in the district of Hor. Therefore, through his father, a Horpa, the young boy was connected with the tribe over which had reigned King Kurkar, of whom he was said to be the reincarnation. For the moment the lad was living as a novice in the Kyirku monastery and wore a monk's habit, which he would be free to give up later, if, when grown up, he did not wish to belong to the clergy.

I did not find anything particularly remarkable about him, unless it were a certain sly look, which shyness and the legend that surrounded him would sufficiently explain.

It was said in proof of his demoniacal origin that some extraordinary facts had accompanied his birth.

According to the good people of the place, the child as soon as he was born had spoken to his mother, saying he wanted bread, and then had set to work to make it himself, kneading the dough and baking it in the cinders.

Later on, his evil nature had revealed itself. He took pleasure in killing birds with stones, in fighting his playmates; and, strange to

---

[1] For details regarding his flight and the reasons that gave rise to it see *My Journey to Lhasa.*

say, the stones that he threw always reached their mark, bringing death to the animal against which they were directed, and the blows that he gave with his infantile fists always produced serious injuries. In short, frightened by these omens and fearing the evil that he might do when he became a man, his family had placed him in the monastery, believing that beneath a monk's habit his bad instincts would be stifled.

There was a question also of another boy, likewise a novice in the same monastery, who was considered to be the reincarnation of another of the former kings of Hor: King Kurser; but the legend connected with him seemed less consistent and less generally accepted.

*　　*　　*

On to the Gesar Epic have been grafted various prophecies, certain of which connect with those that relate to the advent of the coming Buddha. All of them present the return of Gesar as the prelude to a new era. What is to be the distinctive character of this period is not very clearly defined, but it appears that it will be of such a nature as to produce 'more justice' than exists at present on earth.

The expected Gesar is to continue to act in quality of warrior. The ends for which he will strive will be of a social rather than of a religious order, and he will attain them *by force*. All those with whom I was able to talk on the subject of his return expressed the same conviction: Gesar will revive the power of humiliated Asia by driving out the Whites. But, curiously enough, the majority of those who expressed this fervent hope possessed no geographical knowledge of Asia and had never seen a White.

Asia—a term which they never use—represented to these Tibetans, first of all their own country: 'the Country of the Religion', then China, India, Nepal, Mongolia, and, right in the north, the mysterious land of the 'Orossos' (the Russians of Siberia). For them, the Whites were those redoubtable and perverse 'Philings' who govern in India, who have obtruded themselves upon China, and have persuaded the Dalai Lama to exact hitherto unknown taxes from his subjects.[1]

---

[1] In order to divert from the Dalai Lama and themselves the resentment of the Kham people, who were astonished at being taxed more heavily than they had been under the rule of their local chiefs and the suzerainty of China, the officials of the Lhasa Government told them that it was the 'Philings' who had advised the Dalai Lama to increase their taxes.

As for the Russians, considered as Whites they should have been just as odious, but their activity was less apparent; they were less known as enemies. Also were they really Whites, beings of the same species as the 'Philings'? There were doubts on this point. But that which was known was this: beyond the country of the Sogpos (Mongols), on the more northern tracts of land, lived men who were not Whites: lamas, *nangpas* ('insiders', that is, those who belong to the Buddhist faith), who would follow Gesar.

It is interesting and, perhaps, useful also, to discover beneath all this discursiveness, the state of mind of those who entertain such thoughts and become intoxicated by them.

Chang[1] Shambala (the mythical land of the North, the Land of Quietude) holds a big place in the prophecies concerning Gesar's return.

Has Shambala ever been the name of a town or country? Such a thing is possible, but of it there exists no proof.

The Venerable Ekai Kawaguchi, a Japanese who stayed for a time in Lhasa a little more than thirty years ago, thinks that a lama of the 'Yellow' sect was the originator of the legend of Shambala, which he localized in Kashmir and from where, according to him, a conquering prince would rise who would become the master of the world and spread Buddhism throughout it. Later on, according to the same informant, the political envoy of the Tzar, a Siberian Lama Dorjieff, had adroitly used this prophecy to increase Russian influence in Tibet, by declaring that Chang Shambala was Russia.

In supposing that the Tibetans ever had imagined that Shambala was in Kashmir (a fact which I very much doubt and which would contradict the signification of the word *Chang* (north), since Kashmir is south of Tibet) and that, later they had transferred the position of this mysterious country or city to Russia, nothing actually remains of such beliefs. Those (they are far less numerous than certain foreigners seem to think) who, in Tibet, do speak of the hypothetical Shambala take it to be an island lying somewhere in the north, perhaps near Siberia, but certainly not in Russia, the land of the white Orossos.

Three Bön-nag magicians, to whom I had occasion to be of use during a journey and who had camped for some weeks near my tents, told me that among their co-religionists certain ancient traditions were handed down concerning a land of quietude situated in the

[1] *Chang* signifies north.

44

north. Perhaps the origin of Shambala should be sought for in the folk-lore of the primitive Böns of Tibet.

On the other hand, the origin of the Tibetan belief in a Shambala can be explained very simply. In olden times the Indians spoke of a 'land of eternal beatitude', which they called Uttara Kuru: 'the northern land of the Kurus'. The Tibetans, who have borrowed from the Indians their religious books and a number of traditions, may have imported this tradition as well. This fact, however, would not preclude it from having been amalgamated with similar legends already in circulation in Tibet.

Some lamas incline to a mystical conception of Shambala: 'Shambala is in my mind' is a phrase that I have heard several times.

The North is held to be the mystic direction. 'Those who have attained spiritual illumination (those who know Brahma[1]) leave this world, not to return, during the six months that the sun is in the north'[2] say the Hindus; and the Masters of the Tibetan esoteric doctrines teach 'the Paths of the North' that lead the yogi to supreme emancipation.

This spiritual Shambala is probably more interesting than the terrestrial one, but as it is not connected with my subject, I will not linger over it.

It is well to remark that not all the prophecies concerning the return of Gesar mention Shambala. Many of them do not give a name to the place where Gesar will be reborn and where he will muster his former companions-in-arms who will have reincarnated in order to fight again under his orders. Nevertheless, all place it in the north: either in Mongolia, Turkestan, or Siberia. Some think, too, that the prophecies have come to pass in part. According to a few Tibetan 'seers', Gesar and several other personages of the new epic have already been born, and important events, marking the beginning of the Hero's activity, should take place before fifteen years have elapsed.

*   *   *

Unless many large volumes were devoted to it, it would be impossible to give a complete and word for word translation of the Gesar Epic. The interminable preambles that accompany each song:

---

[1] Not the masculine personal God Brahmā, but the neuter Brahma or Brahman, the Absolute of the pantheistic theories of the Vedanta Philosophy.

[2] Bhagavad Gītā.

invocations to the protective deities of the character who is about to speak, enumeration of all his names and titles, the genealogy of this personage, the recounting of his numerous exploits, and the perpetual repetitions of things already said and resaid, in the manner of the Eastern story-teller, would make it a gigantic work.

One of the manuscripts that I possess, which treats of the single episode of Gesar's struggles against King Satham, is seven hundred and forty-eight pages long. I have already said that the bard of Kyirku had sung the poem daily for more than six weeks. His recitals lasted about three hours each and he gave two a day. Moreover I had permitted him to abridge the recitation of those passages in the story upon which some notables of the country, who possessed manuscripts of the poem, had provided me with notes and with which I contented myself by comparing with his version.

However, though the Epic here presented is divested of its tiresome redundances, it nevertheless contains all the chief incidents in the Hero's adventures. I have based my work on manuscripts in my possession, on the notes that I have taken of the substance of other manuscripts, and on those written down by lama Yongden and by me while following the songs of the different bards.

Although bards and manuscripts agree in the main, yet they differ in points of detail. When I have found myself faced by several varying accounts, I have sought to reproduce the one that appears to be the most generally accepted.

*   *   *

In order not to overload the text, I have rarely given the true spelling of the proper nouns and other Tibetan terms used in it. This spelling seldom corresponds to the pronunciation, therefore I have confined myself to transcribing these words phonetically.

I must also give an explanation concerning the way in which I have employed the different persons of the verb during the course of the dialogues. The Tibetans possess a choice of pronouns for all three persons and adopt one or other of them according as to whether they wish to express humility, familiarity, or respect. I will only point out those that are most generally used in conversation.

Khyod, which resembles the old English *thou*, is employed when familiarly addressing equals, and always in addressing inferiors. *Khyed* and *ñid* are more polite forms. A still greater degree of

46

politeness is shown by speaking in the third person and in giving the individual whom one is addressing the title to which his rank or office gives him the right, or, failing a title, in employing the term *Kushog* (Sir or Madam, the same word is used for both sexes).

The pronouns of the third person, *he* and *she*, are respectively *kho* and *mo*; a more polite form is *khong* for both genders. When speaking still more ceremoniously titles are made use of in the same way as with the second person pronouns.

The particle *lags* (which fulfils the same role as the *ji* in the current language of India) can be added to Kushog and to all the titles but that of *rimpoche* (precious), the highest of all. *Lags*, which has no meaning of itself, can be translated when joined to a title by the word 'honourable': *Kushog lags*, 'Honourable Sir'; *Pönpo lags*, 'Honourable Chief'. The majority of the manual and liberal professions can likewise be named by different terms, according as to whether or not one desires to show deference to the person to whom one is speaking.

Lags, when used alone, signifies a sort of polite acquiescence, a kind of *yes*, or it precedes a negative in a respectful denial. The words *yes* and *no* do not exist in Tibetan.

In the impossibility of rendering all these expressions in English, I have contented myself with using *thou* to indicate the *khyod* (the *thou* without politeness) of the Tibetan text, and *you* for all the other kinds of *thou*, polite or respectful.

There are no equivalent terms for the 'respectful' *he* and *she*, so I have been obliged in every case to keep to the pronouns of the third person.

It would have been impossible, in the course of this book, for me to give detailed explanations concerning the religious rites, customs or theories mentioned in the narrative.

For this reason I have been frequently obliged to ask the reader to refer to my previous works for any explanations they might wish to have regarding these.

Prologue

I

A T that time, after having practised in many places perfect giving and boundless charity, the Bodhisattva[1] had retired into the forest to conclude his sacrifice.

Possessing nothing, not even a rag with which to cover himself, he intended to give his very body in alms to the creatures suffering the pangs of hunger. How many times during his successive lives had he not already shown, by similar acts, his complete abnegation, his unconcern of self, and his immeasurable compassion. It is by thus travelling the various stages of this royal road of infinite love that those who desire to become Buddhas, guides, and instructors of beings, advance towards their glorious goal.

Not far from the forest where the Bodhisattva dwelt, lived two women: mother and daughter. Without being really rich, they nevertheless possessed ample means. Their herds of yaks[2] and sheep provided them with much milk, butter, cheese, and meat, also with skins for winter clothing. In addition, these beasts furnished them with a great quantity of wool, which was exchanged for *tsampa*,[3] wheat, rice, utensils, and ornaments.

Both these women had witnessed the extraordinary behaviour of the Bodhisattva, but occupied with their daily tasks, they had not paid much attention to it.

Now it came to pass that, having offered his flesh and blood as food to the insects and birds of prey, the saintly hermit died one evening as the sun was sinking behind the violet peaks that barred

---

[1] A being who has attained a high degree of spiritual perfection and who can become a Buddha in his next existence.

[2] The long-haired grunting ox that lives on the high Tibetan tablelands.

[3] Flour made from roasted barley, the staple food of the Tibetans.

the horizon, beyond which lies the rich and distant country of Nub Palang Chyöd.[1]

At this moment, the elder of the two women was assembling her herds on the mountain. All at once, from afar, she saw a supernatural light shine at the spot where the Bodhisattva lived at the foot of a tree. Astonished and fearful she stood still, and while she remained gazing in wonderment, the light rose above the forest, crossed the sky, and disappeared in the direction of India.

Then, enlightened by sudden intuition, she understood that the eccentric hermit who practised such strange austerities had just ended his present existence, and that his reiterated vows, emphasized by so many heroic acts, were now coming to fulfilment in India, where he would be reborn as a Buddha and where he would turn the 'Wheel of the Law'[2] in order to teach beings the 'Way of deliverance from suffering'.

Bitterly regretting that she had not shown the sage the respect that was his due and had neglected to learn from him the Doctrine that dissipates the darkness of ignorance, this woman, despite her great age, conceived the project of going to India to hear, when the time came, the preaching of the Buddha.

Taken up with this thought, she descended towards the valley without thinking about her beasts; but these, very sensibly, with meditative air, followed her without straying. The lambs did not frolic, as was their custom, but trotted quietly by their mothers; the young yaks usually so turbulent, so ready to fight one another, advanced gravely as do elderly bulls, heads of herds that are conscious of their responsibility. Even, the roar of the torrent changed to a softer note; a great silence enveloped the pastures, and all things lay bathed in an ineffable serenity.

When she reached home, the mother immediately told her daughter about what she had seen and of the resolution she had taken. The good woman never doubted but that her enthusiasm and her pious desire would be shared by her daughter. Therefore, without hesitation, she proposed that they should abandon all they owned and start on the road to India, where, later, the Buddha would preach.

Mothers easily deceive themselves when they imagine that their

---

[1] According to Tibetan geography it is the west country, which is rich in cattle.
[2] 'Turn the wheel of the law' signifies in Buddhist phraseology 'preach the Doctrine'.

desires reflect the natural order of things. They think the children whom they have conceived must resemble them in everything and follow along the path in which they themselves delight. It is not so. Mothers and fathers are each but a cause among many others at work in the bringing about of the birth of a human being. The latter is the fruit of a succession of material and mental acts of which the origins, impossible to discern, lose themselves in the night of time. The child is a passing guest, and the mother the inn where it stops to borrow a garment before continuing its way. Thus diverge the tendencies of the sons from those of the fathers, those of the daughters from the mothers; for these tendencies come from a past that remains veiled to the ignorant.

The thoughts of the old woman's daughter did not rise above the goods of this earth. The idea of abandoning her yaks and sheep and having to sell the corals of her head-dress and the amber beads of her necklaces for food during the journey, appeared insane to her.

'Think well, mother,' she said. 'Does the lot of the *arjopas*[1] appeal to you? Have you not seen them when they have stopped at our door to ask for alms? Dressed in rags, they are numbed and shivering in winter and soaked through in the wet season; famished, without shelter, they sleep in the snow or in the mud. It is all very well for young people to visit the sacred places in this way, but is it the kind of pilgrimage that women who are accustomed to live in comfort should dream of undertaking, and above all, you, at your age?'

While saying this the young woman's tone had grown slightly sarcastic, as if she thought that age had affected her mother's reason.

'What are riches?' replied the mother. 'Smoke that the first puff of wind disperses. As a castle fashioned by clouds, a town risen in a mirage or forms seen in dreams, the illusion of a brief moment, which the next instant carries away, such are the things of the world. So long as one is young it seems as if life could never end, but old age comes apace . . . and then death. Of what use, then, are herds and ornaments? Nothing follows us but our black or white deeds,[2] which lead us to unhappy existences or to paradises.'

And having said this, she added piously: '*Oṁ mani padme hūṁ!* May I be reborn in Nub Dewachen!'[3]

These wise words, the majority of which are drawn from the

---

[1] Mendicant pilgrims.
[2] That is to say bad or good deeds.
[3] The 'Western Paradise of Great Bliss'.

sacred Scriptures, did not make any impression on the young woman. The prospect of a beatific future was a matter of indifference to her.

'The Buddha, his Doctrine, Nub Dewachen or Jol-song[1] are of little importance to me,' she replied. 'It is said that the ascetic who lived near here was once rich. He gave all his possessions in charity, and, when he had nothing left, offered his body for food to the animals; then he died. What good can there be in such extravagant behaviour? It is just self-torture. What benefit has he received from the sufferings he inflicted on himself? I cannot see any. To act thus is pure madness and I shall certainly not imitate him. If, against all reason, you insist on your project, you are free to go, but I shall not follow you.'

After having tried in vain for several days to awaken some better feeling in the heart of her daughter, the old woman realized that all like efforts would be in vain, and, one morning at daybreak, she departed alone.

First she trudged across the great grass desert, where it is possible to walk for days and days without coming across a single dokpa's[2] tent, then along the vast bleak tablelands. She painfully climbed the narrow paths that lead to passes bordering on the clouds, and many times was nearly drowned when crossing rivers. Still, whenever she came across villages or dokpa encampments, the people, on learning the object of her pilgrimage, filled her bag with tsampa and, sometimes, added a little butter, cheese or tea.

In this way, after many years of travel she reached India, and when yet more years had passed, she came one day to the place where the Buddha was preaching to his disciples. By this time the devout pilgrim had attained the extreme limit of old age and could hardly stand. She was not one of those whose mind was capable of seizing the Doctrine of the Jinas[3] in all its subtle depth, but, after listening with respect to that which was expounded to her, she advanced to the entrance of the Path.[4]

Soon after her arrival, she asked the Buddha if she would live much longer.

[1] The worlds of suffering: purgatories. Buddhism does not admit of an everlasting hell.
[2] Literally, 'people of the solitude'. The herdsmen who live in tents among their cattle.
[3] The 'Victors', an appellation of the Buddhas.
[4] In Tibetan Buddhist phraseology this 'path' (thar lam) is the one that leads to liberation. Liberation consists in being freed from ignorance, in attaining spiritual illumination.

'Why should you remain here any longer,' answered the Master. 'Tomorrow, at sunrise, light a lamp,[1] and worship the Buddhas residing in the ten directions[2] while wishing joy to all beings. A light emanating from Amitaba[3] will rest on your head and your spirit,[4] following this luminous path in the sky, shall reach the Western Paradise of Great Bliss (Nub Dewachen).'

The old woman obeyed the order that had been given her. At dawn she lighted a lamp, and, while she remained in meditation, there appeared with the first ray of sunlight the trail of brilliant white light of which she had been told.

Then guided by the tutelary deities that reside in each one of us, her spirit began its ascent from her heart to the crown of her head. When it had reached there, it caught a glimpse along the luminous track of the dwelling-place of the Thirty-three gods,[5] and, beyond it. of the red Amitaba seated on his throne in the Western Paradise, surrounded by a thousand and twenty-two Buddhas. Escaping at that moment from the body with which it had been united, the spirit of the pious pilgrim darted along the path of light and, travelling the space with the rapidity of an eagle, attained the abode of all felicities.

*   *   *

After her mother's departure, the other woman continued her usual occupations, and, in the course of the following years, had three sons.

She had expected to pass her days in peace, rejoicing in the possessions that were so dear to her and that she had preferred to the privilege of hearing the discourses of the Buddha; but a mysterious run of ill-luck relentlessly pursued her. Successive epidemics broke out among the herds, until the last beast died. All that she owned was destroyed, stolen, or taken by creditors whom she was unable to repay. At last, enfeebled by privations, she and her sons fell ill and none came to their aid.

With her eyes always turned towards those who, more fortunate

[1] An altar lamp, similar to those that burn in the temples in front of the statues of gods or saints.
[2] The four cardinal points, the intermediate points, the zenith and the nadir.
[3] The Bodhisattva of the 'Infinite Light', who reigns in the Western Paradise.
[4] I use the word 'spirit', failing another, but it badly expresses the meaning of the Tibetan term *rnamshes* which designates the principle that knows: the 'knower'.
[5] The mention of the Thirty-three gods, the Trāyastrimsha of the Hindu pantheon, reveals the Indian origin of the legend.

than she, possessed the comforts that had been taken from her, she never ceased to curse their selfishness and their hardness, forgetting that when she, herself, had been prosperous, her conduct had been the same as theirs.

Some withhold the riches that the earth produces, she now thought, while others who are deprived of them have no possibility of alleviating their distress by taking what they need from the superfluity of those favoured by fortune. Little would suffice to save my children's lives, but that little I cannot obtain, and we shall die.

Owing to the confusion into which suffering had cast her, she did not remember that she had blamed the saintly anchorite for his excessive compassion. Had she not characterized as folly his sublime charity, and loudly proclaimed her firm intention of not imitating him?

If it had been given to her to hear the preaching of the Buddha, perhaps she would have understood that, owing to a wrong conception of the world and of the nature of beings, the selfish desire for enjoyment leads men reciprocally to inflict suffering upon one another and does not permit any to taste the well-being of a perfect security. All her misfortunes, she believed, were consequent on her refusal to accompany her mother to India to meet the Buddha, who was avenging himself for her lack of zeal and respect. This conviction had bred in her a boundless hatred of the Master and of his Doctrine. Not a day passed but she blasphemed against both, and, when through hunger she lay at the point of death, her last words were imprecations:

'May we,' she said, 'my sons and I, be reborn as rich and powerful kings who will utterly destroy the Doctrine of the Buddha and those who profess it.'

Having expressed this terrible wish, she expired. Her three sons died shortly after her, and all were taken to the cemetery.[1]

---

[1] That is to say, left in a deserted place in the mountains for vultures to eat, as is the Tibetan custom.

Padma Sambhava tries to prevent the demons from incarnating—His plans miscarry—The gods take counsel—One of them consents to incarnate as Gesar and to destroy the demons—He lays down conditions.

PADMA SAMBHAVA was residing at Zangdog Palri when the unhappy mother uttered her impious wish. He heard it, and he also knew that the blasphemer and her sons had died. In great haste he sent for his two wives, Yeshes Tsogyal and Mandara, and explained the situation to them.

'Without doubt,' he said, 'the wish of this woman will be realized if we are not quick in forestalling its baleful consequences. I can avert the peril that menaces the Religion by making a magic circle in which certain portions of the four corpses are placed. Transform yourselves, both of you, into vultures and fly rapidly towards the mountains where the remains have been deposited. Once there, detach the eyes, the heart, some particles of the nails and skin, also a tuft of hair, and without delay bring them to me.'

In the twinkling of an eye the two fairies became two great vultures with enormous wings, and left Zangdog Palri. Endowed with supernatural strength, it only took them a few seconds to reach the distant country where, on a deserted mountain, lay the four dead. Many vultures hovered in the sky, circling above the prey that had fallen to their lot, and others were arriving at full speed from the confines of the horizon; but, a magic influence held them back and not one of them dared approach the bodies offered to their greed. Thus, without any interference, the two great fairy-birds were able to detach the parts that had been indicated to them, and, holding the bloodstained fragments in their claws, flew away to Zangdog Palri.

Suddenly a great wind rose. In spite of the strength of their wings, the two vultures were carried away by the storm and whirled round and round like bits of straw, desperately striving the while to keep hold of the gruesome remains that their lord demanded. The force of the cyclone did not slacken. An unexpected gust, more violent than the preceding ones, overturned the two birds, who let go their macabre burdens. These fell near a village, and were instantly devoured by some dogs.

Then the storm abated and the unhappy fairies were able to regain the abode of their consort.

It is said:

'*As the seed sown in the earth produces the tree and its fruit, so actions and thoughts are the seed from which spring new actions and thoughts. Effect follows cause as the shadows follow the walker.*'

Mighty as he was, Padma Sambhava had been impotent in his attempt to neutralize the effect of the powerful concentration of thought with which the deceased had uttered her wish. The only thing that remained for him to do was to try to avert the danger that would menace the Religion when the four enemies who would implacably strive to destroy it were born.

For sixty years the spirits of the dead woman and her sons wandered in the *bardo*[1] without being able to reach any paradise or purgatory. Then, all four were born on earth. The mother manifested as three simultaneous incarnations and became the three Kur brothers: Kurkar, Kurnag, and Kurser, kings of the three tribes of Hor. The eldest of the three sons became Lutzen, king of the North country, and the two younger ones, Satham and Chingti, kings of states that were situated respectively in the West and in the South.

Padma Sambhava, knowing that the four demoniacal personages were on earth and would soon begin their attack on the Religion, went to the paradise situated in front of Zangdog Palri and asked the gods who inhabited it to come together in order to listen to a communication that he had to make to them.

One hundred and ten magician-sages (*dubthobs*), a thousand and twenty-eight deities, and a great number of fairies (*dakinīs*) assembled and attentively listened to the recounting of the events that had caused the existence of the kings who menaced the Religion. By his

[1] The Tibetans term '*bardo*': a vague phantasmagoric world, a kind of limbo where the spirits of the departed wander in a half-torpid state without being able to get a clear idea of things and are a prey to many illusionary visions. This stage precedes rebirth in a paradise, on earth, or in one of the purgatories; hence the name *bardo* 'between-two', meaning between death and a new birth. The belief in a *bardo* is foreign to original Buddhism.

On the subject of *bardo*, see *The Tibetan Book of the Dead*, by W. Y. Evans-Wentz, and my book, *With Mystics and Magicians in Tibet*, chapter 'Death and the Beyond'.

superior powers of clear-sightedness, Padma Sambhava knew that only one hero in the universe was capable of conquering them, and that this one was among the thousand and ten magician-sages before him. But which of them he was, Padma Sambhava did not know, nor was the magician who possessed this capacity any more conscious of it.

So each god, fairy, and magician present was asked to discover the unknown hero by means of a divinatory practice called *mo*.

Thubpa Gawa, the son of Korle Demchog and Dorje Phagmo (two deities of the Lamaist pantheon), was designated unanimously. This *mo* was verified by two others, which each gave a like result.

Then, Padma Sambhava addressing Thubpa Gawa said: 'Son of gods, the *mo* has pointed to you; therefore to you falls the task of conquering the enemies of the Religion and of humanity. You must incarnate on earth and fight against the demon-kings.'

Greatly distressed at these words, the magician replied: 'Do not hope that I shall leave this happy dwelling-place. Of old, in India, I lived a pure life, practised all the virtues, and assiduously gave myself to meditation. Today I taste the fruit of the efforts that caused me to be born in this blissful abode. Here, with joy, I wear the yellow robe of a member of the *sangha*;[1] to abandon it and go through the world dressed as a layman would be to retrogress and bring me suffering. Do not count upon me; I will not go among men.'

Having spoken thus, he remained seated in silence, resolutely decided not to accede to the request of the great Master. His face shone as pure gold and his monastic robe, although of a brilliant yellow, took on, by contrast, the dull tone of a faded flower.

In order to overcome his resistance, Padma Sambhava repeated in fuller detail the story of the good old woman who had left her home to go and hear the Buddha preach, of her unbelieving and impious daughter, and of all that had followed.[2] Then he adjured him to fulfil the task that had devolved upon him.

'No other save you is capable of overcoming these demons,' he said to him; 'their power increases from day to day. They are the enemies of the Religion and the world. O golden god! do not refuse the glorious mission that has fallen to you. Uphold the true Doctrine by the wonders that you, alone, are capable of performing, protect

---

[1] The Buddhist Order.
[2] The bards, at this point, begin to repeat the whole of the first part of the Prologue.

the beings that the demons wish to afflict, remove their sufferings and let them all rejoice in your exploits.'

It was difficult for Thubpa Gawa to resist the eloquence of Guru Padma and to refuse him his help in a work so necessary and meritorious. Nevertheless, the magician did not surrender at once.

'Before promising anything, I wish to know many things,' he answered. 'Here, in the abode of the gods, my father is the mighty Korle Demchog, my mother is the illustrious Dorje Phagmo, and my name is Thubpa Gawa. If I incarnate in the world of men in what manner shall I be born there? Who will be my father? Who will be my mother? What name shall I bear?

'If I consent to take human form, I demand eighteen things. It is for you to say if you can ensure them to me.

'I desire that my father be a god and my mother a nāgī.[1]

'I desire a horse that death cannot overtake. It must be able to fly across the sky and travel over the four continents of the world[2] in an instant. It must be capable of understanding the languages of men and animals and of speaking to each in his own tongue.

'I desire a magnificent saddle studded with gems.

'I desire a helmet, cuirass, and sword that shall not have been forged by human hands.

'I desire a bow with arrows perfectly adapted to its size. These, too, must not have been made by men; they must have sprung forth miraculously. The arrows must not be made either of wood or the horn of any animal.

'I desire, as companions-in-arms, two heroes, neither very young nor very old, but in the fullness of vigorous manhood and as strong as lhamayins.[3]

'I desire an uncle who is energetic and a clever strategist.

'I desire a wife whose beauty is without equal on earth; who will inflame the passions of all men and incite them to fight for her.

'Finally, I desire that a few of the gods and fairies residing in this paradise shall also incarnate among mortals in order to help me there, and that all the others shall be ready, at all times, to answer my call and to come to my aid.

[1] A feminine being belonging to the species of demi-gods that inhabit the ocean, streams, and lakes and are said to possess fabulous treasures. Nāga, and the feminine nāgī is their Sanskrit name. The Tibetans call them lu (klu), feminine lumo (klumo).

[2] Tibetan geography describes four great continents and eight small ones or intermediate islands.

[3] Literally 'not-gods', kind of warrior-Titans.

'It rests with you now, venerable Master, and with you, sons of the gods, to see if it be possible for you to subscribe to these conditions.'

This said, Thubpa Gawa again remained silent, seated on his beautiful chair ornamented with turquoises and coral. With mind detached and calm, indifferent to the answer that would be given him, knowing that the world and all the events that take place there are but phantasmagoria: the play[1] of shadows projected by ignorance, desire, and action on the immutable background of the Void.

In the meantime, Padma Sambhava and the gods considered, in animated discussion, the means of satisfying the demands of Thubpa Gawa. They all willingly consented to lend him their aid, but they did not see any possibility of being able to procure for him the extraordinary things that he had enumerated.

Then, Guru Padma rose from the high[2] throne covered with priceless carpets and incrusted with gold and precious stones upon which he had been requested to sit. Knowing well how greatly his wisdom and cleverness inspired respect in those around him, he resolved to put an end to their perplexity by assigning to each one his task and by indicating where the different things that fulfilled the conditions made by Thubpa Gawa were to be found.

'Thubpa Gawa,' he said, addressing the magician. 'In what concerns you, no hesitation is possible. It is your duty to fight the demon-kings and to accomplish other tasks tending to the welfare of beings. Your conditions are accepted, and I will explain to you how they will be carried out.

'Tamdrin[3] shall produce a *tulku* who will be your uncle. The white Dolma shall be your wife. Chagna Dorje and Je Sahra Arpa shall be your companions-in-arms. Your father shall be the divine As Kenzo.'

Then, turning to the others, he said: 'All of you who have been named, prepare yourselves from now for the part that you will have to play.'

Once more addressing Thubpa Gawa, he continued: 'The one who will become your mother is not here, because she belongs to the race of nāgas whose palaces stand at the bottom of the ocean. I will see about a way of bringing her on earth.

---

[1] The expression used here is *rolpa*, which signifies play, sport. In Sanskrit, *lila*.
[2] This place of honour had been given to him because, according to the Tibetans, a sage is much superior to a god, who can owe his divine birth simply to his virtues and his piety. Intelligence is held to be far superior to these last.
[3] See Introduction.

'As to the weapons, the helmet, and cuirass, they exist, just as you desire them, in a place named Jigdag Magyalpumra, where long ago I hid them together with a talisman that renders invulnerable the one who wears it. It is for you to take possession of these things.

'It only remains now for me to provide you with the charger you desire. Nangwa Thayais shall produce a *tulku*, which will have the body of a horse, perfect in form and colour, and which will possess all the extraordinary qualities that you have specified. It shall be your mount.

'All the sons of gods, the fairies, the magicians here present will answer your call when you require their aid and will support you in battle. As for me, I shall be your guide and counsellor for as long as your mission lasts.'

When Padma Sambhava had finished speaking and Thubpa Gawa had promised to fulfil the task that had been confided to him, the assembly dispersed.

Soon after, a *tulku* of Tamdrin was born in the country of Ling, where he received the name of Todong.

Chapter 1

Padma Sambhava goes under the ocean to the country of the Nāgas to look for the future mother of Gesar—Her arrival on earth—She becomes a servant in the tent of the King of Ling—He falls in love with her—Jealousy of the Queen—She seeks to kill the nāgī—The gods descend to the nāgī and make her drink a magic potion—Miraculous birth of many deities and of Gesar—Todong and the Queen try to kill the Hero from his birth—The sorcery of a great magician—How Gesar, as child, victoriously protects himself against it—The sorcerer is immured in his retreat—Gesar and his mother are exiled in the desert

AFTER the birth of Todong, Gyatza, and Demasamdong, all three of whom were destined to play a part in Gesar's adventures, Padma Sambhava thought about bringing on earth the nāgī who was to become the mother of Gesar. This undertaking presented many difficulties, but the precious Master (Guru rinpoch'e) 'is expert in all things and his cleverness is without equal.'

He converted his entire supply of ingredients used in magic processes into poisons and poured them into the river that, under the waters of the ocean, runs through the world of the serpent-deities: the nāgas. A strange epidemic very soon declared itself among the latter. The skin of the sick became dry and covered with sores, and a low fever sapped the victims' vitality. Desolation reigned throughout the country.

As this evil continued, the King of the nāgas summoned his ministers, and, together, they performed the divinatory practice called *mo*, in order to discover to which lama or god they must address themselves so that the scourge might be removed. It was declared to them that neither god nor lama was capable of putting an end to the ill from which they suffered: Padma Sambhava alone had this power. A further *mo* indicated the nāga Tsug-na Rinchen as the delegate who must be sent to Padma Sambhava to solicit his help.

Without delay the chosen nāga saddled a grey[1] horse and

---

[1] Literally the adjective *ñonpo* (*sñonpo*) signifies blue, but the Tibetans have the habit of applying this colour to animals that have silver-grey coats. In a similar way, young leaves and new grass are said to be blue and not green, notwithstanding that the word green exists in the Tibetan language. It was one of my amusements, while travelling in Tibet, to hear my horses and mules spoken of as blue, as in a fairy-tale.

departed. He entered the world of men by emerging from Lake Lungser Gokongmar, near Lake Yamdok (a geographical reference that takes us far from Ling; Lake Yamdok is south of Lhasa).

Arrived there, the ambassador felt very perplexed because he did not know where Guru Padma resided and what direction he ought to take. Therefore, after reaching the shore, he respectfully prostrated himself several times, praying Padma Sambhava to guide him that he might accomplish his mission.

The latter, from whom nothing is hid, saw him and commanded two *dākinīs* (fairies): the White Gechong and the Brown Chidag, to go to him and lead him to Zangdog Palri by the path of the white rainbow.

They immediately obeyed, and, on arriving at the border of the lake, saw the nāga. They first of all made quite sure of his identity by asking him questions concerning himself, the country from whence he came, and the object of his voyage. (Tibetans never omit this examination, which they make tiresomely long and detailed, before rendering the least service to a traveller.)

Satisfied with his answers, the *dākinīs* told him that they had been sent as guides and took him by the luminous way. In less than a minute he found himself in front of the Precious Master's throne.

After having bowed down to the ground and offered the rich gifts of which he was the bearer, he made known the miserable condition of the nāgas, who had been stricken with an unknown disease, and ended with the prayer that Padma Sambhava would come and deliver them from it.

Better than anyone else, Guru Padma knew all the details of the affair, for had he not himself caused the illness that attacked the poor nāgas; but, in pursuance of his plan, he pretended to listen with great attention and to be astonished at the sad news communicated to him.

'I sincerely sympathize with your friends in their misfortune,' he replied to the nāga, 'only it would be very difficult for me to accede to their request and undertake such a long journey. I am old, and, moreover, very busy. I shall give you some medicines, which you will distribute among the sick; their effect will be the same as that which you expect from my visit.'

'The difference is great,' replied the ambassador, 'between care received from a doctor in person and medicines that are sent from afar. Your saintly presence, in itself, is capable of effecting a cure.'

Thus, by persuasive words and by manifesting great faith, he strove to lead the Master to view favourably his request.

It was in conformity with Padma Sambhava's plans for him to go to the nāgas, but he had wanted the invitation to come from them, so that it would appear that he was yielding to their earnest entreaties. For this reason he had contaminated their river and produced the epidemic that they implored him to come and put an end to. Therefore, after having once more feigned resistance, he finally surrendered to the appeals of the nāga delegate.

'Since you wish it, I will come myself and see your sick,' he said. 'I have no need of your presents. I only desire one little thing, of no importance.'

Even before he had finished speaking, the envoy had promised him in the name of his Sovereign and of the whole nation of demi-god serpents that, whatever the thing might be for which he wished, it would be given him, if it lay within their power to do so.

Padma Sambhava showed his satisfaction and dismissed his visitor, bidding him return to his country and announce to the people that in seven days he, himself, would come to them.

Whereupon, the *dakīnīs* reconducted Tsug-na to the border of the lake where they had met him, and he, diving into the water, hastened to regain the territory of the nāgas by subterranean ways inaccessible to human beings.

The nāgas were overjoyed at the good news brought them by their envoy. Tsug-na was warmly congratulated at having so ably pleaded their cause, and preparations for the reception of Padma Sambhava were begun at once. Magnificent carpets, richly embroidered tapestries, seats and tables of gold and silver, others of sandalwood incrusted with lapis-lazuli, vases ornamented with jewels, and a thousand other precious articles were brought out from the state treasury. When the decoration of the palace in which the Guru was to dwell was complete, it shone with the united splendour of the sun and moon.

Padma Sambhava appeared on the seventh day after the return of Tsug-na. He was escorted by hundreds of *lamas*, *dakīnīs*, and goddesses, who played various musical instruments and carried umbrellas, garlands of flowers, and vases in which burned fragrant perfumes. This gorgeous procession slowly gained the dwelling that had been prepared for the Guru. The mere sight of the visitors gave rebirth to hope in the hearts of the sick and their sufferings were alleviated.

Guru Padma remained three months with the nāgas, preparing various medicines, which he gave his patients. At the end of that time, all who had been ill were cured and sorrow gave place to joy.

Then Padma Sambhava having announced his intention of returning to Zangdog Palri, the King and the chiefs of the nāgas commanded that all the riches in the kingdom's treasury should be placed before the great Master. Jewels, pearls, corals, turquoises, crystals, amber, rubies, ivories, white shells that are the mouth of the Makara,[1] skins of venomous snakes, tiger skins, blue dragon's eggs, and a great number of other rare and precious objects were heaped in piles as high as mountains. All these things were offered to the Guru in token of their gratitude, while the King and his chiefs asked him:

'Venerable Master, are our presents worthy of your acceptance? Do they please you?'

'Your presents are magnificent,' the Guru answered graciously. 'I am very pleased with your offerings, but I have no need of them. On the other hand, you possess a thing of very small value, which I do not see here. It is that which I desire. Will you give it to me?'

Greatly astonished, the King asked him:

'Illustrious Master, what is this thing? I cannot guess what it is, but whatever it be, it is yours.'

'Very well,' said the Guru. 'I accept it. Nāga Menken is the father of a young girl of whom Durwa is the uncle, it is she who I want.'

A silence followed this declaration, during which the nāgas looked at one another full of surprise.

'What did he say?' murmured Menken, thinking that he had not heard aright.

'He says that he wants our Dzeden,' answered his brother Durwa, who was at his side. 'But he won't have her!'

Durwa had a quick temper, which he controlled with difficulty. He felt a paternal affection for her who, according to custom, was called his 'niece', but who, as the daughter of the wife whom he shared with his elder brother,[2] could be in reality his own child.

[1] A fantastic sea-beast.
[2] A limited form of polyandry within the family circle—one wife for several brothers—is practised in Central Tibet. The children of this common spouse call the eldest of the brothers 'father' and the younger ones 'uncle'.

Anger rose in him at the thought that the old Guru, legitimate husband of two noble ladies and hero of many fantastic extra-matrimonial adventures, now set his eyes on Dzeden.

'The initiates of profound doctrines,' he said, 'assure us that all in this world is but a game and an illusion. They also affirm that the actions of the learned Guru Padma are inspired by transcendent motives that are incomprehensible to the vulgar. But so much knowledge is not for my niece. Whether it be a question of a game, a dream, or a reality, it would be all one to her in the company of a greybeard; it would only bring her unhappiness. The epidemic spared her, must it be for the doctor to harm her?'

Those who stood close to Durwa began to tremble on hearing these bold words. Not but that a few impious ones did approve of them in their hearts, only they feared the anger of the terrible Guru, should the words come to his ears.

As to the nāga chiefs grouped round Padma Sambhava, they did not wait to discuss his wish, but, full of respect for him, decided by common accord to give the young girl to their saviour.

The fury of Durwa reached its height when he heard this resolution. He snatched from a nāga the scarf[1] of white silk the latter was unfolding in readiness for passing round the neck of the nāgī who was to be presented as offering, and, holding it stretched in his hands, he strode towards the great Master.

'All that we possess,' he said savagely to him, 'we have offered to you. We have emptied our treasury in order to lay its contents at your feet. If these gifts do not satisfy you, know that there are no others for you. As to the young girl, do not flatter yourself by thinking that you will get her. For all your power and cleverness, you will not succeed in doing so.

' "Shining in the heavens, the sun and the moon light the world,
     This is admirable!
Sometimes a planet destroys them and darkness covers the universe.
     This is very sad!
When the grain is sown, the corn grows,
     This is admirable!

---

[1] In Tibetan: *Kadag*. These scarves are offered at every turn in Tibet, as a mark of respect, of gratitude, as a welcome to those who arrive and for a good journey to those who depart. They are offered to the statues in the temples, to the sacred books, etc., etc. . . . It is not possible to travel in Tibet without a provision of them. The quality of the texture and the length of the scarf denote the degree of esteem in which the one is held to whom the *Kadag* is presented.

If it hails and it is destroyed,
      This is very sad!
When the lama who wears the habit of the Holy Order preaches the
      Sacred Doctrine and practises it,
      This is admirable!
If he lusts after a woman,
      This is very sad!"

'I have spoken. Nothing is truer than these sayings. You shall not have my niece.'

Padma Sambhava has not an easy temper and it is dangerous to irritate him. With flaming countenance and flashing eyes he rose from his seat. All the nāgās drew back in dismay.

'Thou who art learned in maxims, come here,' he imperiously commanded. 'I can quote thee others in answer to thine:

' "In a village market place a poor wretch was being judged. A passer-by, filled with pity, intervened and obtained his pardon. The other, once more at liberty, forgot the intercessor's kindness".

' "A man was suffering punishment for his crimes in one of the purgatories. A compassionate Bodhisattva removed him from there and took him to a paradise. As soon as he was established in the blissful abode he forgot the one who had rescued him from his tortures".

'When many of you were stricken with the disease, you made appeal to my knowledge. Thou, as the other nāgas, wert willing to grant me whatever I asked in return for my aid. And, now thou, who hast been a victim of the epidemic, dost forget that thou owest thy recovery to me and wouldst retract thy promise. Despicable knave, without honour, thou deservest no pity. I have no need of thy niece. I wish for her no longer. I leave at once. But the ill from which I had delivered you all will return, and you will bewail as before; only, this time, it will be useless to implore my help.'

With a terrible air, Guru Padma took a few steps forward, Lamas, dakīnīs, and goddesses formed themselves in processional order; the white rainbow, the etheric path on which the Master travels, appeared and its end touched the palace roof. The nāgas, trembling and terrified, could not find words with which to appease the anger of the redoubtable magician.

Then Menken, holding in his hand a scarf of white silk, staggered forward, placed it on the feet of the Guru, and, prostrating himself three times, said in a voice suffocated with terror:

65

'O Precious Master, do not be offended, I implore you. My brother has just spoken to you in a reckless manner, but it was not his intention to be lacking in respect. Pardon him, Dzeden is yours. I am her father. She is dependent on me only. . . . I give her to you. Do us the great favour of accepting her.'

'How do you know that you are her father other than by right of seniority . . . ?' began the incorrigible Durwa, but some twenty nāgas threw themselves on him and, thrusting in his mouth the scarf that he still grasped in his hand, dragged him from the palace.

Somewhat pacified, but nevertheless preserving a severe expression, Padma Sambhava briefly responded:

'Very well, I accept her. In seven days, bring Dzeden to the shore of Lake Lungsen-Gokongma. She will find a protector near there.' (Literally: 'She will find a master, a proprietor': *dakpo*, written *bdagpo*.)

Then, having spoken, he raised himself above the crowd of nāgas. Surrounded by his brilliant court, he proceeded along the luminous way that extended right across the sky and soon disappeared amid the clouds.

*　　*　　*

When seven days had elapsed, several hundred nāgas accompanied their young sister to the lake indicated by Guru Padma.

'My daughter,' Menken said to her, 'I must leave thee here. Go into the vast world of men, as our precious Master has commanded, rely on him and have faith. He knows what is necessary to beings and will not abandon thee. I give thee a mare, a cow, a ewe, a she-goat, and a bitch. These animals will be useful to thee wherever thou goest.'

The poor nāgī was crying bitterly; the idea of being left alone in this deserted place, so far from her country, filled her with terror.

'Father,' she sobbed. 'You order me to go, but where am I to go? I know of no way in this foreign land. When I lift my eyes I see the great empty sky, when I lower them I see the vast empty earth.[1] In which direction must I turn my steps? There, is a red road; farther on, a white one; on this side, I perceive a yellow path, and still others stretch in the far distance. Which am I to choose? I do not know. Have pity, let me return to our country; do not abandon me. I cannot leave you. . . .'

---

[1] A description that exactly portrays the immense solitudes of Northern Tibet.

Menken, knowing that it was impossible to do as she asked, tried to lessen the bitterness of the separation by giving her advice that would be useful to her.

'My child,' he said, 'look at that blue road, which, down in the valley, appears as a giant serpent whose scales are made of turquoises. It leads to a country where innumerable lakes, day after day, reflect the blue of an ever-cloudless sky. Do not turn thy steps in that direction. It is the land of hunger and thirst. The water of the lakes is salt and not a tent is pitched on their desert banks.[1]

'See, farther on, the narrow twisting path, so white that it seems to hang on the mountain rocks like a rosary of shells made for the reciting of thousands of *manis*.[2] Keep from following it. This white road leads by arid, wind-swept tablelands to eternal snows that are haunted by demons.

'There, behind thee, that emerald path, studded with flowers, hides a snare under its enchanting aspect, for, at the horizon, it buries itself in vast grassy swamps. The traveller who is overtaken by darkness on this boggy ground, uncertain of his way, slips and sinks in a sea of mud, which closes over him. Do not venture there.

'At the foot of those hills, now golden in the sunlight, that yellow track—thin thread of amber resembling a necklace that might have been dropped from on high by a careless goddess—runs by caverns where live black or white bears dangerous to the lonely passer-by. Keep away from there.

'But, at the end of the plain, canst thou descry the coral-coloured ribbon that gently rises towards a pass where linger the clouds.[3] Follow it. It leads to a peaceful and happy country called Ling, and, there, thou wilt find the protector promised thee by Guru Padma.'

The young nāgī realized that, constrained by a sense of gratitude and the fear of disobeying Padma Sambhava, her father would not let himself be persuaded. She made no reply. Through her tears she fixed her gaze on the red road that mounted towards the pass, upon which clouds formed a curtain whose moving folds hid a troubling mystery. While she remained in contemplation, her father and the other nāgas quietly stole away. When she turned round, she found

---

[1] This description applies to the region near the centre of the Chang Thangs (desert tablelands of the north) where there are many lakes.
[2] 'Manis'—the mantra *Oṁ mani padme hūṁ*.
[3] Apart from the poetical comparisons, all these descriptions correspond to the actual appearance of landscapes in Northern Tibet, and anyone familiar with that country can easily locate them.

herself alone, and, abandoning all hope of regaining her country, she slowly strolled towards the coral path, followed by her animals.

At twilight, she arrived at a house where she asked for hospitality. The people who lived there gave her a kindly welcome and she stayed with them three months. At the end of that time, she inquired the road to the country of Ling and started on her way, guided by the directions she had received.

*   *   *

Todong—the *tulku* of Tamdrin—was then residing in the country of Ling as one of its chiefs. One night he had a strange dream, which made such an impression on him that, at dawn, he sent his servants to the King his brother and to the warriors who inhabited the neighbouring tents to ask them come and listen to an account of it, so as to discover if it did not presage an event of importance for their tribe.

When they were assembled, Todong offered them tea and had dishes containing *tsampa* and butter placed before them. Then, when each guest had eaten a *pā*,[1] he related his dream.

'I saw the grass of the pass of Toyang Shamchema carried away by the wind,' he said, 'and it came and fell on Ling. It took root again here, and each blade became a jewel. Among the gems was an unknown one, the colour of beer; I took it and placed it on a throne. Perhaps some mighty chief or some saintly *lama* is coming to us for the good of our country. We must know. Singlen, my brother, do a *mo*.'

King Singlen sent one of his servants to fetch a book on divination from his tent. The man quickly returned bringing with him the required volume and a little bag containing two dice.

First of all, Singlen invoked the Three Jewels (The Buddha, his Doctrine, and the Order), then he threw the dice, and afterwards

---

[1] The *pā* is made in the following way: you leave a little buttered tea at the bottom of your bowl and pour on it some roasted barley-meal (*tsampa*). The quantity of meal must be sufficient to make a small pyramid that rises much above the rim of the bowl. Carefully, you introduce your forefinger into the middle of the meal and turn it gently in order to moisten it. Then, you use both first and second fingers and, finally, when the meal has become just moist enough to make a sticky paste, you knead it against your palm with the fingers of the same hand. By this means you form a little ball of almost dry meal, which is the *pā*, and you eat it either alone, or with meat, curdled milk, or anything else. When beginning the operation you must be careful not to let any of the dry meal fall out of the bowl, for such an accident is considered a great breach of good manners.

68

consulted the passage in the book corresponding to the number of points shown by the dice.

Those around him remained silent and attentive during these operations, following all his movements with interest. At last the King declared:

'It is neither a *lama* nor a chief who comes to us, but a young girl, who descends from the pass followed by a mare, a cow, a ewe, a she-goat, and a useless bitch. She will arrive here today.'

The men began to laugh, but Todong could not hide his disappointment. The premonitory dream, of which he was so proud, did not then concern any marvellous happening in which he could play an important part. He disliked having to admit such a thing.

'I do not believe that the jewels I saw can have reference to a young girl and a few animals,' he said to his brother; 'perhaps you have not clearly understood the answer given by the *mo*. Anyhow. we shall soon know. Let us hold ourselves in readiness, in any case, If a great personage comes, it is only right that we receive him suitably; if a beggar, that we give him alms.'

Then, after having drunk another bowl of tea, each one returned to his tent. When he reached home, Singlen laughingly recounted to his wife Gyasa what had taken place, making fun of the conceited Todong for the disappointment and ill-humour that he had shown.

A little later, Gyasa, going to the river to get water, saw Dzeden, who was arriving with her animals.

Already informed by her husband of what the *mo* had predicted, she was not very astonished at seeing this strange traveller. Therefore, on coming up to her, she merely asked her where she had come from.

'I come from "Gong yul" (country of the night),' answered the nāgī.

'Are you a native of that country?' Gyasa asked again.

'Yes,' said Dzeden.

It was thus that the name of Gongmo (woman of the country of Gong) was given to her, and, as she did not reveal her own, it was by this that she was called in Ling until the advent of Gesar.

Gyasa invited the new-comer to stay for a few days in her tent so that she might rest herself, and the young girl accepted her invitation.

The nāgas have the power of assuming no matter what form and are particularly clever in taking that of a human being. Nothing in her outward appearance betrayed Dzeden's origin and the *dokpas*, quite naturally, believed her to be one of their race.

When Dzeden had spent a week near her, Gyasa, who liked the young girl, asked her husband's permission to have her as servant. He consented, and the nāgī and her animals remained with them.

*   *   *

Three years had elapsed since the arrival of Dzeden at Ling. During this time she had conscientiously carried out her duties: leading the cattle to pasture on the mountains, churning the butter, drying the yaks' dung (used for fuel in Tibet), and making herself useful in various ways.

In the beginning Singlen had paid no attention to her, then, little by little, he began to notice that she was graceful, well-made, good-looking, and had a charming smile. From this discovery to the desire to possess the fresh young girl who brightened his hearth was but a step. Singlen, in spite of his fifty years, felt his heart grow young within him, and he made his feelings known to his pretty servant.

The nāgī, now the humble Gongmo, also felt for her master an emotion more tender than that of respectful gratitude. She would willingly have become Singlen's second wife, for he was still a fine man and always kind, but Gyasa did not intend to have a rival. Although the customs of the country permitted polygamy as well as polyandry, she maintained that, since she had given her husband a son, he could not state any good reason for taking a second wife.[1]

From then on, the harmony that had reigned up to that time in the chief's tent was troubled by frequent quarrels between mistress and servant. Singlen, seeing things were going wrong, decided that, being no longer young, it would be unwise to compromise the peace of his household, and he abstained from giving way to his desire.

His jealous wife was not at all grateful to him for his sacrifice. Mistrusting him and having come to hate the nāgī, she thought that the most sure way of not being supplanted by her would be to kill her. As it was not possible to murder the girl in the immediate vicinity of the camp, the idea came to Gyasa to have recourse to a ruse by which she would be able to give Gongmo to the demons to devour.

An unforeseen circumstance favoured this wicked plan. Impelled

[1] The customs of the country favour this point of view.

either by his deep piety or by a longing for relief from the amorous desires which he had to renounce, Singlen started on a pilgrimage to distant sacred places.

In order not to rouse the suspicions of the young girl, Gyasa let several months pass, during which she, to all appearances, became reconciled to Dzeden. Then one day she said to her:

'Gongmo, bridle my son Gyatza's horse and take it to graze on the mountain near the Toyang Shamchema Pass. I have read in a book of prophecies that if a horse feeds in this region on turquoise blue grass, it will discover a treasure at southern Chibdag. This treasure, which no man is capable of finding, must be unearthed by a horse digging the ground with its hoofs. Once it has discovered it, its master can carry it away. What a great thing it would be for us, if we could secure it.'

The nāgī made no reply, but she was not taken in by her mistress. There is no treasure to discover, she thought, nor anything written concerning grass the colour of turquoise. This woman has read about no such thing, but through jealousy she wishes to take advantage of Singlen's absence in order to get rid of me. It is well known that the surroundings of the pass where she is sending me are haunted by demons, therefore she counts on my being devoured by them.

Great was her despair, but she dared not disobey Gyasa. So she started, walking slowly and leading the animal by a long cord.

Arrived at the foot-path that led to the pass, Gongmo saw in the distance the horrible forms of several evil spirits. The poor girl, too terrified to go farther, tied the horse to a bush and sat down under the shelter of some rocks. There, she wept bitterly until tiredness overcame her fear and she fell asleep.

Kenzo, who had been designated as father of the future Gesar, saw her from the paradise where he dwelt and thought the occasion favourable for the accomplishment of his mission; so, riding a grey courser, he descended towards her along a golden rainbow. An escort of six hundred gods, carrying flags and umbrellas, accompanied him. This magnificent procession moved in dazzling light.

Awakened by this supernatural brilliance, the young girl saw the resplendent gods assembled round her, and was very afraid.

Kenzo got down from his horse and approached her. He carried a gold vase filled with *dutsi* (Tibetan holy water) in which a bunch of peacock feathers was steeped. The *dubthob* Thubpa Gawa[1] had

---

[1] The one who is to incarnate as Gesar.

looked at himself in this consecrated water, imprinting his image on it.

'Sister Nāgī,' said Kenzo, 'have no fear. If you do not know me, learn that I am As Kenzo sent by Guru Padma. This sacred vase is filled with magic ingredients and contains the Lord of a hundred and ten *dubthobs*. Drink! By this act a kingdom will be founded, the demons will be overcome, you will obtain the fruit of the sublime Doctrine, and all your wishes will be realized.'

Kenzo then poured the holy water in a yellow jade cup ornamented with the eight propitious signs[1] and handed it to the young girl, who drank the contents. Then, without saying anything more, he ascended to the sky on the golden rainbow, followed by the six hundred gods. For a few moments the sound of their instruments and the light about the divine procession still hung in space, then all became again shadow and silence on the mountain, and the nāgī wondered if she had not been dreaming.

At dawn, she went home, taking the horse back to her mistress. When Gyasa saw her servant returning safe and sound, she was greatly troubled, but she made every effort to hide her disappointment. She asked about the horse. Had it grazed? Without questioning her further, she sent Gongmo to have some tea.

During the night following her return the nāgī suffered from violent pains in her head, and for three days she was very ill. The fourth day, as she remained in the same state, her mistress thought she had better pay some attention to her, for, if she did not, the neighbours would say that she was lacking in compassion and would speak badly of her.

She sent for a lama and a doctor. The one performed several religious ceremonies, the other gave the patient medicine. The girl became neither better nor worse.

Singlen's wife, as soon as she had known of her servant's illness, had hoped for her death. The uncertainty in which she remained as to the issue of the malady irritated her and her anger increased as time went on.

One night, unable to restrain herself any longer, she went to the tent where Gongmo was lying.

'Thou half-dead creature,' she said brutally to the invalid, 'is it a

[1] An ornamentation very common in Tibet. The eight signs are: the golden wheel of the Doctrine—the vessel containing the water of immortality—the white conch, the spiral of which turns towards the right—the standard of victory—the curled lasso—the lotus—the goldfish—the royal umbrella.

passionate attachment to something thou canst not resign thyself to leave that keeps thee in this world and prevents thee from dying?[1] Or hast thou in thee a demon that does not let thee recover?'

'Mistress,' answered the poor nāgī, 'there is nothing of the sort. If I do not get better, it is because I am suffering from a serious illness. If I do not die, it is that I have a strong constitution.' And she began to cry.

Gyasa then became ashamed of having spoken in this manner to a sick girl, and, without further remark, returned to her tent.

Not long after Gyasa's departure, the nāgī saw the end of a white rainbow touch her head. At the same time, from her body rose a light that joined the rainbow, and a male child as white as a conch emerged from the summit of her head. He circled round her three times, keeping her on his right, and said:

'Mother, one will come who will recompense you for the goodness you have shown in giving me birth.'

He then flew away in the sky and reached the paradise where Chenrezigs dwells.

The next day, a red gleam coming from the sky rested on the young girl's right shoulder. Out of this shoulder sprang a boy, flame red, who circled round her, said the same words that his brother had uttered, and, in a red light, ascended to the Marmized paradise.

The day after, it was a blue light that touched her left shoulder. Out of it leaped a male child blue as a turquoise. He circled round her and repeated what the other two children had said, then, on a path of blue light, mounted to the paradise of 'Perfect Joy'.

At dawn on the fourth day after the beginning of this strange series of marvels, a ray of sunlight touched the nāgī's heart and, almost at once, a little girl of extreme beauty came from it. She wore a head-dress displaying the images of the five Dhyāni Buddhas and was adorned with necklaces and various other ornaments made from the bones of human beings. She prostrated herself three times before her mother, said the same words as her brothers, and, ascending along the ray of sunlight, went to the Dolma paradise.

[1] The Tibetans believe that a very profound attachment to a person or a thing creates a tie that can defer for a long time the departure of the spirit, without, however, bringing healing to the dying person. This departure can also be delayed, according to them, by the desire to accomplish a particular act, to fulfil a duty before leaving this world. A solemn promise made to the dying person that one will accomplish for him the act that he desires done can put an end to the struggle and allow the spirit to escape from the body.

The fifth day, a faint light showed on the navel of the nāgī and out of it came a sack.

Gongmo's terror had increased as the incomprehensible events succeeded one another; the sight of the inert sack filled her with dismay. What is this thing? she asked herself. Never has a human being been born in this manner. Could it be that I have given birth to one of my own race?

Out of her wits, incapable of any longer enduring the solitude in which her mistress had left her since the night when she had shown herself so unfeeling towards her, the nāgī opened the flap of the tent and called Gyasa. When the latter had come, she showed her the sack lying in a corner.

'What is that?' exclaimed Gyasa, horrified. 'Never have I seen such a thing. Is it a god or a demon that has sent it to you? Who can tell. . . . The sack must be shown to aku[1] Todong and his advice asked.'

'I would never dare to do so,' answered Gongmo, trembling.

'If you do not dare to speak to him, I shall speak to him myself,' retorted Singlen's wife.

In great haste, she ran to her brother-in-law, Todong, and told him of what she had seen.

Todong remained silent, as if before answering he sought to find the possible significance of this strange event. He was connecting it with an ancient prophecy, one that he had read while staying at his residence in Shalogtsang thang, where there was the library belonging to his family. In a manuscript it was written that a young girl would arrive bringing five animals with her, that she would become the mother of several gods, then of a man who, as King of Ling, would conquer many countries.

Todong was unaware, as was also his sister-in-law, of the three gods and the goddess that had issued from the nāgī, but he well remembered her arrival with the five beasts. Perhaps this extraordinary sack was connected with the remainder of the prophecy.

The birth of one who is to become a victorious king can but be a happy event for Ling, he thought, but it will be prejudicial to me. As long as my brother Singlen continues to be King of the tribes of Ling, I am certain to remain one of the chiefs, and my authority,

---

[1] *Aku:* uncle. This title does not always indicate real relationship. It is given by courtesy to an old man, or to a young one as a mark of respect either for his personal position or for that of his family.

indeed, is as great as his. Under another King, this authority will be very greatly reduced, if I am not entirely deprived of it. To lose my power is to lose the profits that are attached to it. The gifts of cattle, wool, butter, and many other things that ensure me my ease will go to another. Ah! this is bad. I must see about it before it is too late.

Todong, coming out of his meditation, assumed a grave and important air. 'I am going to see Gongmo and her sack; but, in my opinion, this strange thing is not of good augury,' he declared.

Gyasa having left, Todong saddled his horse, put on his helmet, thrust several swords under his belt, and, in a very bad temper, went towards the nāgī's tent.

Arrived there, he asked to see the sack. As soon as it was put before him, he manifested profound disgust and great sorrow; then beating his breast, he exclaimed:

'Aka! Aka! What a misfortune. Never was such a thing born of woman, either in China or in Tibet. You are a bad girl, that is why this dreadful thing has come out of you. If this sack remains here any longer it will bring misfortune upon Ling. It must at once be thrown into the river.'

By order of Todong, three lamas, three heads of families, and three married women took the sack to the river's bank and, at sunset, threw it in the water.

That same night, the King of Hor dreamed he saw a jewel that sparkled in the river. When he awoke, he sent for his minister Rigpatarbum, who was a fisherman, and commanded him to bring him whatsoever he should catch in his net, no matter what that thing might be.

During the course of the day Rigpatarbum netted the sack, which had been carried by the current. When it was shown to the King, neither he nor any of those who were with him knew what to think of the strange object. The King sent a request to lama Tirong that he would come and examine it. The latter was a man learned in a number of sciences; as soon as he had caught sight of the sack, he declared:

'This is a human matrix. Let us see what it holds,' and, borrowing a knife from one of the attendants, he cut the sack open.

First, he took out a child, red as flame.

King Kurkar said: 'Give it to me, I want it,' and, enveloping it in a piece of red silk, carried it away.

75

The lama then lifted out a child, blue as a turquoise; and the King's brother, Prince Kurser, saying he would like it, took it away in a scrap of blue silk.

Finally, a black child was found in the sack. Prince Kurnag, another brother, wishing for it, bore it away rolled in swaddling clothes of black silk.

Now, the three chiefs were the three avatars[1] of the woman who, many centuries[2] before, had blasphemed against the Buddha, and had wished to be reborn as one of the mighty ones of the earth so that she might destroy his Doctrine and those who professed it. Not being able to discern the origin of the three children whom they carried away, these chiefs fostered their enemies, for the three boys were *tulkus* of the gods who had promised to help Gesar in his struggle against the Kings of Hor.

The red child was called Dikchen Shenpa; the blue child, Shechen Yundub; and the black child, Thugöd Mebar.

The day following the one on which the sack had been thrown into the river, the nāgī heard a voice that spoke from the upper part of her heart, as if some being was enclosed there.

'Mother,' said the voice, 'is it now time for me to be born? Shall I come out from the summit of your head?'

Poor Gongmo became terror-stricken once more.

'If you are a demon,' she answered, 'come out of my head if it pleases you; I cannot prevent your doing anything. But, if you are a god, I pray you to be born in the natural way. Todong and Gyasa are angry with me. The strange sack, which they have seen, leads them to think that I belong to a race of demons, and, fearing that my presence here will bring misfortune on the country, they may kill me.'

The voice replied:

'Do not fear, they will do you no harm. It is best that I come from your head. But, first, you must study the omens.

'See if the animals that you brought with you have had young. Does a rain of white rice fall from the sky? Have golden flowers blossomed? Is the ground covered with yellow, red, blue, and black snow? Go and see.'

---

[1] It has already been said that, according to the Tibetans, the same person can have several co-existing avatars (*tulkus*).

[2] It has already been said that the spirits of the impious woman and her sons were reborn on earth after sixty years; now, it is a question of many centuries. These discrepancies illustrate that which I pointed out in the Introduction: how both bards and audience pay little attention to contradictions of this kind.

Leaving the tent, Gongmo marvelled at seeing all that the voice speaking within her had described.

Near to each of the beasts that her father Menken the nāga had given her lay a little one just born. A powdering of different coloured snow: yellow, red, blue, and black, out of which rose golden flowers, covered the ground with a fairy carpet; and from the sky fell a rain of white rice, the grains of which sparkled as silver spangles.

For a few moments the nāgī gazed at these wonders, but, rendered uneasy by the voice that she had heard, and understanding that yet another child was to be born in a manner as miraculous as the preceding ones, she went back and hid herself in her tent.

Then out of a white vein, which opened on the top of her head, came a white egg marked with three spots that resembled three eyes.

What a queer thing, thought Gongmo. A few moments ago I heard inside me the voice of a young boy, and it is an egg that comes out! She enveloped it in a rag and put it in her dress.[1] A little while later it broke of itself, and from it emerged a male child with dark skin, the colour of beer.[2] He had three eyes.

This time, the new-born babe did not seem to want to fly away as his brothers had done. The mother looked with sadness at the three eyes in his face, foreseeing that this peculiarity would again excite the anger of Todong and Gyasa and would thus become a fresh source of torment to her. Such a prospect was too hard for her to contemplate, so, with her thumb, she put out the third eye, which was in the centre of the infant's forehead, between the other two. Then, holding the little fellow in her arms, she questioned him.

'Where do you come from? Why are you born of me? Why did my animals have young today?'

The child answered:

'For a great number of years I was an Indian hermit practising unheard of austerities in dense forests. In virtue of these practices I was reborn in the world of gods as the son of Korlo Demchog and Dorje Phagmo, and my name was Thubpa Gawa.

'Many demons who have been born on this earth seek to destroy the Religion. I have come to wage war against them and prevent them

---

[1] The Tibetans, men and women, wear very ample dresses held in at the waist by a belt; the fullness above it forms a kind of pocket on the chest. The Tibetan costume has no other pocket and in this one a variety of things is placed. The women of the people, especially in winter when they wear their fur-lined dresses, carry their children in it, in order to keep them warm.

[2] A curious comparison, because Tibetan beer is scarcely coloured.

from putting into execution their malevolent design. It was necessary for me to have a human body in order to accomplish this task. I took of your substance to form it.

'As to the young of your animals, the mare's foal is a *tulku* of Nangwathayas: he will be my courser and my help in the numerous battles that I shall have to fight. The others are harbingers of good omen.

'The calf of the *di* (the female of the yak) has gold horns, the lamb and the kid come from the herds of the gods. They announce that by conquest I shall acquire cattle that will multiply abundantly in this country. The birth of the dog is a favourable sign, which predicts my victory: the enemy will not take me unawares, but will be conquered by me.

'The blossoming of the golden flowers signifies that a number of sages will be born in Ling. The black snow has reference to Lutzen, the black demon of the North; I shall send an arrow between his two eyes. The yellow snow foretells my victory over Kurkar, King of Hor. I shall place my saddle on his neck, mount him and kill him. Likewise the blue and the red snow respectively indicate the conquest of the kingdoms of Satham and Shingti.

'The white rainbow, the end of which rested on you, is evidence of my relationship with the gods; they will be my counsellors and assistants.'

In the afternoon snow fell heavily. The wonders that the nāgī had looked upon together with the birth of her son had absorbed her attention, making her forget her duties as servant. Towards evening, Gyasa, seeing that Gongmo had neither brushed away the snow that had accumulated in front of the tent, nor had fetched water from the brook, took a stick and went to the girl's tent, thinking to beat her for her laziness.

The nāgī saw her in the distance, through a gap in the curtains, and became very frightened.

'Gyasa is coming here,' she said to her son, 'she has a stick in her hand and her face is convulsed with anger. Certainly she will beat me and perhaps kill me. The best thing for us to do is to run away.'

'Do not be afraid,' answered the little boy. 'I will speak to her. I have come down from the abode of the gods to fight and vanquish several powerful demons; it would be surprising if I could not get the better of a woman.'

'Ah! my son,' cried the poor nāgī, trembling, 'do not be too rash.

78

You do not yet know the women of the human race, and how terrible love and hatred make them.'

'Fear not,' replied the child, 'only put me on the ground.'

Gongmo obeyed, and the first thing that Gyasa saw on entering was the child, standing, a tiny boy of great beauty, with large eyes and long black hair. He looked fixedly and severely at her.

She was terror-struck, and, dropping her stick, remained fascinated without being able to say a word.

'Listen to me,' the boy said to her. 'If you do not know me, I shall tell you who I am.

'On my father's side I am related to Kurkar, King of Hor, and belong, as he does, to the line of the Hachen Hor. My mother is of the race of black demons and the cousin of Lutzen, Monarch of the North. I, myself, am really the demon with nine heads come to destroy China and India. Do not oppose me, because I think of devouring you.'

While saying this, he strode to and fro.

Gyasa, pale with fear, mustering the little strength that remained to her, rushed from the tent and, without re-entering hers, sought refuge in Todong's. When she arrived there, she was as a mad woman. It took some time and many cups of tea before she recovered her power of speech. She then related to her brother-in-law what she had seen and heard, and implored him to have the demon killed.

In the meantime, Todong pondered. The prophecy, written in the family book, was being realized point by point. He could no longer have any doubt on the subject; and the apprehension, which he had already felt, returned with greater intensity. The arrival of the future conqueror, although a blessing for Ling, presaged his own downfall as a chief whose wealth was increasing day by day. It was said that the Hero would be severely just. Todong only appreciated the saints in the tales that were told of an evening round the hearth while drinking bowls of spirit. At too close quarters, these paragons were troublesome people. They usually poked their noses into affairs that were not their concern, and inconvenienced those who wished to make certain of this world's benefits before aspiring to a place in the Beyond among the Blest.

Turning these thoughts over and over again in his mind, he decided to kill the child, thinking that if he did not get rid of him at once he might be incapable of doing so later.

'I will go myself and see this monster,' he said to Gyasa.

Whereupon Todong saddled his horse, put on his helmet, and passed his swords under his belt. Aku Todong, chief of Ling, wished always to appear before those he governed in a manner calculated to inspire them with feelings of respect.

He went straight to the nāgī's tent. Before even dismounting from his horse, he abused the poor girl, shouting angrily.

'Daughter of demons, why have you given birth to this child in our country? Malevolent creature, why did we not kill you the day you came among us!'

Then, seizing the head of the child, whom the mother had put back into her dress, he tried to snatch him away. But Gongmo, grasping her infant by his feet, strove to hold him back; thus, Todong and she pulled him in different directions.

'Let me go, mother,' he said. 'Your tenderness and your anguish make me suffer. Todong cannot hurt me.'

Gongmo let go of the child, and Todong, taking him by one foot, beat his head three times against a stone with all the force of which he was capable. He then let him fall to the ground, thinking he had killed him, but the child picked himself up, laughing mischievously, and fixed his big shining eyes, without a trace of fear in them, on his would-be executioner.

Although astonished and very alarmed, Todong nevertheless forced himself to put a bold face on the matter. With the aid of Gyasa, he bound the boy hand and foot and wrapped him in a rag picked up in a corner. After having made a hole close to the tent, he buried him, first covering the body with thorns, then with earth, and finally placing a heavy flat stone over the grave.

The nāgī had not been able to interfere, but her distress was intense, for she thought her son was dead. As soon as Todong and Gyasa had gone, she went to the place where he was buried and spoke to him:

'Do not be afraid, my poor child,' she said, 'all that which has happened is the effect of previous causes. Go to a paradise. I will send for lamas so that they may celebrate religious rites. . . . I will visit places of pilgrimage, that your spirit may find happiness in a blissful abode.' Great sobs shook Gongmo as she spoke.

Then a voice sounded from under the ground.

'Do not cry, mother,' said the wonder child. 'I am not dead. Death does not exist for me, who am the envoy of the gods. In the ill-treatment I have received at the hands of Todong, there is only happy omen. He has buried me, that denotes that I shall possess the ground where I lie. The big stone that has been placed over me symbolizes my power, which will be as stable as a rock. The rag in which I have been enveloped is the emblem of the royal robes that will clothe me.

'Return home in peace, mother. I go to my brothers the gods; in three days I will be back again with you.'

Full of joy, the nāgī retraced her steps, wondering at the power of the one who had incarnated through her.

When the night came, the *dakīnīs* descended on a path of white light to the child's grave. They lifted the stone, removed the earth, and bore away Thubpa Gawa's *tulku* to the gods of his family.

After his barbarous crime Todong entered Singlen's tent, and, Gyasa having made tea, they drank it together, laughing and rejoicing. 'The demon is really dead this time,' Todong said, and he felt reassured, thinking that he had rendered abortive the prophecies that had disquieted him. As to his sister-in-law, whose jealousy time had not allayed, she thought with secret pleasure that probably sorrow would undermine Gongmo's robust constitution, so that, when Singlen returned from his pilgrimage, he would find her no longer living.

When he had passed some time with Gyasa, Todong went home. There, his fears returned once more.

He was convinced that the prophecy written in his book related to Gongmo's son. He again saw himself beating the boy's head against the rock with such force as would have sufficed to break the skull of a yak. And the little fellow had got up and defied him. However, now that the imp was lying covered with earth and a big stone over him, he must be dead. Certainly any other child belonging to the human race would be, but this one, who, having been born only a few hours before, spoke, walked, and threatened, was surely an incarnated god or demon. . . . Perhaps in spite of everything he still lived?

Todong, unable to reassure himself, remained in his tent, without sleeping, without eating, haunted by the thought that the king who would take the place of the easy-going Singlen would deprive him of his title of chief, or, having asked him awkward questions concerning the source of his wealth, would perhaps dispossess him of it, or at least prevent him from acquiring more.

Three days after taking him from his tomb and bearing him to the gods, the *dakinis* brought the young child back to his mother. She wrapped him in a white silk scarf and placed him in her dress.

Meanwhile Todong, tortured by anxiety, and no longer able to resist the desire to know if he really was rid of his redoubtable rival, went to his sister-in-law and confided to her his fear that the child was still alive.

Lacking the courage to be the first to approach the tomb to see if the stone that closed it had been touched, he invented a pretext for sending Gyasa. She, easily guessing the nature of the feeling that animated him and not being much braver herself, grew still more afraid.

Nevertheless, not daring to disobey her brother-in-law, Gyasa went out. However, she did not go right up to the tomb, but tried to make out its appearance from a distance.

As she stopped she heard the child talking to his mother in the tent. It was useless therefore to examine further; she already knew that the little demon still lived. Without losing an instant she hurried back to tell Todong that Gongmo's son had come back to his mother and was at the moment talking to her.

Todong was not greatly surprised at the news. He was prepared for the worst.

'We shall never succeed in killing this monster,' he said to his sister-in-law. 'Yet, the thing may be possible, but it requires the work of someone more powerful than we are. Gods and demons can only be conquered by magic processes. . . . I will go and consult *gomchen* (hermit) Ratna of the Mutegspa[1] monastery.'

At dawn next day Todong started on horseback for the mountain where the hermit lived. Each year, in spring, the latter left the monastery of which he was the head and settled for the whole of the summer in the cave where previously he had spent a number of years acquiring in solitude and darkness[2] extraordinary powers over beings and things.

Arrived at the hermitage, Todong approached the *gomchen* Ratna with suitable respect. He offered him a long scarf of white silk, on which he placed two magnificent turquoises, and prostrated himself three times.

---

[1] The term *mutegspa* (*mustegspa*) in classical language usually designates Hindu Brahminists or Jains, 'heretics' with respect to Buddhists. In the popular language of the Gesar Epic it, perhaps, applies to those non-Buddhists who are more or less adepts in Nepalese tantrism. Certain passages in the Epic admit of this opinion.

[2] Concerning these retreats (*tshams*) and seclusion in the dark, see *With Mystics and Magicians in Tibet*.

Ratna having invited him to sit on a carpet, they exchanged the usual civilities. The hermit then inquired of Todong the reason for his visit.

'It concerns a very serious matter,' answered the latter, 'one that is of great importance to me. I have a grave subject of worry. If you can deliver me of it, I will give you the half of what I possess.'

The magician smiled graciously. He had acquired the power of subjugating demons and making them his slaves, but not of overcoming his greed, which was insatiable. He knew that Todong was rich, and the prospect of all that he might extort from him roused his cupidity.

'In what way can I be useful to you?' he asked.

Without omitting a single detail, repeating the same thing many times, Todong informed Ratna of all that it was convenient he should know: the arrival of Gongmo, the sack born of her, the child who later came into the world, the fruitless attempts to kill it; all this he told him.

When he had finished, the hermit said in a conceited tone:

'Undoubtedly, for you, it is a serious matter, but, for me, it is a trifle. What is the size of the child?'

'He is still only a very little boy,' answered Todong.

'Very well. Rely on me and do not worry. Tomorrow I shall send three black birds that will rid you of him.'

Having said this, he politely dismissed his visitor, for it was the hour when he had to present offerings to the evil spirits and propitiate them by means of rites and magic words.

On his return that evening, Todong immediately told his sister-in-law the result of his interview with Ratna and of the promise that he had obtained from him. This time, both of them felt completely reassured and awaited the next day with confidence.

Now, the young boy knew of Todong's visit to the hermit magician and what the latter was preparing against him. He said to his mother:

'Do not be afraid of what you will see. Tomorrow enemies will come to me from the valley that opens in front of your tent. Bring me a few birds' feathers and some cypress branches of the length of your two arms when outstretched.'[1]

---

[1] A measure used in Tibet. It is called *dompa*. For example, a piece of material is taken between the fingers of both hands and then both arms are stretched out and back as far as possible: the length of stuff thus held is a *dompa*. Small people try to obtain the assistance of a friend with long arms when they have to buy goods that are measured in this way.

The nāgī, knowing her son to be an incarnated god, hastened to obey him.

With the wood, the child manufactured a bow and arrows. Three hairs, taken from the right side of his mother's head, made the string of the bow, and the feathers served to feather the arrows.

The next morning the birds appeared. In place of plumage, thin blades of iron and copper provided them with shining armour, and each beak was a pointed sword that flashed in the sunlight. Todong and Gyasa, hidden behind the curtains of their tents, watched their coming, eager to witness the drama that was in preparation.

As soon as the young boy caught sight of these monsters, he put an arrow in his bow and went to the entrance of the tent.

Invisible to all others save to the child himself, Padma Sambhava and a celestial army surrounded him. The boy shot three arrows in succession, and the three birds fell on the ground, dead. Then, smiling, he went in again.

Todong and Gyasa remained motionless, petrified with astonishment and fear.

The next day, having somewhat recovered from his agitation, Todong returned to Ratna.

The hermit was sitting in front of his cave. When he saw the chief of Ling coming, he felt certain that the latter was bringing him some handsome present, the precursor of the wealth that had been promised him, and he experienced a lively satisfaction.

As soon as Todong was before him, without waiting for the prescribed courtesies, he said in an assured tone:

'The little fellow is dead.'

Only then did he notice the depressed look on his visitor's face: it was scarcely the expression of one who brings glad tidings.

'No, he is not dead,' Todong answered abruptly. 'He has killed your birds, it only took him an instant to destroy them. He is much more powerful than we are. The best thing we can do is to run away from him.'

Although troubled at the unexpected outcome of his witchcraft, the magician, anxious not to lose importance in the eyes of the chief, feigned confidence.

'It is nothing,' he said, 'nothing at all. . . . Simply a preliminary trial. . . . Its result was known to me beforehand. You "black men" (*mi nag* = laymen) are not capable of grasping the subtlety of our acts and of our words. When I said "The little fellow is dead", that meant that he was living. Living, but dead all the same. . . . In order to understand me, you must be initiated. Do not try to comprehend. It does not befit your position as layman. Do not be disturbed. Send the boy to me tomorrow. I know how to rid ourselves of him.'

Then, changing his tone, he continued:

'You can place your offering on the carpet.'

Todong had to confess that, in his flurry and anxiety at what had occurred, he had forgotten to bring a gift.

The magician scowled.

'It is of little consequence,' he said coldly. And he added, with emphasis: 'He whose thought has dominion over the three worlds is indifferent to the treasures of this earth.'

Fearing to have offended him Todong felt rather uneasy, so continued his excuses and promises; but, without answering, Ratna dismissed him by a gesture and with majestic step walked to his cave.

As soon as he arrived near the tents, Todong called to Gongmo and ordered her to send her son the next day to the hermit Ratna, who wished to see him.

'You know who he is,' he added. 'He is a powerful magician. It will be the worse for you if you do not obey.'

The poor nāgī told her son of the order that she had received from Todong.

'This terrible *mutegspa* will kill you,' she said. 'That is quite certain. Let us hasten to escape and hide ourselves either in China or in India.'

The child smiled.

'You do not understand these things, mother,' he answered gently. 'Why should we fly away? We have nothing to fear from anyone. Our place, here, has been decreed; it is here that happiness will come to us. Remain at home. Tomorrow I will go alone to the *gomchen*.'

The next day he went alone and naked to the magician's hermitage.

He found him arrayed in a long flowing robe that was covered with an apron made of carved human bones, wearing a large black hat ornamented with small death's heads in ivory, and rolling between his fingers a rosary of tiny discs cut from human skulls.

Three great *tormas*[1] had already been placed before the entrance of the cave. When the *gomchen* saw the child, he entrenched himself behind them and addressed him without preamble.

'Son of a demon, where dost thou come from?'

[1] Ritual cakes, sometimes tiny, sometimes as high as twenty feet.

'Is your health good, lama?' the young boy asked politely.

'I am well,' Ratna answered. 'What wast thou in thy previous life?'

'I do not remember,' calmly declared the little fellow. 'But you, who are a great magician, you ought to know these things. Tell me, I pray, what were you in your previous life?'

Ratna did not expect to have his question returned to him. Taken unawares, without having prepared an answer, he let the truth escape:

'I do not know,' he confessed.

'Really, you have no knowledge of it? This is very strange,' retorted the child. 'You are a celebrated hermit who is known to have spent half your life in meditation. For more than three years you lived in this cave with all the openings closed, in complete darkness, without pronouncing or hearing a word, witho ut seeing anyone, not even the servant who brought you your food, and yet you cannot answer me. How can you then hope to find in one who was born only a few days ago knowledge that, in spite of so much deep reflection, you have been unable to acquire?'

'Thou art very bold,' angrily rejoined Ratna. 'Dost thou know what I have done for the good of beings during my long years of retreat?'

'Yes, that I know,' the little naked boy answered quietly, looking the sorcerer straight in the eyes. 'You have not done anything for the good of anyone, but you have been expert in the art of deceiving credulous people and in getting presents out of them. It was at devising such tricks that you passed your time shut up in your cave.'

The rage that mastered the *gomchen* did not allow him to realize how ridiculous it was for a man such as he to discuss with a baby, who looked as if he could be destroyed by a mere flip of the fingers. But the latter's astonishing answers together with what he had learned from Todong convinced him that under the infantile form that he saw before him there existed something other than a human being.

'What!' he exclaimed indignantly. 'I have done nothing for the good of beings?'

'I am young,' the extraordinary child replied, with a smile. 'My age cannot be counted by years or by months, but by days. I know, however, from whence I come, although I did not tell you. I also know that the *arahans* (sages, disciples of Buddha) have taught men the path of paradises and that of supreme liberation (nirvāna), but

86

you and your kind have done nothing but accumulate riches in your monasteries.'

'Is it thus that thou defiest me, demon,' roared Ratna. 'I am accustomed to contend with those of thy race. We will see which of us is the more powerful. Invoke thy protectors. I will call my aids. One of us must perish in the fight.'

Then, in a terrible voice, the magician invoked his tutelary gods.

'All ye who have as weapon the thunder, hasten to me, hasten!' And he pronounced magic formulæ, the least of which would have sufficed to reduce to dust any other than the avatar of the divine Thubpa Gawa.

Then he walked to the table on which he had placed his *tormas*. One of them, which had been dedicated to the planets, was saturated with blood and encircled with human entrails. Another was impregnated with various vital substances. The third had remained in the cave during the three years that the magician had passed enclosed there, and had become stored with a considerable reserve of occult force.

Ratna threw them, one after the other, at the little boy, without any other effect than to see the child receive them on his hand and return them to him, as if he were playing ball.

The *mutegspa's* forehead was beaded with the perspiration of horror. Instinctively he drew back for protection as far as the entrance of his cave.

The child then picked up from the ground a piece of the *torma* that had been thrown at him, and, holding it in his hand, said to the defeated hermit:

'You pretend to be a great master of magic, but you are not. You have just demonstrated the extent of your power. Now see what a child of five days can do.'

He then threw the piece of *torma*, which, turning into a great rock and striking the entrance of the cave, blocked it completely, entombing the sorcerer in his den.

After his victory, the boy went back to his mother.

Todong, who had seen him return safe and sound, began to despair of ever being able to get rid of him. The magician had twice failed in his attempts at doing so, and the old chief did not think of appealing to him again; but, he was eager to learn how the child had made his escape. He therefore returned to the hermitage. As he approached it, some crows flew away with a great beating of wings, whilst others, more bold, finished devouring the remains of the *tormas* scattered on the ground. The seat on which Ratna usually sat was lying overturned near the entrance of the cave, which was now entirely blocked by a rock. There was no need for him to continue his investigations in order to discover the sorcerer's fate.

Todong went home confounded. He no longer had any hope of being able to rid himself, by magic processes, of the one whom he had scoffingly called Choris.[1] He, therefore, resolved to send him with his mother to a far distant and deserted spot. The lack of food, he thought, would serve his purpose better than Ratna's science.

By his orders, the next day, nine lamas, nine heads of families, and nine women led the nāgī and her son to Mamesadalungo; and when, after a journey of many days, this place was reached, they abandoned them there. It was an uninhabited region, only herds of *kyangs* (wild asses) and a few bears wandered over it. The poor mother, finding herself and her son lost in these immense solitudes, could not restrain her tears.

'We cannot remain here,' she said to her child. 'Let us direct our steps towards either China or India before the supply of provisions that they have left us is finished. If we could get to villages we would obtain food.'

The boy replied:

'This country is that of the gods. We shall live happily here. You will dig for *tumas*,[2] and I will hunt for rats.[3] In this way we will not suffer from hunger.'

Thus they abided in Mamesadalungo for three years. And with them were the five female animals belonging to the nāgī and the young males born of them.

---

[1] *Choris* signifies caste, descent. Here, the word is used in abbreviation of *btum pai choris*, 'having honourable ancestors'. Other bards use the word *Jorigs* or *Jerigs*, which means of noble birth. In both cases the nickname, used in derision, refers to the child's origin as the son of a servant and of an unknown father.

[2] A wild root that by reason of its mealy substance and sweet taste resembles the chestnut.

[3] Species of tailless field rats that live in great numbers in the solitudes of Northern and Eastern Tibet. The Tibetans call them *gomchen* (*hermits*) because they spend all the winter shut up in their holes. Some naturalists name them *Lagomys badius*.

Chapter 2

Padma Sambhava rouses Gesar's memory and commands him to get himself elected King of Ling—Ruse employed by the Hero to attain this end—Todong is duped by him—Gesar's marriage—He takes possession of the treasures hidden at Magyalpumra

PADMA SAMBHAVA, looking down from Zangdog Palri, saw with displeasure the miserable life that Lu Dzeden, the beautiful nāgī, and her son were leading. He left his palace and went to the paradise where many years before, at a council of the gods, Thubpa Gawa had been chosen as the future destroyer of the enemies of the Religion.

He was received with due reverence, and, after having exchanged with the various inhabitants of the place the usual scarves and felicitations, he requested them to sit with him so that he might make known the purpose of his visit.

When each one had taken his place according to his rank, either on a pile of cushions, more or less high, or on a simple carpet, Padma Sambhava began to speak.

'None of you,' he said, 'can have forgotten the meeting we had here to discuss a means of averting the peril that threatens the Religion. We consulted fate by means of repeated *mos*, and these uniformly pointed to Thubpa Gawa as the one who was destined to fulfil the difficult task of fighting and overcoming the demon enemies of the Sacred Doctrine.

'In obedience to these directions, Thubpa Gawa produced a *tulku*, which has been born of the nāgī Dzeden. The *tulku* has already triumphed over those who have sought to kill him and has shown his power in different ways. Nevertheless, having been exiled with his mother in the solitudes of Mamesadalungo, he is reduced to a state of extreme poverty and obliged to feed on rats.

'Is it thus that he will become King of Ling, will conquer the powerful Lutzen, the sovereign of Hor, and the Kings Satham and Shingti, as the oracles require?'

The gods could not but recognize the justice of Padma Sambhava's remarks and acknowledge that they had neglected their duty.

Guru Padma resumed:

'Without further delay I shall go to the *tulku*, and will waken in him the consciousness of the task that is incumbent on him. All of you who have promised him your aid, be watchful and ready to help him at his first call.'

The words of the Precious Master were applauded by his listeners, who protested their zeal for the meritorious enterprise of which their brother Thubpa Gawa was the leader. Then Padma Sambhava, folding a rainbow in the shape of a tent, entered it and descended to the place where the young boy dwelt.

'Precious son of a god,' he said to him, 'formerly, in one of the blest celestial abodes, thou wert the *dubthob* Thubpa Gawa. I, Padma Sambhava, exhorted thee to incarnate among men in order to perform the important work of destroying the demons who there impede the happiness of beings. Those to whom thou owest thy birth are the god Kenzo, thy father, and the nāgī Dzeden, thy mother. It is now three years that thou hast lived here in misery and inaction, thou must do so no longer. Remember thine origin and the reasons that brought thee into the world of men.

'Henceforth thy name is Gesar, King of Ling. Become conscious of thy strength and of the destiny to which thou art called. Go and take possession of thy throne. The people of Ling must all become thy subjects and the brave among them thy warriors. In order to attain this end use all the resources that wisdom and ability offer thee.

'At the assembly of the gods where thine incarnation was decided upon, thou didst ask me for various things. On the obtaining of these depended thy consent to undertake the mission for which thou hadst been chosen. Thou already possessest several. Thy father, As Kenzo, is a god, and thy mother, Dzeden, is a nāgī, as thou didst ask. Thy colt, born the same day as thou wert, is gifted with all the qualities of the courser that thou didst describe. Other things also have been given thee, of which thou art unaware at present. But to begin with, thou must take possession of the eight treasures hidden at Jigdag Magyalpumra.

'The first of these answers the request that thou madest concerning the preservation of thy life. Thou didst wish that no accident could cause thy death. Thou wilt therefore find the knots of life (*tsedus*)[1] that were tied by the thousand gods of the auspicious period while uttering powerful incantations; the water of life (*tsechu*) consecrated by the Divine Queen who holds life itself; and the pills of life made by the Supreme Protector called Infinite Life.

'The other things are a helmet, a thunderbolt sceptre (*dorje*), and a sword that were made in the heavens by Dolma and by her thrown on earth, where I found them and hid them. Then ninety-eight arrows that have been made from a three-noded bamboo and painted with a composition of powdered coral. These arrows are feathered with turquoises instead of the usual feathers. The heads are of "iron fallen from the sky" (a meteorite) and are fastened to the bamboo sticks by means of a gold ring. The bow, which thou wilt find with the arrows, is made of Kyon's horn.[2]

'Finally thou wilt find a whip in the handle of which a jewelled charm is inset, and a spear ornamented with turquoises, which is called "the conqueror of the three worlds".

'Listen further:

'A man named Tampagyaltsen lives in the land of Ga:[3] he possesses incalculable riches and his daughter is a *tulku* of the goddess Chomden Dolma (Dolma the conqueress). Thou must wed her.

'Her father's treasures include many precious statues. Three of these are giant figures in pure gold, which respectively personify the Spirit, the Word, and the Form. The rest consist of a bronze statue representing Chenrezigs, the Great Compassionate One of penetrating vision, a coral statue representing Odpamed, infinite light, a turquoise statue representing Dolma, the mysterious mother of beings, an iron statue representing Mahakala, the redoubtable protector of the Religion, and an agate[4] statue representing the terrible Palden Lhamo, whose mount has for saddle a blood-stained human skin.

'Tampagyaltsen possesses also the twelve volumes of the Bum (the Prajñā Pāramitā in a hundred thousand verses), a gold drum as large as a sun,[5] two *ragdongs* (Tibetan trumpets) each measuring

---

[1] Narrow strips of material that a lama has knotted while pronouncing ritual words. They are supposed to preserve the life of the one who wears them fastened to his neck.

[2] Fabulous bird: the Garuda of the Hindus.

[3] N.E. of Tibet, region of Jakyendo.

[4] The stone that the Tibetans call *gzig*.

[5] The rich Tibetans, specially the great lamas, have their gold beaten in the form of discs or drums, and they keep it in this way in their treasury. Some of these gold wheels are very large. It is a precautionary measure against theft, for the weight of these discs renders their transport very difficult.

seven *dompas*,[1] many silver *gyalings* (hautboys), a pair of gold vases for holding incense sticks, various copper vases on which are engraved the images of the five Dhyāni-Buddhas, two turquoise plates, a hundred and twenty-four cases full of rice, one hundred and eighty great chests filled with barley, twenty-four thousand sheep, eighty thousand horses, and a hundred and thirty thousand yaks.

'All these things must become thine.'

Having spoken thus, Padma Sambhava shut himself into his marvellous tent and slowly rose into the sky. For a few moments the light that surrounded him traced a luminous path amid the clouds, then faded in the distance. While the Precious Guru returned to Zangdog Palri, the young boy to whom he had given the name of Gesar found himself once more alone in the desert, dreaming of what he had just heard.

While he was listening to the Great Master, the mist that had enveloped his memory dispersed. He was now fully conscious of his personality and of the task that he had to accomplish.

The Guru's first command concerned the objects that were hidden at Magyalpumra. He must have these things in order to set to work, but how was he to get possession of them . . . ?

The people of Ling, he thought, know of the existence of a treasure in this place. There is mention of it in their prophetic writings. The learned lamas also preserve a tradition on the subject. It is said that he for whom the treasure is destined will one day come to take it and that, any other than he, even if he were to discover it, would not be able to carry it away.

If Todong or another from Ling should see me make for Magyalpumra, he would guess my intention and prevent me from continuing my way. I must resort to an artifice.

Gesar pondered long, and, this time, in full possession of his intelligence and divine insight, which had been reawakened through the intervention of Padma Sambhava. He finally resolved on a plan.

He knew that before his birth as son of the one whom, at Ling, they called Gongmo the servant, Padma Sambhava and many gods were wont to counsel Todong and send him their messages by ravens. He decided therefore to transform himself into a raven and mislead Todong.

At midnight, under this form, he reached the balcony of the room where the chief was sleeping. First of all he woke him by

[1] See footnote, Chapter 1.

repeated cawings, then, when he saw him look his way, called out:

'Todong! Listen, pay attention; I have important tidings to give thee.

'The gods have decided to make thee owner of the treasures that are hidden at Magyalpumra as well as of those that belong to Tampagyaltsen, who also must give thee his daughter in marriage.

'Now listen to the advice that they in their wisdom send thee so that thou mayest enter into possession of all these riches and enjoy them in peace, without exciting the displeasure of the people of Ling and provoking quarrels.

'Thou must first draw the attention of the chiefs and elders of the council to the long absence of King Singlen, who, gone on a pilgrimage several years ago, has not returned. Thou must say that Padma Sambhava and the gods have made it known to thee that he has passed into a better world and that, consequently, it is expedient to install another king in his place.

'Thou shalt also say that, by further order of the Precious Guru and the gods, a race must be organized in which all horsemen, whoever they may be, young or old, servants, beggars, or sons of good family, shall be allowed to take part, without exception. The first who will arrive at the throne, placed as winning-post, and sit on it shall be proclaimed King of Ling, the treasures that he will discover at Magyalpumra shall become his exclusive property, and Tampagyaltsen shall give him his daughter in marriage.

'Choose thy best horse; the gods are with thee. Thou shalt be the winner.'

Todong was overjoyed.

This bird that speaks so wisely cannot be just a simple messenger of the gods, he thought, but must himself be a god, who appreciates my great qualities and who has taken this form in order to counsel me, incognito. Proud of his perspicacity, he poured the contents of a bowl full of turquoises and coral beads into a bag, and, protesting his gratitude, respectfully offered it to the raven.

The latter accepted the bag with a kindly air of protection, then, holding it in his beak, flew away towards Mamesadalungo, where, once again taking human form, he gave his astonished mother the magnificent gift he had received from the all-too-credulous Todong.

After the departure of the marvellous bird, the ambitious chief

93

of Ling was too greatly moved by what he had just heard to be able to sleep again. Sitting on his couch in the darkness, he soliloquized:

'The gods are with me,' he muttered. 'That is certain . . . the raven has told me so. Their superior intelligence could not fail to appreciate my value. Now I am definitely protected from the demon's son who seemed to defy me. He probably lies dead in the desert. . . .

'Singlen has found his virtue's reward in the course of his pious pilgrimage. He did well to undertake it. My worthy brother is now an inhabitant of one or other of the blest paradises. Such an arrangement is admirably suited to him. . . . He was too soft for the proper exercise of authority. . . . The clear-sighted gods, becoming aware of this, are giving to each of us the part that best befits him. I bless them for their justice and admire their wisdom. . . . I was made to be a king.'

Nevertheless, even more than the prospect of the power and riches that were to be his, the thought of marrying the beautiful Sechang Dugmo filled Todong with joy.

There was nothing of the ascetic about the old fellow. He was a glutton, and his thirst was only quenched when, intoxicated, he lay stretched inert on the thick cushions of his couch. But, above all, he remained, in spite of his age, an incorrigible rake. Always seeking after young girls, he continually swore at his wife, who had become too mature for his taste and who with detestable shrewdness would often thwart his wanton projects.

What arguments would the old Karza Sartog bring forward now? The mandate of the gods was explicit. He would be the happy husband of a second wife, the most beautiful woman in Ling; as to the other, she could grumble to her heart's content in the kitchen.

Yes, it would be thus. But, for the moment, solitude weighed on him. He was consumed with the desire to reveal to someone the brilliant future that had been promised him and to be congratulated upon it.

'Cham! Cham!'[1] he cried.

He called his wife, because he was accustomed to confide in her and also because, at the moment, only she was within call.

[1] *Cham* is a polite form of address when speaking to married women of good family who have not the right to the superior title of *lha cham kuchog*, which is reserved for those belonging to the nobility. It is not polite in Tibet for the husband to call his wife by her name and, still less, for the wife to call her husband by his.

He had to shout several times, for the good lady was fast asleep. At last she came running from the adjoining room and inquired:

'What is it, Kushog?[1] Are you ill?'

'I am very well,' answered Todong. 'That is not the question. Listen:

'The precious Guru and the gods have just given me proof of their good will by sending a messenger to me.'

Then he proudly repeated to his wife what the bird had said to him, omitting that which concerned his second marriage, but adding other details of his own invention designed to increase his importance.

Karza Sertog was a cautious woman and full of common sense. While her husband was speaking, she pondered deeply, and her thoughts were not in agreement with the enthusiasm manifested by him. When he had finished, she shook her head.

'It is true,' she said, 'that formerly you received visits from birds that brought you messages from Guru Padma, but for three years they have ceased to come. Is the one that you have just seen an envoy of the same kind? . . . I doubt it. I fear that he may be an emissary of some enemy and that his communication is intended to deceive you. In future, the best thing that you can do will be to sleep quietly and keep your possessions instead of distributing them to ravens who may be malevolent demons. It will be difficult for you to secure the treasures of Magyalpumra.'

On hearing these remarks, Todong became violently angry.

'Shut up, you foolish old woman,' he cried. 'What do you understand of these things? You are not worthy to become queen; the gods are well advised. You are only fit to be my servant. I shall marry the girl Sechang Dugmo. Adorned with all her jewels she will resemble a brilliant star by my throne. Refrain from adding another word to your childish ravings, if you do not wish to be beaten.'

While speaking he shook his great fist at her.

The poor woman ran away crying.

As soon as it was dawn, Todong sent his servants in all directions to summon the men of Ling. They were told to assemble at a place called Ling Dutsi Tagtongtamo to hear a very important announcement that he had to make to them.

They were all there the next day. Todong, as the principal chief, took the highest seat. At his right was Tarpin, the second chief, and on his left Singlen's son Gyatza, the third chief. Before them sat the

[1] *Kushog*, written *skushog*, means sir.

men from a thousand tent encampments. Without delaying, Todong began to speak:

'The Precious Guru and the gods have shed their blessings on us,' he said, 'and, in their goodness, sent a messenger to instruct me regarding the following matters:

'First of all, know that our *gyalpo* (king) Singlen, my honoured and well-beloved brother, has been favoured by the gods in the course of his pilgrimage; they have carried him away from this world of misery and have admitted him to a place among them.

'Further, I have been told that the treasures hidden at Magyalpumra will not go out of our country. They are destined for one of us.

'As the three tribes of Ling possess the ground of Magyalpumra in common, this is what Guru Padma and the gods have decreed in order that no dispute shall divide us and that we may continue to live at peace.

'All the men born in the land of Ling, whosoever they may be, nobles or beggars, shall be allowed to take part in a race, the winning-post of which will be marked by a throne. The first rider to reach it and to sit on it shall become King of Ling. We three chiefs shall hand over our authority to him. Once become King, he will be at liberty to search for the treasures and, if he discovers them, they shall belong to him unconditionally.'

Then, turning towards Tampagyaltsen, whose riches procured him a place of honour by the side of the chiefs, he added:

'Thou, Uncle[1] Tampagyaltsen, the gods command thee to give thy daughter to the winner.'

Tampagyaltsen consented willingly. He was the richest man in Ling and did not know how to find a son-in-law worthy of him. The happy possessor of the Magyalpumra treasures, who would make his daughter a queen, appeared indeed to have been sent by the gods.

The rest of the people also readily accepted Padma Sambhava's decree. An ancient prophecy foretold that a King of Ling would conquer many countries and that, during his reign, his subjects would enjoy a prosperity hitherto unknown. This victorious monarch, who was to enrich them all, must surely be the one that the test instituted by the gods would reveal.

Therefore, they all separated joyously, and the happiest man amongst them was Todong.

---

[1] A polite mode of address among the people, which does not necessarily indicate real relationship.

96

The day fixed for the race arrived. Each qualified competitor had trained his swiftest horse and decorated it to the best of his ability. With their tails divided into several long plaits interwoven with thin red cord, multi-coloured ribbons hanging from their manes, bells tinkling at their necks, a saddle covered with a beautiful carpet[1] on their backs, the beasts appeared as proud and vain as their masters; just as if they, too, fostered the hope of ruling over Ling.

More gorgeous than any other candidate was old Todong. He wore a robe of fine dark blue *puruk* (cloth), which showed at the opening a waistcoat of turquoise blue silk edged with a wide piping of gold cloth. His fine bay horse with black tail[2] and mane carried a magnificent saddle covered with lizard skin and ornamented with arabesques in gold and silver.

Certain as to the result of the race, he already looked with the eye of an enamoured master at the beautiful Sechang Dugmo, who was adorned with so many jewels that she bent under their weight. The prettiest and most resplendent among the crowd of gorgeously dressed women, she shone forth as a goddess.

The riders had begun to head for the starting-post, when up came young Chori: the son of Singlen and his servant Gongmo as he was thought to be by the people of Ling, who were unaware of his true identity.

He was clad in a rough sheepskin robe and rode bareback the chestnut horse foaled of the mare that his mother had brought with her to Ling.

Some laughed when they saw him line up for the race, others were inclined to be angry, but the elders silenced them. The conditions of the test had been fixed by the gods and voluntarily accepted by all the people, therefore nothing could be changed but at the risk of bringing Padma Sambhava's anger down upon the country; everyone, without distinction, had a right to compete.

The men willingly accepted the rebuke. The majority of them saw only a subject for amusement and jesting in the young boy's participation in the race. But Todong knew Chori's power better than they did, and he was seized with painful misgiving; however, he soon threw it off as lacking foundation after what the raven had said to him.

[1] Tibetan saddles are made of wood and are padded. It is customary to cover them with a carpet, more or less rich. The front of the saddle, which curves upwards, is ornamented.

[2] Horses of this colour with black tail and mane are greatly prized in Tibet.

A glance cast at the throne and another at Sechang Dugmo sufficed to give him back his self-confidence, and he went with the others to line up at the end of the plain.

The signal was given and the horses sprang forward. In a second Chori-Gesar's steed had outstripped the rest. It flew rather than galloped, its feet seemed scarcely to touch the ground. Before the fastest of the other competitors had run half the course, Gesar had reached the goal and was seated on the throne, directing to the astonished and speechless crowd the calm and steady gaze of a divine master.

His victory could not be contested. Therefore all those who were present began to file past him, placing at his feet the scarves of congratulation and respectful homage that they held ready for the winner of the race.

Todong came last. His horse, usually so docile, had behaved strangely and thrown him exactly in front of the tent where Sechang Dugmo was seated. Very uncharitably the pretty girl laughed with her companions at him.

In spite of his bitter disappointment, the ambitious old fool was forced to approach Gesar with a scarf and to acknowledge him as King, handing over at the same time, as it had been agreed, the authority that he hitherto exercised.

The memory of his inhuman conduct towards the one who was now his sovereign came vividly to his mind, and he trembled greatly at the thought of the punishment the winner would inflict on him. But Gesar affected not to notice anything, and the old fellow was able to go quietly away and in solitude to deplore his foolish credulity. He no longer doubted that it was Gesar himself who had tricked him by speaking to him under the form of a raven, and he sorely repented of not having listened to the wise advice of his wife. But these were vain regrets.

Tampagyaltsen, although somewhat surprised at the unexpected son-in-law that the gods had reserved for him, could not go back on his word. Besides he did not think of doing so. Yesterday, Chori, a poor, miserable little boy, might have been an object of contempt, but today, as Gesar King of Ling, soon to be in possession of the treasures of Magyalpumra, he was a very different person. Without any feeling of constraint, he led his daughter to him, and she, sharing her father's sentiments, sat down contentedly at the foot of the throne as Queen of Ling.

Meanwhile, unseen by all save the Hero, fairies gathered round him, while Padma Sambhava entrusted him with a magic *dorje*[1] with which to open the subterranean palaces that contained the treasures.

The days that followed passed in rejoicings. Presents were brought to Gesar from every tent. Sechang Dugmo's father celebrated the royal nuptials with sumptuous banquets. The women of Ling dressed themselves each day in their holiday garments and the lips of the men, constantly dipped in beer or spirits, had never time to dry.

For all that, little by little, life resumed its normal course. Gesar had a palace built where he lived with his wife and his mother, surrounded by many servants. The weeks and months glided by and everyone was happy.

*   *   *

Then, one night, while Gesar was sleeping, Manene appeared in his room and wakened him. She rode a white lion, and led a buffalo in leash behind her; in one hand she held a bow, in the other a mirror.

'Gesar,' she said, 'I am Manene, she who conveys the decisions of the gods and is the counsellor whom they have given thee.

'The time has come for thee to take possession of the treasures that have been reserved for thee. Thou wilt find among them the things of which thou hast need for the accomplishing of thy mission and very many other things besides. When they become thine, show thy generosity by liberally distributing a portion of them among the Ling warriors; they will be useful to them.'

Having spoken thus, the goddess disappeared, and for a long time the room remained illuminated by the brilliance that she left behind her.

In the morning, Gesar told his wife about the apparition of Manene and of what she had said to him. He also despatched messengers in every direction to beat the drum of the law to assemble the men.

Meanwhile Sechang Dugmo and her servants made great preparations for the forthcoming gathering.

Hundreds of carpets were spread on the ground: some of tiger skin, others of leopard skin; some from China woven of the finest wool, others made of Tibetan *thigma*.[2] In this way, each guest, according to his rank, could find a sitting-place.

[1] Ritual sceptre.
[2] Woollen material on which is printed a design in the form of a cross.

Gold and silver vases were taken from the treasury, and many low tables, supporting pyramids of *tsampa*[1] and butter, were placed in front of the carpets.

A few days later, the men belonging to the different Ling tribes came together and feasted with their King.

During the banquet Gesar told them of the message that the goddess had brought him, and his listeners manifested great enthusiasm at the idea of securing the hidden treasures.

A whole week was devoted to preparing for the expedition. When the day of departure arrived, the men, in military formation, rushed from the palace precincts with the impetuosity of a torrent. The horses reared and curvetted, their riders' bows and lances clashed, and, like a flock of sheep, the infantry scurried after the cavalry.

The earth trembled; the stones resounded under the tread of man and beast; and, overhead, flags floated in the wind, some red, some yellow, some multi-coloured.

The dust raised by the marching army rose as high as the summits of the loftiest mountains, darkening the sky and enveloping the warriors in a dense cloud.

At Magyalpumra, they pitched many white tents, all of which were highly ornamented with blue and red designs. The one belonging to Gesar contained his gold throne, resplendent as the sun.

For three days the great lama, surrounded by his *trapas* (monks), celebrated various ceremonies, glorifying the gods and subjugating the demons.

The following day, which was that of the full moon, Gesar assumed the appearance of an air spirit and went to the mountain. There, among sombre rocks whence flames escaped, stood one of pure crystal having the shape of a gigantic *bumpa* (ritual vase for holding consecrated water). The Hero approached it, and, grasping in his hand the ritual dagger (*phurba*), traced the *mudra* (magic sign) of anger, while he said in a voice of thunder:

'Here are the treasures hidden by Padma Sambhava. They are guarded by the twelve goddesses of the earth. I, Gesar, son of gods, am the legitimate owner of them. According to the bidding of Manene, I come to claim them.'

Animated by the full force of his will, he knocked on the crystal

[1] Barley flour: the grain of the barley having been roasted before it was ground. It is the staple food of the Tibetans.

rock with the gold *dorje* that Padma Sambhava had given him. The rock opened at once.

Stepping through the door-like opening, Gesar entered a magnificent hall where, on a large gold throne, lay a *mandala* (a magic pentacle). In the centre of this shone the vessel containing the water of immortality, which bubbled up and overflowed; a happy portent for Ling and its King. Around the vessel were ranged the knots and pills of life, a number of other magic charms, and the supernatural armour destined for Gesar.

At the foot of the throne countless bows, arrows, helmets, and lances formed the outer circles of the *mandala*. The whole was bathed in dazzling light of surpassing intensity: the splendour of the sun united with that of the moon.

Gesar directed the removal of the treasure, which took a whole week to complete. While it was being done, Manene appeared to the Hero and told him to be on his guard, for bad spirits prowled the neighbourhood with the intention of killing him and his companions.

In fact, very soon, these foes made their presence known. First they loosed a black wind, which darkened the sky and fell as a waterspout upon the Ling encampment, knocking down in the temple-tent three sacred bows, one of which had the 'life'[1] of the people attached to it. Gesar threw at the ink-coloured cloud a *dorje* made of iron fallen from the skies, which he had found among his treasures. It immediately dispersed and the wind dropped suddenly.

Nevertheless the warriors were dismayed at the fall of the bows, for such an occurrence was of ill-omen. Gesar revived their courage by declaring that he had killed the demons that were in the cloud, but he exhorted his men still to keep careful watch.

Other bad spirits then manifested themselves in the guise of animals. First, it was a musk-deer of fantastic gait, which the warrior Tema pierced with an arrow. Then, a 'cemetery' boar terrified the camp with its blood-curdling cries; it was killed by a well-directed stone. Finally, an extraordinary monkey appeared during the night, when the watchers were drowsy, and began plundering the place; but the divine horse, Kyang Gö Karkar, recognizing it to be a demon, killed it with a kick.

Whereupon the hostile beings ceased their attacks. The lamas

[1] Frequently, in Tibet, the 'life' of an individual or of a group is said to reside in a mountain, a tree, or an inanimate object, the deterioration or destruction of which brings illness or death to the being whose 'life' is attached to it. Thus, the 'life' of Tibet is said to be attached to the Lake Yamdok.

burned a number of incense sticks in honour of the local deities and laid pure offerings before them. Gesar left Magyalpumra at the head of his soldiers, who carried the treasure.

As the army started, Padma Sambhava appeared in the sky, surrounded by a great many gods and fairies, who waved flags, carried umbrellas, and rained down flowers and rice upon the earth. In an ecstasy of joy, the people of Ling shouted: 'Victory to the gods! The demons are overcome!' and their acclamations filled the valleys as the rolling of thunder.

The treasure was carried with great pomp to Gesar's palace, and magnificent banquets took place while the arms were being apportioned to the warriors.

Surrounded by his clergy, the great lama distributed the charms and the pills and 'knots' of life that had been found with the treasures. In addition, everyone received a few drops of the water of immortality from the miraculous vessel that never empties, and, on this occasion, an *angkur*[1] was conferred upon all the people of the country.

When at last the joyous excitement had abated and the members of the royal household were once more abandoning themselves to the pleasures of idleness, Gesar shut himself up in a secluded part of the palace for a long period of retreat. There he remained deep in meditation for many years, seeing no one but his wife, who brought him his meals, and the ministers, who sometimes solicited his advice regarding the country's affairs.

In this manner he attained his fourteenth year.

---

[1] I have given the explanation and description of the initiatory rites called Angkur in *With Mystics and Magicians in Tibet*, and in *Initiations and Initiates in Tibet*.

Chapter 3

Extraordinary adventures in the land of the Mutegspa magicians—Gesar exterminates them and secures the precious medicines that they were withholding—He miraculously saves their Chief's daughter and gives her in marriage to an Indian king.

ONE morning at dawn, the King's room became suddenly illuminated by a light that paled that of the rising sun, and Manene appeared before him.

'Gesar,' she said, 'thy rest has lasted long enough. Much work awaits thee; it is time that thou didst begin it. Thou drawest near to thy fifteenth year, the one during which thou hast to pierce with an arrow the forehead of Lutzen, the black demon of the north, and to subdue his numerous subjects. But before thou dost start thy task, it is necessary that thou shouldst have knowledge of the region inhabited by him and of the perils that confront whosoever attacks him.

'Lutzen's kingdom is a gloomy country, unvisited by the sun. Its sombre mountains of bare rock reach to a dark sky from which falls ceaselessly a heavy rain of blood. Pestilential mists fill the depths of its barren valleys and creep up the steep slopes, carrying death with them. No one, if he be not provided with powerful medicines, can withstand their destructive effects. Know, also, that Lutzen, by his magic, is able to drive these deadly vapours beyond his frontiers and can at will poison the men and animals of neighbouring states.

'In Tibet, there are only medicines that are extracted from the rocks. But in India, medicinal flowers of all colours cover the ground like an immense rainbow, while trees with trunks as big as cascades (*sic*) and overflowing with healing sap form, above them, an impenetrable roof of healing leaves.

'The Mutegspas (Brahmins or Jains) possess *arura*, the king of medicaments, *parura* and *kyurura*, which are his ministers, and *gurgum, gabur, dzati, lichi, tsenden*,[1] which, in the great family of

---

[1] *Arura* = myrobalan. *Parura* (Tib. ortho. *barura*), another kind of myrobalan. *Kyurura* (Tib. ortho. *skyurura*), a fruit used as a depurative medicine. *Gurgum* = saffron, used in liver diseases. *Dzati* = nutmeg. *Lichi* = cloves. *Tsenden* (Tib. ortho. *tsandan*) = sandal-wood.

medicines, represent respectively the virgin, the youth, the doctor, the reverend, and life. They have in addition a thousand other drugs, all exceedingly precious, whose possession would be of more use to man than all the gold in the world. These valuable medicines, however, are jealously guarded by the Mutegspas, who forbid their exportation.

'This monopoly will continue so long as the disciples of Lungjags Nagpo exist, because their prosperity depends upon the retention of these excellent medicines. The quintessence of these, the life jewel of the Mutegspas, is enclosed in a sandal-wood box, the turquoise key of which is in the keeping of Lungjags' daughter. The latter is the *tulku* of a Yeshes Kahdoma (celestial fairy). Remember this fact, that it may help thee in devising a plan by which to secure the casket's contents, for while it remains in the monastery, Lungjags and his followers will continue to be invincible.

'Listen further: the chief of the Mutegspas and his Kashmirian and Nepalese disciples all preach false doctrines and spread the religion of the demons. They worship the nine-headed Brahmā, invoke the sun and the moon, and offer them blood sacrifices. Their minds are versatile; by turn they profess one or other of the four extreme teachings and make them the subject of their meditations.[1]

'They are expert magicians and by their cunning impose on the Tibetans, many of whom become their adepts, and are thus led along the path of perdition. If thou dost not put an end to the activity of these false masters, they will end by corrupting the Religion.

'Meanwhile, in a doorless fortress built in bronze, the Mutegspas keep secreted the Sacred Writings. Of these they possess a complete collection, which includes the Sutras, the Prajñā-pāramitā, and the commentaries and discourses of lama-sages. Thou must secure these precious teachings, that they may be spread and become known throughout India and Tibet.

'In order to breach the fort's walls it will suffice if thou shoot at them one of thy magic arrows; but, the way that leads there is long and fraught with danger. Thou must pass through narrow gorges where tigers, leopards, and, what are more formidable still, cannibal demons lie in ambush. In a human body thou couldst never succeed

---

[1] These four extreme theories, in Tibetan *mu hji*, concern: (1) birth-cessation; (2) permanence-discontinuity; (3) existence-non-existence; (4) manifested universe (the phenomenal world)—the Void.

in passing these. Therefore transform thy divine courser into the king of vultures and, mounted on him, follow a route above that of the birds; in an instant thou wilt be in India.

'First of all thou must conquer the tutelary gods of the Mutegspas. Know that Lungjags Nagpo's vital essence[1] resides in a terrible nine-headed serpent, which, by magic means, has entered a sandal-tree, where it makes its home. The vital essence of his disciples is concentrated in a nine-headed tortoise, as high as a tower. This monster lives in a nine-storied iron grotto. Thou canst reduce it to powder by throwing at it thy ritual dagger of celestial iron (made from an aerolite).

'What further there will be to do, is for thee to consider. If thou hast understood my counsels, they shall be to thee as sweet as sugar. If thou hast not grasped their meaning, I shall have spoken in vain. Bear in mind all that I have said.'

At these words the goddess ascended into the sky and disappeared.

The same day Gesar repeated to the assembled people of Ling that which Manene had told him.

'I have already given you arms,' he said, 'that you may defend yourselves against your enemies. Our protectress now wishes to provide us with medicines that will ensure us against disease. It is essential that my expedition be concluded within three months. I cannot take a companion, and I must start without delay.'

When the King had ceased speaking, the people and the warriors broke into clamorous protestations. They could not bear the thought of their chief, under whose rule they were so perfectly happy, undertaking alone, in a distant land, such a perilous enterprise. More than any one, Sechang Dugmo was opposed to her husband's project. Tearfully, she pleaded that it was cruel of him to abandon her, for her father was now too old to act as her protector.

While they all continued to lament, an old man, the Chipön Gyalpo (chief equerry), stood up, and, addressing Gesar, said:

'Precious nephew,[2] what you have told us exactly agrees with certain ancient predictions that are known to our lama-sages and recorded in our prophetic writings. It was foretold that you would introduce into Tibet the medicines used by the Mutegspas. We, therefore, cannot oppose your charitable intention. Only vouchsafe

[1] See footnote near the end of Chapter 2.
[2] Affectionate mode of address used by an old man to a younger, and one which does not necessarily imply real relationship.

105

to wish happiness to Ling before you leave; we will then patiently await your return.'

Whereupon the people, understanding that the commands of Padma Sambhava and the gods were conclusive, ceased their objections. They thanked Gesar for his great kindness, and, after the latter had wished them happiness and prosperity, they dispersed to their respective tents.

Two days later, Gesar transformed his horse into a gigantic bird: the king of vultures. Then, when he had partaken of the farewell repast with which his wife served him, he assumed a divine form and, majestically sitting on his winged mount, flew high into the sky surrounded by an escort of gods and fairies. In the twinkling of an eye he reached the region called Menling Gongma,[1] where meet the frontiers of Kashmir, Nepal, and Tibet.

Near the spot at which he alighted was a crystal grotto called the 'luminous sunlit cave'. In very ancient times Guru Shenrabs,[2] and then the Buddha, had sojourned and meditated there. Later, Padma Sambhava had practised the eight different austerities within it, and, because of the spiritual illumination to which he attained, the further name of 'cave of the Liberated Vision' was given to it. There, Gesar lived hidden for two months, during which time he remained unperceived by either gods, men, or demons. His horse abandoned its bird-like form and, assuming that of a man, became his servant.

During his retreat the Hero propitiated Vajra Kila and Shinje,[3] the lord of the three worlds, and, with their aid, he completely subjugated the two great gods of the Mutegspas, Angchug Chenpo[4] and Tugri Nagbar, by capturing them with the 'lasso of concentrated thought' and the 'hook of compassion'.[5] When these gods were under his power, and before he liberated them, he made them take the solemn vow of the Chöskyongs, defenders of Buddhism. As they were, now, obliged to support the Doctrine of the Buddha and his followers, the protection that they had hitherto given to the Mutegspas

---

[1] 'Upper valley of medicines.' (Tib. ortho. *smen gling gong ma*.)

[2] Shenrabs was the founder of the Bön religion. The sojourn of the historical Buddha in this region is a fantastic invention.

[3] Kila: one of the names of Shiva; Shinje is the Tibetan name of Yama, the god of the infernal regions in Hindu mythology.

[4] Angchug (*dbang phyug*) is another name for Shiva. I have already pointed out that the various Hindu gods, on being adopted by the Tibetans, have completely changed in character; their different names have also created, in Tibet, as many different personalities. Tugri Nagbar (*dug ri nag bar*) 'the black mountain of poison that burns', appears to be the name of a local deity.

[5] Mystic phraseology.

ceased of itself, leaving these last without adequate defence before Gesar.

Then the King of Ling thought of the nine-headed tortoise and the venomous snake, whose retreats were not far from his cave. That of the tortoise was situated at the foot of the very mountain on which he dwelt. Calling to his tutelary gods for aid, he threw a ritual dagger made of iron from the heavens at the nine-storied cave. The tortoise was pulverized together with its dwelling. Only the terrible lightning flashing gem that it carried in its skull remained intact and was taken possession of by the Hero.

Two days later, Gesar and his divine steed[1] each produced a phantom (*tulku*), that is an emanation from himself, which, in the present case, resembled its creator perfectly. These two magic creatures, on reaching the frontier between India and Nepal, came to a mountain covered with dense forests of terrifying aspect, upon which was stretched an eightfold layer of shadow (*sic*).

There, deeply embedded in the heart of an immense sandal tree, was the giant reptile whose dreadful roaring (*sic*) sounded as the clashing of heaven and earth in conflict.

Invoking his protector gods, Gesar's phantom shot a magic arrow at the monster's forehead and the beast expired immediately. The victor then cut off its luminous horns, removed its eyes, the pupils of which were of iron, and cut out its blazing heart; all three were magic jewels.

The same day, in the monastery fortress of the Mutegspas, omens of evil portent made their appearance. Blood flowed from the white conch neck of the gold vase that held holy water. The wind rent the banner made of human skin that stood before the sanctuary. The bottom of the cauldron, in which the tea for the breakfast of the assembled monks was being boiled, suddenly fell away. The kitchen was flooded although it had not rained.

Very alarmed, the Mutegspas gathered together in the great hall of the monastery, and there pondered over these signs for a long time, without being able to discern their meaning. They finally decided to leave it to their god to enlighten them on the matter, in dream; and they all retired to rest.

During the night, Manene appeared to Gesar and said to him:

'Beware, O Hero! The Mutegspas' magic skill is about to manifest

[1] It will be remembered that the horse was an avatar of a deity. Concerning *tulkus* and *tulpas* see *With Mystics and Magicians in Tibet*, p. 113.

itself effectively. Assume, without delay, the form of the god of their maternal ancestors (*mo lha*); that is, of a young seer astride a *khyung*;[1] thy horse will take on the appearance of this bird. Thus shalt thou go to Lungjags Nagpo and endeavour to mislead him by thy predictions. If thou dost not succeed in deceiving him with false prophecies, thou wilt never be able to defeat him. Pay great attention to my counsels and be happy.'

Having uttered these words, the goddess disappeared.

Gesar immediately took on the features of the divine Tungkar (white conch) who foretells the future. He resembled a young boy of eight years, gorgeously apparelled and adorned with magnificent jewels, riding the king of birds.

He found Lungjags Nagpo asleep, and awoke him by singing an invocation to the nine-faced Brahmā and the goddess Uma.

He then said to him: 'I am the son of the great prophet of the gods. Rouse thyself from sleep, O mighty Magician, listen to me and let thy fears be dissipated.

'Yesterday, when the omens appeared, thy disciples' minds became confused, and now the most irrational thoughts are surging in them. Five hundred of thy pupils have assembled and have supplicated their gods to make known to them, in dream, the meaning of the signs that they have witnessed. It is in answer to their prayer that I have been sent.

'Thou must not be in any doubt as to the nature of the presages: they foretell no danger; on the contrary, all are auspicious. I will disclose their meaning to thee.

'The blood flowing from the vase of holy water betokens that the celestial Mother Uma regards thee with favour. Whatever the end may be that thou seekest, thou shalt happily attain it.

'The tearing of the skin banner by the wind signifies that thou wilt bring under thy power the god who holds in his hand the lasso that controls the wind.[2]

'The falling away of the bottom of the tea-cauldron denotes that the Doctrine of Buddha declines and will end by disappearing from Tibet.

---

[1] A mythical bird: the garuda of the Hindus.
[2] The Tibetans believe that the wind is caused by a god mounted on a galloping horse. By slinging stones in the direction of the horse, it is possible, if its legs are hit, to impede its gallop. If it can be caught with a lasso, the wind ceases. This difficult task, it is said, is only accomplished by a special god or by a very great magician, whereas many lamaist sorcerers think they are clever at throwing stones at the legs of the invisible courser.

'The water that flooded the kitchen indicates that Brahmā is pleased with thee. If thou drinkest of this water, thy desires shall be satisfied.

'Prosperity and glory for the Mutegspas, this is what has been foreshown by the signs that have troubled thee. Do not be cast down, O great Sage, do not distort the meaning of oracles, the truth of which time will justify. There is no need to verify them by *mos* (divinatory practices). The minister of the nine-headed god will come shortly and make things clear to you all and advise you. Do not doubt my word, prepare for his reception, and remember what thou hast just heard.'

And the apparition faded.

Lungjags, his fears entirely dispelled, was filled with joy. He hastened to have the gong sounded to summon his disciples and, as soon as they were gathered in the assembly hall, he repeated to them the reassuring words of the young god. A general light-heartedness ensued, and, without loss of time, preparations were begun for the reception of the nine-headed Brahmā's ambassador.

Gesar, having once again changed his appearance, arrived about midday. He now resembled the expected minister-god and was mounted on a nine-headed elephant, which had for saddle a blood-stained human skin.

As soon as the sentries gave warning of his approach, the Mutegspas, eager to see him, rushed to the dreadful ramparts of their fortress-monastery, which were decorated with severed heads and flags of human skin.

Disdaining the door which was opened to him, Gesar flew with his elephant over the outside wall and landed in the court of the great temple.

During this time, the Mutegspas played various musical instruments, advanced in procession carrying banners and umbrellas, and filled the air with joyous exclamations and praises in honour of their divine visitor.

Gesar tied his elephant to the door of the building, where the choicest food was immediately placed before it. Then he entered the great hall, conducted by Lungjags and followed by the latter's disciples.

As soon as the so-called minister of the nine-headed Brahmā was seated on the throne that had been prepared for him, the leading Mutegspas told him of the omens they had witnessed and all pressed closely round him in their desire to hear his explanation of them.

Alone, among them, the aged Guru Nopa did not entirely share in the general confidence. To him the god who had descended in their midst appeared suspect; he thought, by certain signs, to recognize him as an illusory creation of Buddhist magicians. Doubt preyed upon the old man's mind.

Affecting profound respect and assuming the candid air of a man who desires to be instructed, he approached Gesar and put several questions to him concerning the doctrine of the Mutegspas and its origin. The Hero's tutelary deities, who surrounded him, invisible to his listeners, dictated the answers. He completely satisfied the suspicious Nopa and, in addition, even expatiated upon other points than those that had been put before him, and concerning which the spiritual Master was entirely ignorant. Overwhelmed by such a display of knowledge, Nopa could not do otherwise than join in the praise that was chorused by the learned Mutegspas, who were amazed at the god's brilliant intelligence.

Some of the disciples then brought in the articles used for consulting fate by means of *mos*, and, setting them down in front of him, begged that he would read the future.

Whereupon the pseudo-minister of Brahmā graciously smiled his approval, and said:

"There is nothing better. This is the true means by which to dispel your fears and to know with certitude what destiny has in store for you. I am the *mopa* of Brahmā, who never fails to consult me before undertaking important business or in the event of omens appearing to him. I learnt my art from an illustrious master, a diviner venerated by all the gods. My *mos* are infallible. I have done hundreds of them, and all, without exception, have proved true. Moreover, I did not come here of my own accord, but by order of Brahmā, who, out of his great kindness towards you his servants, directed me to do so. Therefore let us begin without further delay.'

This speech greatly pleased the Mutegspas. They hastened to spread out a tanned skin before Gesar on which several designs representing dwellings and various localities were traced, and to place near it a goblet three parts full of different coloured pebbles. The *mopa* had to shake the goblet until either a single stone, or several at the same time, fell from it, then the drawing on which these fell would reveal to him the secret of the future.

First, a white stone dropped in the house of the gods.

'This signifies that Brahmā will continue to extend his powerful protection to you,' declared Gesar.

The test had begun well, a murmur of satisfaction ran round the vast hall, and the *mopa* proceeded with his interpretation.

Two speckled stones fall in the 'terrible place'.

'The people of the agricultural regions will become powerful.'

Three pebbles of different colours fall into the home of the nāgas:

'The learned Mutegspa Masters will enjoy long life.'

Four black pebbles fall in the centre of the drawing:

'Buddhism will decline and disappear from Tibet.'

A tiny little stone ricochets along the skin and falls off it:

'Guru Nopa, who questioned me a few minutes ago, has doubted my personality and my mission. He must apologize.'

Six pebbles scatter in falling and touch the four corners of a drawing:

'Danger threatens you; it comes from Tibet and Shang Shung.'[1]

Gesar stops. He pretends to consider attentively the drawing. The Mutegspas are all attention:

'Danger,' he repeats, 'a very great danger too. It must be averted forthwith.'

He ponders again.

'Bring out from your stores,' he says at last, 'great quantities of medicinal plants and trees from which drugs are extracted. Pile them up inside your citadel walls, leaving only sufficient room in which to move about. Let the heaps reach to the height of the ramparts. Of your four gates, wall in three of them and let the opening of the fourth be reduced to the dimensions sufficient for one man to pass through at a time. As regards yourselves, remain within the fortifications for fear of hostile encounters, and let only the water carriers have permission to go out for the needs of their service.

'Carefully guard yourselves. Brahmā has placed in your hands the medicine treasure of India, do not share it with any one else. Do not allow the Tibetans to seize it.

'You must propitiate the gods by unceasing religious ceremonies. A mighty chief is coming from Tibet. If you do not succeed in stopping him, he will burn your reserves of medicines, your religion will degenerate, and your very existence will be in peril.'

[1] Shang Shung is the ancient name of a country situated in the region of Ngari Korsum, south-west of Tibet. It was the native land of Guru Shenrabs, who holds among the Bönpos the place that is occupied by the Buddha Gautama with the Buddhists.

He again shakes the goblet and nine black pebbles fall in one direction. He resumes:

'The Mutegspas do not understand the meaning of the oracles they deliver. For this reason, the rites they practise for averting evil are worthless. These merely bring them under the power of the demons whom they invoke. In order for you, Masters and disciples, to become instructed in this matter, you must be initiated in the knowledge of the origin of divinatory practices by a *mopa* such as I. This initiation is the spreading of Angchug's religious mantle (*zen*) over you.' [1]

Gesar, once more, shakes the goblet. Several stones escape from it and fall into the centre of the stretched skin.

'One person only amongst you honours the Buddhist gods. She is Padma Chös Tso (lotus ocean of religion).[2] Because of the link she has with them, she will respond to the magic influences that the Buddhists will direct towards her so that this night she may have bad dreams. If you pay attention to them, you will give yourselves to your enemies.

'Remember my words. It is now expedient for me to leave you. It is not well for many diviners (*mopas*) to remain long together, such a proceeding is prejudicial to the respect that they owe to one another.'[3]

All the Mutegspas marvelled at the great wisdom of Brahmā's minister, and, although he had foretold impending danger, they did not doubt but that by following his advice they would be able to avert it. With a chorus of thanks, they offered the false *mopa* costly presents, which he placed on his nine-headed elephant and forthwith departed.

The Mutegspas escorted him for a time, but soon it became impossible for them to keep up with the rapid strides of the giant animal, and before long it disappeared with its divine rider from their sight.

In an instant Gesar regained the cave that he had chosen for his dwelling and, after dissolving the magic forms that had served to deceive the Mutegspas, he became absorbed in meditation.

Upon the departure of their celestial counsellor, the Mutegspas began piling the medicinal plants into enormous heaps along the

[1] In token of protection.
[2] The daughter of Lungjags Nagpo.
[3] Tibetan proverb equivalent to the saying 'Two soothsayers cannot look one another in the face without laughing.'

monastery streets.[1] Branches and trunks of trees were also brought, from outside, into the interior of the monastic citadel. Meanwhile, those who were skilled in the celebrating of rites gathered together to offer sacrifices to the gods, to recite appropriate offices, and to celebrate various religious ceremonies, as they had been directed to do by 'Brahmā's minister'.

In the great assembly hall, Lungjags and five hundred learned priests sat surrounded by a crowd of other Mutegspas of lesser degree. They shook their bells and their little drums, while cymbals and big drums marked the rhythm of the liturgical phrases. They chanted loudly, uttering with great force the ritual cries of Ha! ha! ho! ho!, which rolled under the ceiling with the sound of thunder. Victims had been slaughtered, and their blood, filling many silver vases, was placed before the statues of the four-headed Brahmā and the nine-headed Brahmā, as well as in many magic pentacles.

During the night, while the priests were thus assembled, Padma Chös Tso, Lungjags Nagpo's daughter, had sinister dreams. As soon as she awoke, she went to the great hall to tell them to her father and the other Mutegspa chiefs, who were continuing the ceremonies in honour of the gods.

'Father,' she said, 'and you, learned divines, deign to listen to me, the *tulku* of a *dakīni* (fairy) who speaks to you in this land of India. Pray hearken!

'Last night, in my dreams, I saw many omens of evil portent. I will describe them to you.

'You were sitting in this place wearing copper hats. The hall was on fire and, soon, nothing was left but ashes. The roofs of the fortified towers that stand at the four corners of the ramparts fell in, and the stones from their crumbling walls rolled to the foot of the mountain. The snow on the high peak behind the monastery melted in the sun. At the foot of the mountain an arrow flew through the green wooded valley where the roaring tigers sport, and it became a dusty desert. You were all wearing cotton garments; I, alone, kept my silken apparel. A red wind,[2] carrying thunder, destroyed the vast kingdom of the Mutegspas.

'Now that I have recounted my terrible dreams, tell me how you interpret them.'

[1] It will be remembered that the Tibetan monasteries are veritable towns. See descriptions and illustrations in *My Journey to Lhasa* and *Magic and Mystery in Tibet*.
[2] Red wind: *Lung mar* does not literally mean that the wind is red in colour. It is the term used to signify a violent hurricane.

While the young girl was speaking, Lungjags Nagpo and his colleagues nodded their heads and smilingly exchanged knowing looks. When she had finished speaking, her father answered her in a pompous tone.

'My daughter, do not talk so much. Who would wish to injure us without a reason? Enemies do not spring up without a cause.'

Padma Chös Tso resumed:

'Listen to me again, I also saw the *mopa*, the minister of Brahmā who was here yesterday. He held a lasso in his hand, which he threw over the flag of victory (*gyaltsen*) that is set up on the ramparts and, lifting it, carried it away. This *mopa* is a mighty magician. Examine carefully my dreams and ponder over them.'

In a voice of suppressed irritation, Lungjags Nagpo replied:

'My child, this *mopa*, from whom the future has no secrets, warned us that thou wouldst have bad dreams. These bear the impress of the Tibetan Buddhists and of the Bönpos of Shang Shung, who have sent them to thee. The discerning minister of Brahmā strongly recommended us not to pay attention to them; but, of course, thou didst not hear what he said to us on the subject.

'Now, leave this hall where thou hast no place. Return to thine apartments. For thine amusement, array thyself in pretty, soft silken dresses, eat of dishes that are sweet and agreeable to thy taste, but do not again relate thy visions to us. Thou worshippest the Buddhist gods, that is why unpleasant dreams visit thee.'

Nevertheless, some among those who were gathered there thought that Lungjags was perhaps too prompt in ignoring, as unworthy of attention, the omens seen by the young girl. They knew her to be an incarnated *dakīnī*, expert in magic; for this reason they deemed it prudent to take into account the warnings that she had just voiced.

They therefore respectfully represented to their chief that too great haste in such a serious matter might bring about regrettable consequences, and requested he would permit Padma Chös Tso's dreams to be examined in their relation to the premonitory signs that they themselves had witnessed during the previous days and any correspondence to be studied by the most competent of their Masters.

Lungjags refused to listen.

'The *mopa* who was sent to us by Brahmā has interpreted all these omens,' he answered, 'and in addition, he has cautioned us concerning the dreams that my daughter would have. All has come to pass as he predicted. Do not let us waste time in idle discussion. Brahmā might get irritated at seeing us doubt the word of his Messenger.'

The authority of Lungjags was firmly established with the Mutegspas; not one of them dared further to oppose his decision. The office continued, and, when it was ended, they all retired to their respective quarters, where they were to remain in seclusion for several days, repeating the names of their tutelary gods, keeping the lamps alight before their images, and celebrating magic rites.

Meanwhile, Gesar transformed his horse into a crystal *dorje* and himself into a beautiful goddess of the Padma Sambhava paradise. Under the guise of this engaging feminine personality, the Hero rode through the air on the translucent *dorje* to the Mutegspa fortress and presented himself before Padma Chös Tso.

'Sister,' he said to her, 'I come from Zandog Palri. Our spiritual father, the Precious Master, has deputed me to give you, on his behalf, this crystal *dorje*. Treasure it carefully. It is a male courser (*sic*); you will need it. Above all else, it will be useful to you one day.

'In Padma Sambhava's kingdom, my mother is Dewa Tungk-yong, your celestial mother's sister. Do not be distressed at having been born among the Mutegspas; you were destined to accomplish a necessary task, and the Precious Guru informs you that you have only a few more days to live here.'

Padma Chös Tso was overjoyed on hearing these words. To begin with, she was enchanted at possessing the crystal *dorje*, then, mistaking the meaning of Gesar's last statement, she thought she was soon to die in this world to be born again in the paradise where she had lived in her previous life.

The sham goddess continued:

'I know that the Mutegspas possess medicines of immortality that are concealed in a sandal-wood box, the turquoise key of which is in your keeping. The Precious Master has told me that whosoever looks upon them and pays them homage is freed from the cause of death (becomes immortal). I beg that you will let me see them before I go back to Zandog Palri.'

'You shall do so,' answered the young girl. 'Our mothers are sisters, therefore we are also sisters.[1] Moreover, you have been sent here by our spiritual father; these are sufficient reasons why I should

---

[1] In Tibet, cousins and second cousins call each other sister or brother and are considered as such. Marriage between them is regarded as incest.

willingly accede to your request. Know, however, that no other but you would make me open the casket that contains these medicines. They hold the vital essence of the one who, in this world, is my father: Lungjags Nagpo, and nobody has ever been permitted to look upon them. Nevertheless, it is written in the books of prophecies that the Tibetans will one day seize them; but no doubt that day is still far distant.

'Now, have a meal with me and then I will take you to the room where the sandal-wood box lies. However, be very careful that no one becomes aware of your presence here.'

Padma Chös Tso served the goddess with many and varied dishes, sweet and pleasing to the taste. She afterwards led her to the casket, which she opened with its turquoise key, and, lifting a piece of embroidered silk, exposed the medicines to view.

By means of his magic power Gesar seized them without their young guardian becoming aware of the fact, and left perfect imitations in their place.

When Padma Chös Tso had relocked the casket, now emptied of its treasure, she returned to her room with her celestial relation and, placing in the latter's hands a superb turquoise, asked her to offer it on her behalf to Padma Sambhava to thank him for the crystal *dorje* that he had sent her.

'This turquoise,' she explained, 'is one of the ornaments of the nine-headed Brahmā[1]; it is one of the rarest jewels that the Mutegspas possess. Place it at the feet of our spiritual father and tell him Padma Chös Tso prostrates herself before him and asks his blessing.'

The goddess took the jewel, and, carrying hidden on her the medicines that she had stolen, rose in the sky and in the twinkling of an eye reached the 'luminous sunlit cave', where she once more became Gesar.

Three days later, the Hero created five phantoms (*tulkus*) by his mind, his word, his body, his knowledge and his actions. Four of these respectively placed themselves in front of the four gates of the Mutegspa citadel: at the eastern gate stood the *tulku* of the Body, at the northern gate that of the Word, at the western gate that of the Mind, at the southern gate that of the Knowledge. They collected a considerable number of sandal shrubs, piled a portion of them against the monastery walls, and threw the rest over it into the enclosure where the Mutegspas had heaped the medicines and

[1] As decoration of the statue.

medicinal trees. Meanwhile, the *tulku* of the Actions sought Padma Chös Tso in order to warn her and prepare her for flight.

At the four cardinal points, the *tulkus* that mounted guard before the citadel gates chanted a song in honour of their tutelary deities. Their sonorous voices shook the skies, but by Gesar's magic power the ears of the Mutegspas were closed, and they heard not the song.

The *tulkus* sang:[1]

Lu ta la la! A la la la! Ta la la!
I invoke you father Lama, Yidams, Kahdos,
Graciously hear me.
Bless me from the beginning and may your benedictions remain with me for ever!

Today I have taken the Mutegspa fortress at Menling Marcham.
I stand before its gate, I, the *tulku* of Tigsum Gompo, the chief of twenty-four divine heroes, the spiritual son of Guru Shenrabs, the enemy of the Mutegspa demons.
Ki ki ki la! Bu swa! Ki ki ki la!
I call to you, O Gods!

I invoke the Gods of the tenth paradise,
Those of the eleventh, of the twelfth, of the thirteenth, and those that are above them!

.   .

In the palace of the Supreme Victory, in a multi-coloured tent,
Ka ra ra!
He sits on a throne of white conch,
Ki li li!
On his head is a conch helmet,
He is clad in white conch armour
And carries a conch shield on his back,
     Ga ra ra!
On his right is a conch arrow,
On his left a conch bow,
On his right is a dadar,[2]
On his left is a halberd,
On his right is a tiger's mane,

---

[1] That which follows can give an idea of the heroic songs of the land of Kham (Eastern Tibet). These abound in the Gesar Epic, of which they continually interrupt the action. A number of them have been borrowed from the Bönpos.

[2] A ritual instrument: an arrow wrapped in many different coloured pieces of silk.

On his left a spotted leopard's skin
And in front of him a white conch horse
　　　Chib, chib, chib!

O thou, whom all the gods of the high paradises surround,
Sever the ropes of the Mutegspas who scale the skies,
Unloose the fierce summit winds to strike them to earth.

　　　　　　　.　.

In the palace where battle the wind and the clouds
The white mountain of the gods rises on the right,
The blue mountain of the Nāgas on the left;
In the centre is the red mount of the Lhamayins (Titans)
And in the heart of Ri rab[1] are jewels without number.

On the gold throne's yellow carpet
He sits wearing a gold helmet,
Clad in yellow gold armour
　　　Chi li li!
With a gold shield on his back
　　　Gni li li!
On his right is a gold arrow
　　　Cha ra ra!
On his left a gold bow
　　　Chi li li!
On his right is a dadar,
On his left a halberd,
On his right is a tiger's mane,
On his left a spotted leopard's skin
And, in front of him, a yellow gold horse
　　　Chib, chib, chib!
O illustrious Docha Ksertzog!
Bring the god who oversets our enemies,
Bar the way to the Mutegspas, that not one escape
Throw thy lasso over them!
　　　　　　.　.

In the shining palace of the Nāgas,
Seated on a throne of turquoise,
He is wearing a helmet of turquoise,
Clad in blue armour of turquoise
　　　Chi li li!

[1] Mount Meru of the Hindu cosmography.

118

With a shield of turquoise on his back.
    Ghi li li!
On his right is an arrow in turquoise
    Cha ra ra!
On his left a bow in turquoise
    Chi li li!
On his right is a hook,
On his left a lasso made from a serpent,
On his right is a tiger's mane,
On his left a spotted leopard's skin
And, in front of him, a blue horse in turquoise.
    Chib, chib, chib!

O Mighty Mathö, send the wind from under the earth to burn the Mutegspas; fan the flame that will destroy them!

Gods, ye who confound our enemies, hasten to us a hundred thousand strong.

In the four directions bar the roads to the Mutegspas, that not one escape and may their race be exterminated to its roots.

God of the burning Shang Shung Mountain, give strength to the wings of the flames that they may rise to the sky.

Great Hero, Tiger-God of destroying fire,
Fling thy lasso of flame over them,
Burn, today, the Mutegspas.
God of the winds, hasten here, blow upon the furnace,
Burn today the Mutegspas.

.   .

At the eastern tower of the flaming tongues of hatred,
O Wisdom, kindle the fire,
Still the pain of birth.

At the northern tower of the dark wind of anger,
O Wisdom, kindle the fire,
Still the pain of old age.

At the western tower of the billows of lust,
O Wisdom, kindle the fire,
Still the pain of disease.

At the southern tower of the immense cavern of pride,
O Wisdom, kindle the fire,
Still the pain of death.

Then, having composed themselves, the *tulkus* representing Gesar concentrated their minds on the *phowa*;[1] the mystic process by which the malevolent force that animated the Mutegspas would be transmuted into benevolent energy and their reincarnated spirits transported on to the path that leads to spiritual illumination.

When this rite was ended, Gesar, through the agency of the *tulkus* emanated from him, set fire to the monastery fortress at its four corners. The conflagration immediately assumed alarming proportions. The roar of the flames filled the ten divisions[2] of space with its sound. The enormous tongues of fire rose until they licked the sky, and the smoke, carried by the wind, darkened all the regions of the world.

Not a Mutegspa escaped, but by Gesar's powerful wish, their spirits were led to the abode of the Buddha of Medicine.[3]

While the Mutegspas ran madly hither and thither, vainly seeking an exit from the burning citadel, the fifth *tulku* formed by Gesar had rejoined Padma Chös Tso to safeguard her. The shrieks of the Mutegspas and the glare of the blaze made all explanations unnecessary. The young girl understood why the crystal *dorje* had been sent to her, and, mounting it, she rose above the flames. In an instant she reached Gesar's cave.

The *dorje* once more assumed the form of a horse, and the five *tulkus*, reuniting, were reabsorbed by Gesar, who alone remained visible with his courser.

Padma Chös Tso was petrified with astonishment.

'Since thou dost not know me,' the Hero then said to her, 'know that I possess the magic powers of Guru Padma Sambhava. My name is Gesar. I am monarch of the world, the protector of the Religion, and foremost among the conquerors of heretics. Formerly, in our paradisal home, we were linked in friendship. I have not forgotten it.

'I came from Ling to secure the healing drugs that the Mutegspas retained in their country and to put an end to their false teaching. I will make thee guardian of the collection of Sacred Writings that we shall find in the bronze palace.'

Padma Chös Tso humbly apologized for not having recognized Thubpa Gawa,[4] a son of gods, under his various forms.

---

[1] Details concerning the *phowa* will be found in the chapter entitled 'Death and the Beyond', in *With Mystics and Magicians in Tibet*.
[2] The four cardinal points, the four intermediate ones, and the zenith and nadir.
[3] A mythological being of the Lamaist pantheon.
[4] The divine being of whom Gesar was the avatar in this world. See Prologue.

She passed a week with the Hero, hidden in the 'luminous sunlit cave', each of them absorbed in meditation. At the end of that time Gesar commanded the people of the country to build many chörtens[1] on the site of the burnt monastery in order to prevent the Mutegspas from reappearing and preaching their false doctrines.

He then breached the great bronze wall by shooting at it one of his magic arrows, as Manene had directed him to do. In the interior of the palace, he found 'The Great Words' in one hundred and eight volumes and countless treatises of the 'Little Words'.[2]

Gesar, having assumed the appearance of a pandit,[3] preached among the Indians, Nepalese, and Kashmiris for twenty-five days. He gave Padma Chös Tso in marriage to King Dharma Mani, and confided to their care half of the Sacred Writings found by him, that they might spread the teachings contained in them.

In the meantime, Gesar had commanded a great quantity of medicines to be collected. There were sixty thousand different kinds, which he had packed in a thousand bales. He was about to consider how he could get them to Ling, when some Indian magicians and fairies offered of their own accord to effect the transport. They transformed themselves into five hundred vultures, and, grasping the packages in their talons, bore them away and by night deposited them on the roof of Gesar's palace.

Before the Hero's departure, magnificent presents were offered to him by the inhabitants of the country and the adjoining regions. After receiving their farewells, Gesar once more set off across the sky, mounted on his divine courser. His absence from Ling had lasted three months.

Gesar's subjects welcomed him with great demonstrations of joy. Nevertheless everyone marvelled, within himself, at seeing the King return alone and empty-handed, but restrained by the respect he inspired, not one of them dared question him on the subject.

The King, who knew their thoughts, invited his ministers on to the roof terrace of the palace. The chiefs, seeing it covered with bales, uttered exclamations of surprise and shouted to the crowd assembled

---

[1] Religious monuments.

[2] The 'Great Words' represent here the collection of canonical Writings that forms the Kahgyur (bkahgyur). The 'Little Words' must be the 'commentaries', namely: the Tengyur collection (bstengyur) and other philosophical treatises.

[3] A Brahman versed in philosophy.

at the foot of the residence. The people loudly blessed Gesar and the gods for the gift of the medicines, although they were unable to guess the mode of their arrival.

For many weeks, games, festivals, and banquets followed one after the other without interruption, then, having made a liberal distribution of medicines, Gesar once more retired to a secluded part of the palace.

Chapter 4

Gesar goes to the 'North Country' to kill King Lutzen—Lutzen's wife betrays
her husband in order to help Gesar—Murder of Lutzen—His wife falls in
love with Gesar—Gesar is bewitched.

SOME months passed during which Gesar remained in complete
seclusion, then, one midday, a ray of light coming from Zandog
Palri illumined his room and Padma Sambhava appeared before
him.

'Gesar,' he said, 'thy fifteenth year is drawing to its close.
Remember the task that thou hast to perform. Set about it without
further delay. Thou must start tomorrow for Lutzen's kingdom.'

However the Hero replied:

'How can I hope to conquer Lutzen, that giant whose tongue is
a living flame? He is known to be an expert and redoubtable
magician. His subjects, who are of the race of demons, are his
powerful supporters. To attempt to defy him would be useless.'

'Lutzen is a terrible adversary,' conceded Guru Padma, 'but thy
mission must be accomplished. It was in order to overcome him that
thou didst incarnate among men. The gods have promised thee their
aid, they will not forsake thee, and I, myself, will stand invisible at thy
side. Start at once.'

He disappeared enveloped in light, and, though the sun was
shining in all its splendour, the room he had left seemed plunged in
shadow.

Gesar immediately sent for his wife and told her of the command
that he had just received.

'For a long time,' he said to her, 'I have known of the task that
is incumbent on me concerning the King of the North. The moment
has now come to carry it into effect and to rid the earth of this
monster whose malevolent power increases day by day.

'I must start at once and, in order to avoid delay, I shall leave the
palace without informing the neighbouring tribal chiefs of my
departure. Go and quickly harness Kyang Gö Karkar with his gold

123

saddle and his bridle ornamented with turquoises. Do not lose a moment.'

Sechang Dugmo was greatly distressed at learning that her husband intended to leave her again for the purpose of undertaking an expedition so fraught with danger; nevertheless, she obeyed him.

When she had finished bridling the horse, she lighted lamps and burned incense on the altar in the 'room of the gods' (*lhakang*). Then, before Gesar rode away, she laid her hands on his courser's shining saddle and, invoking all her husband's tutelary gods, wished for his success. After which she opened the heavy courtyard door and the Hero went away alone, without having been seen by anyone.

The next day, however, news of his departure was rumoured abroad. When his mother and the Ling chiefs heard that he had quitted his apartment and had left the palace on Kyang Gö Karkar, they realized that he was on his way to attack the formidable Lutzen. Immediately they set out in pursuit of their King, hoping to prevent him from continuing his journey. But, as not one of their horses could rival Gesar's in speed, they were not able to overtake him until after thirteen days, and then only because he had stopped to meditate upon a plan of action.

Coming up with him, they at once surrounded him and, manifesting their great anxiety, tried to persuade him to give up his too daring project.

'Just think of your age,' said one; 'you are not yet fifteen.'

'Lutzen is a giant,' said another, 'his head reaches the sky while his feet remain touching the earth.'

'His tongue is a serpentine flame, as that of lightning,' continued a third. 'He will lick you, and you will be burned and swallowed in an instant.'

And they clamorously implored him to return with them to Ling.

Gesar silenced them and, in a tone that did not admit of rejoinder, declared:

'I came down from the abode of the gods expressly to destroy the enemies of the Religion. I received the order from Padma Sambhava and I cannot evade my task. It is useless to try and stop me.'

Then Lumo Dzeden (his mother the nāgī) spoke:

'O Gesar, golden god, what you say is the exact truth. The precious Guru came himself to the country of the Nāgas, and made me leave it in order to become your mother.

'One night, near Toyang Chamchema, a god descended from the

heavens and gave me a magic potion to drink. I miraculously became the mother of several gods, who vanished as soon as they were born. Then you came into the world one morning, when golden flowers blossomed through the multi-coloured snow that covered the table-land. Many times people have tried to kill you, but, always, even when you were buried in a deep pit, you have reappeared alive.

'We have both been destined for a work that we must accomplish. Go and be victorious.'

Placing her hand on her son's saddle, the nāgī silently and earnestly wished him success. Then she turned with the others towards Ling, while Gesar continued his way, alone.

Urging on his horse, he arrived next day near Mount Hachong Tsigu, where, in the distance, he perceived King Lutzen, who was wandering through the solitudes in search of a being to devour for his meal. I have never seen Lutzen, thought Gesar, I shall not kill him today, but I would like to examine him.

He transformed his horse as well as himself into a cairn, such as there are many along the mountain paths, and Lutzen, unsuspecting, passed near the two heaps of stones.

Directly he had gone, Gesar remounted his horse and, under their natural forms, man and steed reached the King's fortress.

The Queen, Dumo Mesang Bumche, was alone at the moment. The great door of the courtyard stood ajar, and Gesar, seeing her through the opening, called to her.

The Queen hastened along the balcony, which circled the court, to a window that overlooked the road to see who it was who dared to hail her thus.

Extremely surprised at seeing an unknown warrior, she questioned him:

'Who are you, O Chief with a shining helmet? Which is your country and what brings you here? How is it that the King has not devoured you? Around this castle no bird flies in the sky, no insect exists, and never a human being has reached here alive. How did you succeed in doing so?'

'It is a mystery that none must know,' answered Gesar. 'I cannot explain it to you in a loud voice for I might be heard. Come down to me and you shall learn all.'

The Queen, impelled by curiosity, left her balcony, thinking to join the stranger outside; but while she was descending the steps, he had entered the courtyard.

Dumo, more and more astonished at his audacity, remained dumbfounded before the calm majesty and imperious bearing of the unknown warrior.

'I am Gesar, King of Ling and Sovereign of the world,' declared the Hero, 'the son of Korlo Demchog and Dorji Phagmo.[1] Leaving the abode of the gods where I was Thubpa Gawa, chief of the magician sages, I incarnated by command of Padma Sambhava for the purpose of destroying the enemies of the Religion. Lutzen must perish by my hand; the hour has come and nothing can save him. O Queen, thou canst secure him an easier death by helping me in my purpose. Tell me what I must do that I may slay him at one blow.'

Trembling, Dumo replied:

'I know there exists an ancient prophecy according to which Lutzen will be killed by Gesar. He, himself, is aware of it. Nevertheless, I pray you spare him. He is my husband and my support; who will provide for me when he is dead? Go, that will be best. The King, he too, has powerful protectors. And the meaning of oracles is always doubtful. If you remain here, you will certainly be devoured by him when he returns home.'

Gesar drew close to her.

'Dumo,' he said in an insinuating voice, 'I possess incalculable riches. I am of the race of gods . . . a god myself, and an adept in the true Religion.

'I will take thee to my country. There thou shalt pass thy days in happiness and wealth, and when thou diest thou shalt go with me and rejoice in the felicities of the Western Paradise.

'Who knows what risks thou dost run in remaining here. Lutzen can cease to love thee; he is violent and cruel. . . . Once his love for thee disappears, thy life will mean little to him. Hast thou never thought that thy husband, this cannibal demon, might one day devour thee?'

Dumo felt tempted. The fear that Gesar had cleverly suggested to her, the prospect of a comfortable security with a king who was of divine extraction and fabulously rich, and, after her death, the joys of paradise to crown her agreeable existence, all these things combined in affecting her mind and undermining her conjugal fidelity.

'Are you telling me the truth?' she asked. 'If I were convinced of it, I could be useful to you; there is a sure way of killing the King and I would reveal it to you.'

'Dumo,' answered Gesar in a coaxing tone, 'dost thou not know

[1] These are the celestial parents of Thubpa Gawa who incarnated as Gesar.

that thou art beautiful, and that one cannot see thee without loving thee? . . . I have seen thee and I love thee. I am rich, powerful, and a hundred times handsomer than thy husband. Thou shalt be my wife in this life and, later, my companion for centuries without number in the lotus gardens of the blessed Paradise.'

The beloved of a divine hero, riches, sovereign state, paradisal delights . . . poor Dumo had never dreamed of such things. Her head was turned. Gesar gazed at her with his big black eyes, an enchanting smile on his lips. . . . The Queen was conquered.

'Come,' she said to the Hero. 'Come and rest.'

When Gesar was seated in the King's chamber, Dumo served him with tea, *tsampa*, and dried meat, and they talked amicably together. As soon as her guest had finished his meal, the Queen said:

'Now I must hide you. Lutzen is learned in divinatory practices (*mo*), and if by his science he should discover your presence here, he would immediately devour you.'

She dug a hole in the corner of the kitchen[1] and made Gesar get into it; then placing a copper cauldron over his head, she heaped stones and tangled brushwood round and about to conceal the cavity.

Near to the kitchen was a dark room, a kind of stable with iron doors. She shut Kyang Gö Karkar in there.

Dumo had hardly finished these arrangements when Lutzen returned. On hearing the sound of his horse's hoofs, she went down into the courtyard, took the animal by the bridle and led it to the foot of the steps, welcoming her husband the while, as is the custom.

'Here you are returned, Sir. Have you undergone hardship?[2] Have you had a pleasant ride?'

The King was in a very bad temper. He had come back furious from hunting. Not having found even the smallest living being that he could make his prey, his empty stomach cried famine. He sat himself down on his cushions and said to Dumo:

'Woman, today is a bad day. I could not find anything to eat. An inexplicable sadness weighs on my mind and, last night, I had a bad dream.

'I want to know if Gesar of Ling's power is increasing. Give me the box containing the dice and the books on *mos*.'

'What would you do if he became more powerful than you and

---

[1] Here, as it does in many Tibetan dwellings, beaten earth took the place of flooring. The kitchen appears to have been on the ground floor.

[2] *Kuchog la ogyais*, current expression.

invaded your kingdom?' asked Dumo, hoping in this way to divert her husband's thoughts from the *mos*.

'There exists a prophecy on the subject,' answered the King. 'Gesar will come here and I shall be conquered by him in a year of the Dog.[1] This is a year of the Dog; but is this the one indicated in the prediction, or is it the one that will come in twelve years' time, or the one that will come in twenty-four years' time, or one of those that will come in a more distant future? . . . Bring me the box so that I may question destiny.'

Lutzen's insistence filled the Queen with terror. She knew her husband to be a skilful *mopa* and did not doubt but that he would discover Gesar's presence in his home. All the same she was forced to obey, so she fetched the box, striving hard to conceal her agitation.

'Open it,' ordered Lutzen, 'and arrange the necessary articles before me. Above all, be careful not to let any wish, either good or bad, form in your mind during the time I am occupied with the *mo*. Such thoughts would influence and alter the result.'

Dumo's excessive fear turned into anger and she retorted irritably:

'All this is senseless. You do not understand anything about prophecies and *mos*.'

Nevertheless she took the books, dice, rosary, and other accessories out of the box and set them down on the table in front of her husband, wishing with all her might that he should not succeed in knowing of Gesar's presence in the palace.

Some moments passed, then the King pensively shook his head:

'The *mo* is bad,' he declared, 'absolutely bad. There is certainly an enemy hidden in the house. We must visit every hole and corner of it, and examine the earth in all the rooms. You will dig on one side and I on the other.'

Dumo felt death stalking her. If Gesar were discovered, she could expect no mercy from her cruel husband. She made another effort to avert the danger.

'What is the good of taking that trouble,' she rejoined, pretending to be still in a bad temper. 'It is not under the earth that one finds enemies. Yours is at Ling. Do another *mo* to see whether you have others elsewhere.'

Lutzen took her advice and on finishing the *mo*, declared:

'This one is in my favour (that is to say he has no enemies other than Gesar), but the first *mo* was thoroughly bad.'

[1] Denomination according to the Tibetan calendar.

Once more he threw the dice on the subject of Gesar, and the answer was bad again.

Is he alive or dead, he thought. If he is dead I have nothing further to fear, but I must make certain. And he continued to do *mos*.

'It is strange,' he said to Dumo after a time. 'I see Gesar in a dark place where the wind does not blow. On his head is a copper cauldron and a mass of maggots swarm about his feet. I cannot discern if he be dead or alive. . . . Perhaps he is being tortured by the King of the infernal regions.'[1]

Dumo feigned intense admiration.

'What a wonderful *mo*!' she exclaimed. 'There can be now no further doubt. Gesar is dead. The gloomy spot is one of the tenebrous hells, the cauldron is that in which the wicked are boiled, and the worms are those that devour their bodies: just as it is shown in our Temple frescoes.'

Lutzen agreed that this must be the meaning of the *mo*. Husband and wife then had some tea and afterwards went to bed. Dumo pretended to doze, but remained awake. In the night, when the King was in a deep sleep, she rose and went down to Gesar. She asked him to go up.

'What is Lutzen doing?' he asked.

'He sleeps,' replied the Queen.

Whereupon Gesar put on his helmet and magic armour, placed one of his magic arrows in his bow, and followed his accomplice to the first floor.

'Listen,' she said to him. 'On Lutzen's forehead there is a very white round mark, that is his vital spot. Shoot your arrow at it and he will die instantly.'

Gesar entered the room, which was feebly lighted by the lamp that burnt before the statues of the deities. His first arrow went straight into the white mark that the perfidious wife had described to him. The demon's head clove in two and he expired immediately.

Then Dumo, who, from the threshold, had witnessed the drama, interceded with Gesar on behalf of the spirit[2] of the dead.

'Lutzen,' she said, 'was always good to me. When he ate human

---

[1] The *nyalwas* are more properly purgatories than hells, for their inhabitants die and are reborn in other places. The Buddhists do not admit of the idea of an everlasting hell.

[2] This is not the soul as understood by Christians. It is impossible, here, to give explanations of the term that I translate approximately by 'spirit', but which more accurately signifies one of the multiple 'consciousnesses' catalogued by the lamaists. Explanations on this subject can be found in my previous books.

flesh, he gave me mutton for my meals. When he drank blood, he gave me milk. He provided for all my needs. I received from him dresses made of fine cloth, beautiful Chinese brocade, and cloth of gold, also ornaments for the hair and necklaces of precious stones. You declared that he was an enemy of the Religion, that is why I have helped you to kill him; but my intention was to permit you only to destroy his body. I crave pardon for his "spirit" and beg you to send him to the Western Paradise.'

'That shall be done,' answered Gesar. 'It is part of my mission to do so. The spirits of the demons whom I conquer must be enlightened and purified; good must take the place of evil.'

Then he approached Lutzen's inert body, whose 'spirit' at that moment was entering the *Bardo*,[1] and called to it. The latter, recognizing Gesar, came immediately.

'Son of good family,[2] listen to me attentively,' he said to him. 'Thou art near to the misty region, which is full of misleading illusions, and where, for want of guidance, some wander for an immeasureable time[3] without finding the way out. Fear not, let thyself be led.

'Do not make for the purgatories towards which thy affinities, the result of thy bad actions, would draw thee. Do violence to the tendencies that urge thee to take this misty road, which, to thee, seems the easiest to follow. It leads to the worlds of suffering.

'Thou hast left thy body of flesh and blood; thy personality is no longer the same. Looking at this body, it now appears to thee as a wall with nine openings. Beware of entering any of them, mistaking them for the doors of various dwellings. Do not pass into the veins of the two legs, which resemble two twin trees lying on the ground. Descend not, raise thyself!

'Do not penetrate into the blue path of waters (the urethral canal). Raise thyself!

'Do not get entangled in the abdomen, which to thee seems as a marsh where winds an interminable road (the intestines). Raise thyself!

---

[1] According to the Tibetans, it is the condition in which the 'spirit' finds itself during the time between death and the new rebirth. A state in which it contemplates subjective visions. See chapter entitled 'Death and its Beyond', in *With Mystics and Magicians in Tibet*.

[2] Polite form of address borrowed from the language of Buddhist Writings.

[3] Opinions differ regarding the duration of the stay in the *Bardo*, some believe it cannot be for a longer period than thirty-nine days, others say forty-nine days, and, as seen from the above, there are still other views on the matter.

'Do not take the path of either of the two hands, which thou seest as valleys. Raise thyself!

'Do not climb the neck, which has the appearance of a wall against which leans a ladder (the vertebral column). Raise thyself!

'Do not creep into the mouth, which looks to thee as a half-open door that is lit up by the sun. Raise thyself!

'Do not venture into the region of the nose, full of crags and ravines. Raise thyself!

'Do not enter into the ears, which seem to be two copper caverns. Raise thyself!

'Three arteries are before thee. Do not make a mistake. *Uma, Roma, Kyangma* lead to different places. *Roma* does not go beyond the *Bardo*, do not follow it. *Kyangma* is a magic creation of the "Great Void", turn away from it. *Uma* is unlike the other two and is the best road. White on the exterior and red in the interior, it is without turnings, straight as the bamboo that grows on the mountains and, like it, has three nodes. On each of these sits a deity.

'Below, is the terrible Machig. Blue of complexion, she sits cross-legged, arrayed in a silk robe of many colours and adorned with "cemetery bone ornaments". In her right hand she holds a hand drum, in her left a sweet sounding bell. Lutzen, may thy spirit unite with her and, with her, rise to the second node.

'There, dwells the victorious white Dolma. Whiter than the whitest conch, covered with sparkling jewels, she is seated in the lotus position; with her right hand she points to the earth, placing the world in subjection, and in her left she holds a blue lotus and a crystal rosary. May thy spirit unite with her and, with her, rise to the third node.

'There, sits the Universal Mother. Her complexion is red. Her red hair, divided in four parts, hangs down her back, over her two shoulders, and over her face. At the top of her head burns a red flame. In her right hand she holds a blood-stained human skin, and with her left she puts to her lips a *kangling*,[1] from which she produces terrifying sounds. Her skirt is a tiger skin and her tunic is of red silk. Upright on an elephant, she dances frantically. May thy spirit unite with her. From her dwelling-place starts the path that leads to the Western paradise where reigns the red Amitaba. Proceed that way.'[2]

[1] Trumpet made from a human femur.
[2] The poem, in the whole of the preceding exhortation, has followed the liturgic wording of a lamaist office that is celebrated near the dying and immediately after the person's death.

Lutzen's spirit obeyed Gesar's instructions, point by point, as they were given. By this means he reached one by one the various stages indicated by his guide, and, transmuting his bad sentiments into beneficent ones, happily attained the Paradise of the Great Beatitude.

When he had arrived there, Gesar said to the Queen:

'Look! Thy husband is now among the blest inhabitants of the Western Paradise.'

And, by his supernatural power, he made her see Lutzen.

Duma prostrated herself at the feet of the Hero, exclaiming:

'O wonder of wonders! How great is your might, Lord. Deign now, also, to remember the promises that you made to me and to conduct me, afterwards, to this beatific abode.'

'Thy hour has not yet come, woman,' answered Gesar gravely. 'I shall consider, later, if it be possible or not for thee to follow the path that leads to beatitude. For the moment, I intend to remain here for some days.'

Dumo rose, crestfallen. The King of Ling had spoken coldly to her, from a height, as a master, and no amorous flame lighted his severe black eyes.

The next day Lutzen's warriors, who had learned that their King had been killed by Gesar, gathered in great numbers round the castle, intending to avenge their sovereign and to put his murderer to death.

Dumo, seeing them advance, anxiously inquired of Gesar what he was going to do.

'Saddle my horse and bring me my magic weapons,' he said. 'I am not of those who can be conquered.'

As soon as he was in the saddle, his divine courser rose with him into the sky and they appeared high above the warriors, who were filled with consternation at the sight.

Never can we kill such a magician, they thought despairingly. However, remaining faithful to their dead master, they attempted to avenge him by shooting poisoned arrows at the Hero. Not one of these reached him; but he, carried away by anger, drew his sword of flame from its scabbard.

Terrified at the sight of this supernatural weapon, the warriors prostrated themselves in token of submission, protesting their readiness to become his subjects and to accept the Religion.

Gesar spared them. The next day he distributed holy water and conferred an initiation on them.

All the people now desired to keep the Hero of Ling in the North Country and to have him for their King. Dumo, who was in love with him, wished it more than any of her subjects. As for the victor, his only thought was to evade the promise that he had given to make her his wife.

However, while he still lingered at the castle, the warriors found opportunities for slipping under his pillow some cushions on which they had sat and rested their feet[1] and some bits of straw with which they had stuffed their shoes. Various impure substances were also thrown into his tea and, because of their defiling effect, Gesar's mind became clouded. He forgot Ling, his mission, his own personality. Each night, he created a magic emanation, which resembled him exactly and which shared the Queen's couch; while she lived in happiness, believing that she possessed the Hero's love.[2]

Six years elapsed. By means of their spells Dumo and the warrior chiefs maintained Gesar's mental stupor, and in this way were able to keep him captive.

[1] To place one's head on a cushion, carpet, or on any other article upon which another person has sat or rested his feet appears abominable to the Tibetans. They look upon it as a serious offence to deceive anyone by giving him such a pillow, which they consider to be impure. According to them, the use of it can produce deterioration that can lead to illness or mental trouble. Many Tibetans even refuse to use as a pillow any cushion upon which they *themselves* have sat.

[2] According to the version sung in Ladak, Gesar really becomes Dumo's husband, and she has a daughter by him.

Chapter 5

Chenrezigs dissipates the effect of the spells that were keeping Gesar in the 'North Country'—He starts for Ling—Meeting with the ghost of his friend Gyatza, who had been killed by the Horpas—The Hero learns of the invasion of Ling by the Horpas, of Todong's treachery and the carrying away of Sechang Dugmo—He finds Singlen and his mother, the Nāgī, reduced to slavery by the traitor Todong—Gesar leaves for Hor in order to destroy the three demon-kings and avenge the defeat of Ling

GESAR would never have accomplished the remainder of his mission had not Chenrezigs the Compassionate appeared to him and, by means of a special *angkur*,[1] dissipated the effect of the spells that were darkening his mind.

The Hero awoke as from a long dream, and, deaf to the entreaties of those around him and to Dumo's weeping, at once started on his horse for Ling.[2]

When he arrived at the Zamling pass, he noticed with astonishment a number of *chörtens* that had not been there when he had passed over the mountain on his way to the 'North Country' six years before. These monuments, he thought, are those that are erected at the death of chiefs, lamas, or men of superior rank to contain their *tsa-tsas*.[3] Why are there so many? . . . Who then has died in Ling? . . .

While he was plunged in these reflections, a headless hawk flew

[1] Initiation, transmission of energy. See *With Mystics and Magicians in Tibet* and *Initiates and Initiations in Tibet*.

[2] In the Ladak version the way in which Gesar is delivered from the effects of the spells that have caused his loss of memory is told differently. Instead of receiving an *angkur* from Chenrezigs, two crows let their excrements drop into his mouth while he is in a faint. This makes him vomit, and in this manner he rids himself of the noxious drugs that Dumo had made him absorb. He leaves for Ling and Dumo follows him with her daughter. Arriving at a ford, she clings to the tail of Gesar's horse and the child clings to her. In the middle of the river the horse starts kicking and flings them both on to the bank from which they have just come, while Gesar lands on the opposite bank. In her anger Dumo kills her child and, dividing the body into two parts, throws the upper half to Gesar, telling him to eat it. She herself devours the lower half. Gesar burns the portion of the corpse that has been given to him and builds a monument over the ashes.

[3] These are miniature *chörtens* made in clay, with which, sometimes, as in the above cases, powdered bones of the dead have been mixed.

134

from the top of one of the *chörtens* and alighted for a moment on his head, then returned to its place on the tomb.

How very impudent of this strange bird, thought Gesar, and he placed an arrow in his bow.

'Dost thou not recognize me?' said the bird.

Gesar was extremely surprised; the torpor produced by the spells to which he had been subjected still overshadowed his mind, notwithstanding the *angkur* that he had received from Chenrezigs, and he failed to recognize who it was who was speaking to him.

However, his divine horse, which had laid itself on the ground, said in a sad tone:

'O Gesar, we have both been sent on earth by the gods to accomplish a mission that requires the exercise of a superior intelligence. And lo! you are unable to discern in this headless hawk the spirit of Gyatza, son of Singlen, with whom, in Ling, you were united by fraternal affection. What difference is there between you and an ordinary man? . . .

'The *chörten* on which the bird is perched has been raised to the memory of Gyatza, whose head has been carried off to Hor. You, living, do not recognize your friend; but he, dead, has recognized you. You have not said one single friendly word to him. Instead, you have wished to kill him. . . . Call him, and he will tell you about Ling's misfortunes and what has taken place there while you remained in the North Country.'

Gesar hastened to call the bird and, weeping, presented him with a white silk scarf, asking his forgiveness for not having realized who it was who had appeared in this strange guise. Then, he told him how, in the land of the demons, he had been the victim of witchcraft.

The hawk came at once and perched itself on Kyang Gö Karkar's saddle.

'So,' continued the Hero, 'thou art dead, my brother Gyatza. But why dost thou wander in the *Bardo*? Why did thy spirit not proceed to one of the paradises, or, if it could not obtain a divine body, why did it not reincarnate in a human form? Even if thou hadst by necessity to be reborn among the birds, surely there are many not wanting in grace and fine plumage. Why a hawk, and why one without a head?'

'Brother,' replied Gyatza, 'do not grieve over me. I did not reincarnate in a human form because such a body would have been of no use to me. I could have gone straight to the Western Paradise, but I wanted to await thy return, to see thee again, and to make certain that thou wouldst avenge the men of Ling who were killed by the Horpas. During the war that they made on us, many belonging to Hor also fell in battle and their deeds have led them to be reborn as rats. In becoming a hawk, their natural enemy, I have been able to destroy a great number of them. . . . But listen to what I have to tell thee.

'Soon after thy departure from Ling, Kurkar, the King of Hor, invaded our country at the head of a powerful army. Thy men resisted bravely and made a great massacre of their foes; but being vastly outnumbered, they were finally obliged to yield. I, myself, was killed at the door of thy home. Kurkar cut off my head and carried it away. It now hangs as a trophy on his palace walls; that is why thou seest this bird without a head.

'For some time Kurkar remained in the country, installed in thine apartments and revelling in his triumph.

'Thy wife valiantly defended herself against the conqueror, who claimed her as part of the booty. Not being able to defy him openly, she resorted to various ruses.

'She told Kurkar that before she could become his, she had, in order to fulfil a vow, to construct a *chörten* in *rima* (sheep and goats' droppings). She never succeeded in her task, because the dried *rimas* rolled and that which she built fell to pieces in the working. She hoped that during the time she was deceiving her captor thou wouldst return, but it was not so.

'Then, Todong, believing that Lutzen had devoured thee and that thou wouldst never return, thought it would be to his advantage to curry favour with the conqueror.

' "Do you not see", he said to him, "that this woman is trying to deceive you. Tell her to soak the *rimas* in wax, and they will stick together."

'It was the same with many other devices that Sechang Dugmo invented; Todong always hinted at a way by which to outwit her.

'In the end, Kurkar returned to his country taking thy wife with him as part of the spoil. And now Todong, after having ignominiously surrendered on every occasion, reigns over Ling as Kurkar's delegate and vassal.

'Notwithstanding his great age, my father Singlen[1] has bravely

<hr />

[1] Singlen, the King of Ling, had gone on a pilgrimage before the birth of Gesar and had passed for dead (see chapters I and II). When had he come back? . . . The very fact of the poem being sung in detached fragments permits the bards to dispense with any logical sequence of events. Singlen reappears and seems to have

withstood the Horpas and has not ceased to encourage the people of Ling to hope for thy return. Such behaviour enrages Todong, who finds it much to his advantage to reign under Kurkar's suzerainty. Also he treats his old brother shamefully; and, as to thy mother, he makes a servant of her.'

Gesar was overcome by sadness on hearing this account of Ling's misfortunes. But he soon recovered his assurance and said affectionately to his friend:

'Do not grieve any more, Gyatza, the brave warriors of Ling shall be avenged. I swear it, and Kurkar shall pay dearly for his temerity. I will not rest until I have destroyed him and the chiefs of his army.

'Now, my brother, leave this miserable bird's body, and go to whatever happy world it pleases thee to choose.'

Gyatza's spirit, reassured by the oath that Gesar had just made and certain that Ling would recover its independence, quitted the hawk's body (which fell inert upon the ground) and was immediately born again in the Paradise of the Great Beatitude.

After this encounter, Gesar continued his way to Ling. When he arrived at the place called Achenchunglung, he saw at a little distance a small boy who was busy skinning a wild goat that he had just killed. He watched him with pleasure; the child was pretty and worked with amusing intentness.

I do not remember ever to have seen this boy, thought Gesar, but it is six years since I left the country, and this little hunter must have been very young at that time. Gyatza had a son, he must now be about this youngster's age. Perhaps it is he? I will find out.

He took on the appearance of the dead Lutzen: a gigantic body resembling a mountain, a terrible countenance, and an enormous mouth out of which shot a tongue of flame. Transformed thus, he advanced towards the lad.

The latter looked at him without manifesting any fear, without even interrupting his work. He simply asked him:

'Where do you come from?'

---

been in regular intercourse with Gesar before the latter's departure for Lutzen's kingdom. It is possible that other bards than those I have heard, or other manuscripts than those I possess, mention circumstances connected with the return of Singlen to Ling and his relations with Gesar, who had become King in his stead. The information that I have gathered on this subject is vague. Therefore, provisionally, we must content ourselves with the knowledge that Singlen had returned to Ling and that he, as well as his son, Gyatza, had been on very friendly terms with Gezar.

'I come from the "North Country",' answered the demon.

'What is your name?'

'I am Lutzen.'

The boy looked at him with greater interest.

'Our Prince,' he said, 'set out a long time ago to kill you. Did you ever meet him?'

'I saw him and devoured him.'

'Where are you going to now?' continued the little man, without losing his calm.

'I am going to wander over Ling and eat its inhabitants.'

Only then did the young hunter abandon his goat. With quiet courage he placed an arrow in his bow.

'You have devoured my King,' he said, 'and now you also want to feed on my compatriots. I shall kill you.'

And he shot the arrow so expertly that it entered the giant's mouth.

The gigantic form of Lutzen was only a magic illusion. Gesar, on hearing himself threatened with death, quickly reduced his real being (textually 'his vital principle') to the dimensions of a silk thread. Notwithstanding this precaution, the arrow passed so near to it that the Hero nearly perished. He immediately made the phantom disappear and himself invisible.

Certainly, he thought, this extraordinary child must be the son of my dear Gyatza, whose bravery surpassed that of all the Ling warriors, and who would have faced no matter what god or devil. However, men gifted with such courage must possess a charitable heart in order to be useful in the world. Let us see if this lad has any kindness in his.

Gesar went away, still invisible, but reappeared at the turning of a valley in the guise of a poor pilgrim lama.

The young boy had not been excessively astonished at the sudden disappearance of him whom he took for Lutzen. This demon, he thought, is a clever magician, it must be impossible for a man to kill him.

When he saw the pilgrim coming, he never suspected that the same Gesar was returning to him under another form. This one had all the appearance of a *naljorpa* (an ascetic—a *yogin*) who was travelling for the purpose of meditating and celebrating the rite of *Chod*[1] in a hundred and eight cemeteries and other places of terrifying

---

[1] See the chapter concerning this curious rite in *Magic and Mystery in Tibet*.

aspect. He leaned on a stick surmounted by a trident, and a trumpet made from a human femur was passed under his belt. On his back he carried a little tent, a hand-drum, and a sack that held other articles used in the performance of rites.

'My provisions are exhausted,' he said to the lad. 'Give me something to eat. I shall read a book of the Sacred Writings in your intention.'

'My father has been killed by the men of Hor,' answered the child, 'and a demon has devoured my uncle,[1] our King. I am going to give you this shoulder of goat. Please recite the office for the dead and guide their spirits to the Western Paradise.'

The boy has a kind heart, thought Gesar, very glad that it was so. All the same, he just gave him a nod, took the meat, and appeared to continue his way.

* * *

Precisely as Gyatza's spirit had told Gesar, Todong was then reigning over the tribes of Ling. After the defeat of his compatriots, he had applied himself to the task of gaining the conqueror's favour, and the latter, in return for Todong's servility, had reinstated him in all the privileges that the ex-chief had been obliged to abandon upon the advent of Gesar.

Todong had never recovered from the loss of his supremacy, and the bitterness that he still nursed against Gesar held chief place among the reasons that had induced him to approach his enemy. Become the vassal of a distant sovereign, in reality a chief independent and absolute provided he sent the annual tribute demanded of the conquered, he was perfectly satisfied with his position, and his most fervent wish was that Gesar should never return. The fears that he had felt regarding the latter's possible reappearance had been gradually allayed. It was more than six years since the Hero had gone to attack the terrible Lutzen and from that time no one had had any news of him. Everything pointed to his having been killed, and the traitor's tranquility was almost assured.

Gesar, retaining the appearance of a religious mendicant, arrived in Ling. He found Singlen looking after the horses on the mountain and his mother gathering *tumas* (edible roots).

---

[1] Gesar, to whom Singlen's servant gave birth a little after the King's departure, passed as Singlen's son and the brother of Gyatza. Consequently, Gyatza's son regarded Gesar as his paternal uncle. The Hero afterwards adopted the boy and the present King of Ling claims to be the latter's descendant.

Without making himself known, he approached her and begged for some *tumas*, promising in exchange to recite a passage from the Sacred Writings. Lumo Dzeden politely inquired the purpose of his journey and, after both had exchanged the customary compliments, she said to him:

'It is now many years since my son Gesar left this country. Will he come back? Please do me a *mo* on the subject, and I will give you some *tumas*.'

'Very well, old mother,' answered Gesar, 'I will do a *mo*.'

After a sham rite, Gesar declared:

'A sign will be given to you. Throw into the air the sack in which you put your *tumas*. Your son will be at the place where it falls.'

The nāgī immediately thought that this unknown lama might be her son. She knew that he was skilled in magic, and that to change form was but child's play to him. She threw her sack into the air and, naturally, it fell at the pilgrim's feet. Now, almost certain that Gesar stood before her, but wishing to have the assurance from him, himself, she said pleadingly:

'I pray you tell me if you be Gesar. Many years I have wept for my child, not knowing if I should ever see him again. Why leave me in suspense?'

Gesar was keenly affected by his mother's sorrow and the tears she shed. . . . Suddenly, he showed himself dressed in his shining armour and carrying his celestial weapons.

The nāgī was overcome with joy, but soon the remembrance of all that had happened during his absence came to her mind: Gesar was no longer King, his kingdom belonged to Kurkar of Hor, and Todong exercised authority in the conqueror's name.

Thinking that perhaps her son was unaware of these sad events, she told him of the invasion of Ling by the Horpas, of the death of Gyatza and the thirteen other chiefs, of the carrying away of Sechang Dugmo by Kurkar, and of the plundering of all his possessions, which had been removed to Hor.[1]

When she had finished her story, she asked the Hero:

'What are you going to do now, you who are a god's son and the messenger of Guru Padma? Will you revenge yourself? Will you retake that of which Kurkar has despoiled you, or will you suffer this loss without attempting to recover it? . . . Oh! why were you so long

[1] When the poem is recited all these details are retold at length.

in coming back? You were to stay only one year in the "North Country", and you have remained away six years.'

'What you say is true, Mother,' answered Gesar, 'but when I had killed Lutzen, Dumo, the Queen, and the warrior chiefs wished to keep me. They gave me good things to eat and surrounded me with comfort. At the same time, by the power of their demoniacal sorcery, my memory became veiled. I forgot who I was. This year, Chenrezigs broke their spells, and on regaining my memory I left at once for here.

'Do not think any more about the sad past, Mother; Kurkar will not retain for long what he has stolen. As to you, return to your tent, and prepare me a meal and a bed. I will rejoin you soon, but first I must see Singlen.'

As soon as Lumo Dzeden had gone, Gesar took the form of a high-born chief, and produced some phantom men to act as his escort and servants. Thus disguised, he returned to the plain where he had caught sight of Singlen. On reaching there, they all (Gesar and his phantoms) got down from their horses, and the servants prepared tea.[1] When this had boiled sufficiently, Gesar hailed Singlen from afar:

'Hi! old father! Come and drink some tea!'

The old man approached and, having politely saluted and thanked the stranger, whom he took to be a foreign chief, said he had not his *phorba* on him.[2]

'That does not matter,' answered Gesar. 'I will lend thee one.'

He handed him a wooden bowl, which a servant hastened to fill with tea.

Singlen, instead of drinking, gazed at the *phorba*, struck by its resemblance to one that he had often seen Gesar use. A vague hope awoke in him and he smiled.

Gesar, who was watching, questioned him:

'Why dost thou look with a smile at my *phorba* instead of drinking thy tea, old father?'

'It reminds me of another,' answered Singlen.

And then, he related all that he knew about the childhood of the

[1] These *tulpas* or *tulkus*, magic creations, are capable, so the Tibetans say, of performing all the acts of which the person or the animal that they represent is himself capable.

[2] The Tibetans have the habit, when they travel or are out for the day, of carrying with them a bowl from which to drink tea. It is repugnant to them to drink from a bowl that another has used, and they only do so exceptionally. *Phorba* is pronounced *porba*.

one whom he called the great King of Ling,[1] never dreaming that the Hero himself was listening to him.

He recounted how Gesar had become King, the discovery of the treasures at Magyalpumra, the King's departure for the 'North Country', the invasion of the Horpas, the conquest of Ling. Then he went on to tell of his own misfortune and that of Lumo Dzeden, and the cruelty of Todong, now become their master. He concluded by saying that the resemblance of the *phorba* to one that had formerly belonged to the King seemed to presage Gesar's return.

The Hero appeared to listen with interest to the old man. But when the latter had finished, he shook his head, saying:

'If Gesar had been coming back, he would not have stayed away so long. My poor old father, there only remains for thee to recite some *mani* for him. He has most certainly been devoured by Lutzen.'

Singlen was greatly distressed at these words. The traveller, he thought, has probably seen Lutzen kill Gesar, or, perhaps, he has heard of his sad end from other witnesses, and he has chosen this indirect way of telling me about it. He began to cry and to beg the chief to tell him if he had seen Gesar die.

'I did not,' answered the Hero, 'but I am convinced that, as thou hast had no news of him for so many years, he is dead.'

'If that be so, there is no hope for us,' said the poor man, and his tears increased.

Gesar was filled with pity at the sight of such great anguish.

'Go and collect thy horses,' he commanded, 'it is late; then come to me again for a moment before taking them to their stables, I have something further to say to thee.'

The old man obeyed. When he came back with his horses, he saw, in place of the stranger with his suite, only Gesar, just as he had known him.

In an access of joy, he clung to the Hero's garments, saying a thousand incoherent things, crying and laughing at the same time, unwilling to let him go from him.

'My dear father,' Gesar said, 'you must return to Todong. In a few days you will see me again, but until then do not tell anyone that you have seen me.'

Singlen promised this; but, in spite of all his endeavours, he could not resume his habitual air of dejection. Laughing quietly to

[1] The same remark applies here as before; all the details are repeated once again.

himself, his eyes shining and his head held high, he returned to Todong, mounted on the latter's finest horse.

Todong, who was on his roof-terrace, saw him coming and was struck by his changed appearance.

Whatever can have happened to Singlen, he asked himself. One thing alone is capable of rendering him so joyous and triumphant: the return of Gesar. Can Gesar have come back? . . . Does my brother know of it? . . . That must be so. . . . What will the former King think if he sees that I send the one whom he treated as Father to look after my horses?

Todong was far from brave, and dared not assume the responsibility of his bad actions. He was seized with terror at the idea of the punishment the Hero could inflict on him if he came back. His only thought was to escape it. As quickly as his great stoutness permitted him, he descended the stairs and went to meet his brother.

Assuming his most gracious air, he welcomed him with these words:

'I am really pained, *ajo* (elder brother), at seeing you leading these horses. Do not be angry with me; I have not many servants and they have much to do, yet it is necessary to send the horses to graze. But it really tires you too much. In future, you will stay at home. Come up and sit with me and have some tea.'

He made Singlen enter his room, where he piled several cushions for him to sit on; then looking at him said:

'Your robe, *ajo*, is good enough for the mountains, but not for the house. I want you to be dressed as I am and for us to live on a footing of equality, as it befits real brothers.'

Whereupon he ordered his wife to bring one of his silk robes, and made Singlen put it on.

For three days the programme marked out by Todong was scrupulously adhered to. Singlen was overwhelmed with attentions. At meal-times they served him with huge pieces of boiled meat, his tea was plentifully buttered, and he drank a good number of cups of spirit during the day.

When Gesar arrives, thought the artful Todong, he cannot fail to be satisfied at seeing his adoptive father so well treated. He will take this fact into account, and I have great need of his clemency because of my relations with his enemy, the King of Hor.

Gesar, however, did not appear. Todong was puzzled. Could the joy that he had remarked in his brother have arisen from another cause than the one that he had taken for granted. He questioned him:

'The other day *ajo*, I saw you ride my horse and laugh as you entered here. Is it that Gesar is coming back soon?'

Singlen remembered the command he had received. He affected a sorrowful mien.

'Alas!' he answered, 'I have no news of him. Such a long time has elapsed since his departure that I have come to believe him dead. Sorrow troubles my mind. Do not be displeased about it, chief Todong, but I often laugh or do a thing without knowing it.'

This is quite possible, thought Todong. People who become a prey to great grief sometimes go half mad. It is probably the case with this idiot. And I, believing that Gesar would arrive shortly, have fed him as a king, installed him in my own room, and clad him in my most beautiful robes.

Anger seized him. Furious at having been his own dupe, he tore his robe off Singlen, kicked him up from the cushions on which he was seated, and railed at him unmercifully.

'Ah!' he cried, 'beggar, good for nothing fool! thou didst permit thyself to ride my best horse. I shall have thee fastened to the gate with my dogs, and thou shalt share their food.'

He pushed the poor wretch outside, and, in accordance with his orders, the latter was fastened to a stake beside the watch dogs.

Gesar had waited for this moment. Singlen had been chained up barely an hour when, clad in his shining armour and carrying all his divine weapons, the Hero appeared before the house of Kurkar's vassal.

Todong's wife, Kartzog Sertog, ran in haste to warn her husband.

'This will be my undoing!' he exclaimed. 'I was right in my surmise. Singlen knew of Gesar's return, and now Gesar has seen his adoptive father chained up near the dogs.'

He thought of running away, but it was too late. The Hero's horse had just stopped before the front steps. There was nothing left for the miserable coward to do but to hide. Instructing his wife to say that he was absent, he hastily undressed, threw his voluminous clothes into a corner, and crept, naked, into one of those big leather sacks in which flour or grain is kept.

Todong's daughter had meanwhile unfastened Singlen, whom Gesar pretended not to have seen; and Kartzog Sertog, after loosely tying the opening of the sack in which Todong was hidden, hurried down to welcome the King with a white scarf in her hand.

'I beg you to come upstairs,' she said.

As soon as he was in the room, Gesar inquired after Todong.

'Please seat yourself on the gilt seat,' said the woman. '*Kushog* has left for Hor. . . . Rest and drink some tea.'

'Very well,' assented Gesar without questioning her further. Then, as he ate and drank of what had been prepared on a table in front of him, he added:

'I come from a distant country, and I am tired. I will pass the night in the little house that you have close by, facing the plain. I will arrange my bed myself. I want it to be soft, so that I can rest well.'

'Why should you go to that little house,' protested Kartzog Sertog. 'It is dirty, for quite recently some goats were shut up in it. . . . Please stay here and sleep on the sandalwood bed. It is Kushog's. I shall arrange the cushions myself and you will be very comfortable.'

'Never!' exclaimed the Hero. 'How could I do such a thing? Todong is an avatar of Tamdrin;[1] if I were so lacking in respect towards him as to put my foot on his couch, such an act would bring me misfortune. No, no. . . . Look, these sacks will do very well, I can use them as a mattress.'[2]

Refusing to listen to any objections, Gesar began to push the sacks roughly about, rolling some of them towards the door.

'Let us be careful that the "mouths" (openings) are well closed,' he said, 'so that the grain does not escape.'

And, saying this, he more securely fastened the mouth of the one that contained Todong. He then seized it, carried it off, bumped it from side to side as he went down the stairs, and called to the servants whom he found in the yard to bring along the other sacks.

When he arrived at the little house, he had it swept; after which he arranged the sacks in the form of a bed, being careful to place the one with Todong inside at his feet. This done, he lay down to sleep, not without having first well kicked the miserable wretch, while pretending to roll himself up in his blankets.

During the night, a few vigorous kicks reminded the traitor of the reality of the situation, even supposing he could have forgotten it as he dozed, huddled up, half-suffocated, breathing through only a tiny tear that he had made with his nail in a spot where the leather had worn thin.

[1] See Prologue and Introduction.
[2] In Tibet, it is quite usual on long journeys, when provisions are carried, to use sacks containing grain or flour as a mattress in the tent. Poor people who have no cushions do the same in their homes.

As soon as it was dawn, Kartzog and her daughter, followed by several servants, brought tea, butter, *tsampa*, dried meat, curds, and placed them before Gesar, begging him to breakfast.

The two women, prey to a terrible anxiety, had not been able to close their eyes all night. They hoped that, if Todong had not come out of the sack and had not obtained Gesar's pardon, they could hasten their guest's departure, or, at least, get him away from the house so as to be able to release the unhappy captive. But Gesar, having amiably thanked them for the good meal that they had brought him, breakfasted slowly, stopping to chat between each mouthful, thus adding to the agony of his suffering hostesses.

When at last he had finished eating, he turned to Kartzog Sertog, saying:

'The soles of my boots are in holes. Please give me some leather, some thread, and two needles that I may sew on new ones.'[1]

'Do not take that trouble,' entreated Todong's wife. 'Come up to us and rest while you have some tea. You can give me your boots; I will repair them myself.'

'What are you saying, *aji lags* (honourable elder sister, courtesy title),' exclaimed Gesar, simulating great respect. 'Are you not Todong's wife? Never would I dare to put on boots that your hand had touched. No! No! I will remain here, only please send me what I need.'

There was nothing to do but to obey.

When he had the needles, Gesar pretended to examine the points.

'Are they strong enough to pierce the leather?' he said. 'Let us see . . .'

And he sharply dug both needles into the sack where Todong was hiding.

By a supreme effort the latter refrained from crying out, but he could not keep from moving. Gesar immediately leaped to his feet, and, staring at the sack, shouted:

'Wonder of wonders! Miracle! A sack of grain that moves! . . . Come and see all of you. The demons of Hor are here!'

Then seizing a club, he struck great blows again and again at the sack.

This time, Todong was unable to restrain himself, and he began to howl: 'Mercy! Mercy! Have pity. . . . Do not kill me.'

[1] Travellers often resole their own footgear while on a journey.

Kartzog Sertog, his daughter, and all those present fell at Gesar's feet, imploring him to spare the poor man.

Gesar, reseating himself, commanded: 'Pull him out of the sack.'

They hastened to obey him, and big-bellied Todong, naked, congested, half-suffocated, and trembling in all his limbs, was extracted from his prison.

'Miserable knave, liar, impostor, coward, and traitor!' exclaimed the Hero. 'It would have been better had you never been born. A man such as you is incapable of living according to the rules of the pure Doctrine (Buddhism). Yes, indeed, as incapable as is an animal.'

'Bind him,' he said to the men, 'and shut him up in the prison.'

In his quality of chief, Todong had in his house a room with thick walls and a heavily barred door that served as jail. It was there that he was confined by his own servants.

Gesar then left the hut where he had passed the night and returned to Todong's house. This time he installed himself comfortably on his host's bed and on the most beautiful of the cushions upon which he put his feet without troubling in the least about the respect due to an *avatar* of Tamdrin.

That night when the Hero was sleeping peacefully, he was awakened by a great light, which illuminated the whole room. Manene stood before him wearing a head-dress bearing the images of the five mystical Buddhas and adorned with flashing jewels.

'Gesar,' she said, 'I am Dolma.[1] Listen attentively to my words. Do not leave Todong in prison. He is Tamdrin's *tulku*: his power is great. Be circumspect in thy treatment of him. He either can be of great service to thee or he can place obstacles in thy way. Thou wilt act wisely in releasing him.

'Prepare to leave for Hor without delay. The road that leads to Kurkar's territory is dangerous; it is guarded by ferocious demons. Thou wilt only be able to advance step by step, by exterminating one by one those who oppose thy passage. Kurkar and his two brothers, Kurnag and Kurser (Kur the white, Kur the black, Kur the yellow), kings respectively of the three Horpa tribes, have sworn to destroy the true Doctrine and its followers. If these brothers are not killed by thee, the Good Law will disappear from the world.

---

[1] It has already been seen that Manene signifies grandmother and is a title, not a name. Therefore we have here: the grandmother Dolma. Dolma is the principal goddess in the Lamaist pantheon. She is the goddess Tara of the Hindus.

Remember the mission that thou hast accepted and fulfil it gloriously.'

Day was dawning. Manene disappeared.

Gesar immediately called Todong's wife and ordered her to bring her husband before him. The latter, set free, presented himself with a silk scarf in his hand. He offered it to the Hero, bowing politely as the custom required, but nothing in his bearing denoted contrition; the old rascal had already regained his assurance. During his confinement he had pondered over matters and had come to the conclusion that, since the King of Ling had neither had him put to death nor had him flogged, he would probably come out of the adventure without other difficulties than those he had already experienced.

'Why did you maltreat me and have me imprisoned, nephew?'[1] he asked quietly, and began to laugh.

Gesar replied in a severe tone.

'He who commits bad actions receives punishment in return. The wicked go to the worlds of pain (purgatories). Think it over. Nevertheless, today, I give thee back thy liberty. Assemble the chiefs and warriors. I wish to speak to them.'

Todong gave the necessary orders. The servants beat the drum that stood above the main door and decorated the walls with banners.

By degrees, the men made for Todong's house, wondering what could be the reason for this summons. The people were as yet unaware of Gesar's return.

When they beheld him, their joy was unbounded; they never doubted but that now the hour for vengeance had come.

With the chiefs came Chipön Gyalpo, who was five hundred years old.[2] He wore a robe of yellow silk and a Mongol hat ornamented with a plume and a ruby. When he walked, he leaned on a gold stick. He was a rich man and a wise one, who was much listened to at the gatherings of the chiefs and respected by the people.

He sent for some jewels, which he offered to Gesar, and inquired the cause of his long absence. He then related to him the unfortunate events[3] that had taken place at Ling and the sorrow of the people at

---

[1] *Tsao:* A term at once familiar and affectionate that is used by a man addressing another who is younger than he. It does not necessarily imply true relationship.

[2] We have already known him speak at the time of Gesar's departure for the kingdom of the North, then however this extraordinary age was not attributed to him.

[3] A fresh recital of all these events is given here.

their inability to withstand the onslaught of the immense forces belonging to the three Kings of Hor.

After he had listened, Gesar addressed those present, exhorting them to take courage.

'Manene appeared to me last night,' he said. 'Guru Padma and the gods are with us. They command us to start without delay for Hor. You must recapture the Queen Sechang Dugmo, that will be a good omen.

'The Kings of Hor, beginning with Kurkar, the most powerful of the three brothers, must be killed, together with their ministers and their demoniacal army. If they remain in this world, they will leave no place for the Religion and its followers.

'Let everyone prepare in haste. We will start tomorrow at dawn.

'The chiefs and the warriors shall all take part in the expedition, but not the other men. These last shall remain in Ling with the women and the herds.'

Chipön Gyalpo asked:

'Are all the chiefs to go without exception?'

Gesar considered:

'No,' he answered. 'Some shall remain with the people. To begin with, father, thou art permitted not to accompany me on account of thy great age. From among the others, only Chaikyu Kongpathagyal and Serwapönpo shall come with me. They will bring a hundred horsemen.'

The men then dispersed, each one to his tent. The rest of the day they spent in looking to their weapons, their clothes and their horses' harness, while the women packed the provisions.

The next day, before sunrise, the little troop of men and horses left Ling and, the same evening, reached the frontier of Hor.

Chapter 6

Gesar and his horsemen reach Hor territory—With the help of several gods, the hero kills a demon-bull that bars his way—Infidelity of Gesar's wife—Todong gives way to his greediness and is captured by a demon—Gesar drowns a hundred and twenty-eight boatmen—The phantom caravan.

THE boundary between the territories of Ling and Hor is marked by a *latza* (cairn), which is placed at the summit of the Hor Konkartao Pass. As Gesar and his men climbed the incline they saw an enormous *dong*[1] barring their road. The beast looked in their direction and appeared to be waiting for them. Its body had the dimensions of a mountain; its horns were of copper and emitted a flame at each point; and its tail, which the animal held raised in an attitude of anger, hung in mid-heaven like a dark thunder cloud.

Gesar immediately knew this fantastic creature to be a demon and that it would be useless to attempt to destroy it by any human means. He halted his little troop.

'Remain here,' he said to them, 'it is not for you to fight against such a being. I, the ambassador of Padma Sambhava, will attack it with the help of the gods and will slay it with my magic weapons.'

His men dismounted, tethered their horses, and sat down on the ground; while Gesar, riding Kyang Gö Karkar, rose high in the sky, sending forth cries of appeal to his tutelary deities.

Instantly, the three gods: Tung Chiung Karpo, Mital Marpo, and Lutug Ödzer, appeared. They were Gesar's brothers, who had been born respectively out of the head and the two shoulders of the nāgī, his mother.[2] Lha Tsangpa Gyaljin[3] accompanied them. Each of them held a lasso.

---

[1] Wild male yak. A huge beast which, in fact, is formidable looking. There still exist wild yaks in the grass deserts of Northern Tibet. These animals live in herds under the leadership of an old bull.

[2] See Chapter 1.

[3] The great Brahmā, who, in the poem, is differentiated from the nine-headed Brahma.

Tung Chiung went to the right of the beast, Mital to its left, Lutug in front of it, and Gesar behind it. Lha Tsangpa hovered above its horns. Together they threw their lassoes. Lha Tsangpa caught the monster's head, Tung Chiung its right foreleg, Lutug its left foreleg, Gesar its right hind leg, and Mitag its left hind leg. Then they all pulled, each at his own rope. The ground rocked beneath the animal's frantic efforts to free itself. Great masses of rock fell and rolled in all directions; the earth trembled and re-echoed as if an internal thunder had been unchained. In the end, with his bones broken, the demon sank down like the subsiding of a mountain.

The hundred horsemen, who had never ceased to look towards the top of the pass, saw the animal fall and Gesar call to them by signs. They hastened to him. With their swords and lances they gave the finishing strokes to the diabolical *dong*, skinned it, and divided the meat for carrying away.

After crossing the pass, they descended the other side and pitched their tents in a grassy valley, near a high peak of red rock at the foot of which meandered a stream.

'Do not light any fires,' commanded Gesar. 'The smoke might betray our presence here and announce our arrival to those at Hor. Abstain also from eating; if you take food you will be thirsty and you will not be able to resist the desire to drink. Then, in order to quench your thirst, you will go to the stream for water, and the bad spirits who inhabit the red rock will fall on you and devour you.'

The next day, before dawn, Gesar and four chiefs left the camp to reconnoitre the route, leaving the others behind.

Arrived at the top of a pass, they saw in front of them Mount Dorje Tse Gu (the *dorje* with nine summits). Some years before, after the defeat of Ling, when Sechang Dugmo had been carried away by Kurkar, she had taken with her several vases made for containing holy water and, while crossing this mountain, had secretly hidden them in a cavity in the rock. When Gesar comes, she had thought, if he finds these vases, it will be a good omen, one that will mean that he will conquer Kurkar and take me back to Ling.

At that time, Sechang Dugmo had loved her husband and had ardently desired his return, but as the years passed her feelings underwent a change. She became enamoured of her abductor, the mighty King of Hor, and had a son by him. Far from still desiring Gesar's return, she then persuaded herself that he had perished in his attempt to destroy Lutzen, and very restful and agreeable she found the certainty that he would not disturb the tranquillity she now enjoyed. . . . As to the vases hidden by her on Mount Dorje Tse Gu, she had forgotten all about them.

As soon as the mountain came into view, Gesar, by his divine clear-sightedness, knew of their presence. He dismounted and commanded those who accompanied him to go and fetch them.

'Look,' he said, pointing to a distant spot. 'You see that bluish rock close to the other very white one? Between them, you will find the *bompas*. I will await you here. Take my horse, and fasten the vases to his saddle.'

The four chiefs went to the place indicated, found the vases, placed them on the saddle, and retraced their steps. But, at a turning on the path, Kurkar perceived them from his palace and, pointing them out to those near him, said:

'Who can those people be who are passing up there leading a bay horse?'

All who were present looked out of the window, and Dikchen Shenpa[1] recognized the horse as Gesar's and the men as Ling Chiefs, but he remained silent.

A colleague of Dikchen Shenpa, Thonatsigö, another of Kurkar's ministers, likewise recognized the travellers.

'They are Ling Chiefs,' he declared, 'and I even know one of them personally, he who is leading the horse.'

Sechang Dugmo, who had also come to the window, exclaimed as she glanced at the mountain:

'It is Gesar's horse! . . . Gesar must be back! . . . '

Then, becoming suddenly afraid, she ceased speaking, for she knew her husband's great power and feared his vengeance.

'Have you any idea what it is that the horse is carrying?' Kurnag, the King's brother, asked her.

Dugmo realized that, according to the direction from which the travellers had come, they must have passed Mount Dorje Tse Gu. The memory came back to her of the *bompas* she had hidden there

---

[1] Dikchen Shenpa was Gesar's brother, one of the three children found in the sack that issued from the nāgī's navel. See Chapter I. He had been brought up by Kurkar and had later become his minister. I would remind the reader that the bard who recited the Gesar Epic to me, in Jakyendo, pretended to be a reincarnation of this Dikchen Shenpa.

and she related the incident, but said nothing about the sentiment that had prompted her to act as she had done.

Kurkar was very annoyed.

'Why have you never told me of these vases?' he asked his wife. 'I would have had them brought here. Perhaps there is some magic virtue inherent in them, which Gesar can use against me.'

The ministers counselled the King to dispatch troops immediately to mount guard on the surrounding heights, for they foresaw that it would not be long before the warriors of Ling showed themselves. Kurkar, however, decided against such precipitate action.

'It is not at all certain that the people of Ling think of attacking us. Perhaps they have simply come to retrieve those *bompas*, which, by some means or another, they discovered to have been deposited in that mountain. It will be sufficient to have their tracks secretly followed.'

While he was speaking, the four chiefs passed out of sight on their way to rejoin Gesar.

During the absence of the latter, the troops in camp, who had been fasting for more than twenty-four hours, were experiencing very unpleasant sensations. Their stomachs burned as if they were on fire, nevertheless they dared not disobey Gesar's orders.

Todong and a man named Kadar Chognie had remained in the Hero's tent and were as famished as their companions. They both loudly bewailed their lot and called the gods to witness their miserable plight. At length fat and greedy Todong could stand it no longer.

'There is some dried cream in Gesar's *tsampa* sack,' he said to Kadar Chognie, 'let us eat it.'

'What are you thinking about?' replied the other, panic-stricken. 'Our King is omniscient, he will know at once of our disobedience and theft. . . . Without doubt he has already heard what you have proposed to me.'

And he began to tremble, looking from right to left to see if Gesar, or some terrible deity in his service, was not appearing for the purpose of punishing them.

'Bah!' replied Todong, 'thou art a coward. The King is no more omniscient than I am. Did he know, while he lingered in Lutzen's kingdom, that Kurkar was carrying off his wife?'

'You are right, Chief,' answered Kadar Chognie. 'It is certain that he knew nothing about it.'

'Then go and fetch the sack.'

Todong's reasoning was not without force, but more forceful still were the terrible pangs of hunger suffered by his companion. The sack was opened, the dried cream voraciously eaten; then the two accomplices, replete, rolled themselves up in their blankets to sleep.

Towards the middle of the night, they both woke with a dry mouth. 'Go and bring me some water from the stream,' commanded Todong.

'Oh!' exclaimed the other. 'Have you forgotten about the demons who lie in wait in the red rock? They will devour me if I go near there.'

Todong again tried the effect of a few convincing arguments by way of inducing the warrior to go to the stream, but this time he failed in his purpose. Chief as he was, his subordinate absolutely refused to face the demons just to please him.

Bravery was not Todong's strong point; he did not care himself to venture near the dangerous spot. Once again, he rolled himself up in his blankets and strove hard to sleep, but he did not succeed any more than did Kadar Chognie. At last, unable to bear the discomfort any longer, he affected a confident tone and said to the latter:

'Come! I am Tamdrin's *tulku*, the demons will not dare to attack me; and, moreover, I possess magic powers capable of mastering them should they take such a liberty.'

Relying on his chief's assertions, Kadar Chognie followed him. As they gained the bank of the stream, the demon Sherigonchen, who was watching them, threw a lasso, caught both of them in its noose, and began to haul them up to his cave. The poor wretches, knocking here, rebounding there on the sharp surface of the rock, felt their ribs breaking.

Their desperate shrieks resounded as far as the camp, and everyone there understood that some of them had been seized by the demons of the rock, but no one had the courage to go to their rescue, for fear of sharing the same fate.

Meanwhile, profiting by the light lavished by a full moon, Gesar had continued his march during the night, and, on approaching the camp, heard the cries of distress. That is Todong, he thought, recognizing the chief's voice. He must have eaten my cream, and, on going to drink at the stream, have been seized by the devil of the rock.

With lightning speed he went to the paradise where his three brothers resided, obtained from there a thunder-bolt (magic *dorje*), and let it fall on the rock, which was immediately pulverized.

Sherigonchen and his two victims were flung among the rocky fragments. Gesar descended from the sky on his divine courser and touched the ground with the majesty of an eagle. The demon, as soon as he perceived him, fled in the direction of Hor, and was pursued by the Hero, who held in his hand his magic lance. Sherigonchen, seeing that he could not escape, threw his lasso at him, but missed his aim. Gesar laughed.

'Know,' he said, 'that I am Gesar of godly race, King of Ling and Sovereign of the Universe. The lance that I have in my hand has not its equal in any world. I am going this instant to slay thee with it.'

As he said this, he thrust the lance with such force that the devil was cloven in two.

The Hero then went back to his camp and said to the men:

'We cannot be seen from Hor in this place, therefore light the fires and make tea. You can now go in safety to get water from the stream.'

'O precious King!' cried the people of Ling, 'how great is your power, and how fortunate that you came in time to save Todong and Kadar. Without you, they certainly would have perished.'

'Did I not forbid you to eat anything, in order that you might avoid thirst and the temptation to go and drink at the stream?' replied Gesar. 'But these two fools have disobeyed me, they have dared to open my sack and eat my cream; also speedily have they paid the penalty of their bad actions. Be sure that whoever disobeys my commands will be severely punished.'

Then they all assembled round the lighted fires, drinking tea and eating *tsampa* and butter. As for Todong and Kadar Chognie, they retreated into the corner of a tent, unable to stand upright, aching in all their bones, and very ashamed of the humiliating results of their gluttony.

The men passed the next day in eating and resting. Towards evening, Gesar called the chiefs to his tent.

'We are going to continue our march to the capital of Hor,' he said, 'but we will not all start together. I shall go first. On the other side of the pass a steep descent leads to the bank of a big river, the surroundings of which are haunted by malevolent beings. It is necessary that I first destroy these enemies, for you would not succeed in overcoming them.

'Remain here, ready to leave, and as soon as you see a white rainbow appear in the sky, hasten to rejoin me. This sign will denote that the road is clear.'

Gesar left at dawn next day. When he was out of sight of the camp, he took on the appearance of a pilgrim lama who carried a little drum on his back. He also created a herd of phantom animals: horses, mules, yaks, all laden with merchandise, and, driving these in front of him, proceeded on his way.

Arrived at the river, he stopped at the landing-place, where leather boats were kept for the purpose of ferrying travellers across. He unloaded his beasts and asked passage for himself and his merchandise.[1]

At this spot there was a hamlet inhabited by one hundred and twenty-eight boatmen. They were greatly surprised at seeing so many beasts of burden driven by one man. Some of them thought the fact suspicious and reminded their colleagues that a prediction existed according to which Gesar, after having vanquished Lutzen, would conquer Hor. And they added:

'May not this strange lama be Gesar himself, disguised?'

Some of them went up to the stranger and asked him:

'Where do you come from, lama? What is your country?'

'I am a native of Tsang and a disciple of Lama Ödzer Gyaltsen,' answered Gesar. 'King Kurkar is his benefactor (*jindag*), and, in return for the gifts that my Master has received from him, he is sending him various presents.'

Lama Ödzer Gyaltsen's name was known to all the Horpas. But one of the boatmen retorted:

'The precious Lama Ödzer Gyaltsen is rich and powerful, how is it that his messenger travels alone and without servants? We will not ferry you gratis to the other shore. How much will you pay us for your passage?'

'I am not alone,' replied Gesar. 'I am simply in advance of the others. Eight great merchants accompany me. They will reach here shortly and will settle the cost of the transport.'

The boatman seemed satisfied with this arrangement.

---

[1] As is the custom in Tibet, the unloaded and unsaddled beasts have to swim across the river.

'All right,' he said, 'we will ask our Chief's permission to take you across.'

Accordingly he went to find Sangyais Chab, the Chief, to inform him of the arrival of a caravan sent by Lama Ödzer.

Now, Sangyais Chab was the *tulku* of one of the *dubthobs* (magician sages), friends of Gesar, in the paradise that the latter had left in order to incarnate on earth. He had assisted at the meeting presided over by Padma Sambhava, during which Gesar's present incarnation and his own had been decided upon. He also knew of the prophecies that announced the conquest of Hor by the Hero, and he wondered if this lama who was leading so many animals might not be Gesar carrying out a stratagem.

'I will see to this affair myself,' he said to the boatman, and he went to the bank of the river, followed by his ferrymen.

After having exchanged with him the usual civilities, Gesar repeated the same story that he had already told the men. Sangyais Chab appeared to listen attentively, but on looking at the speaker he had noticed, between his eyebrows, a little round white mark, from which grew a single hair, straight as an incense-stick. It was the faint trace left of the third eye that Gesar had had when he was born and that his mother had put out with her thumb. This mark was not visible to the boatmen, who belonged to a race of demons, but the *dubthob*, by his clearsightedness, had immediately discerned it, and, becoming certain that Gesar was before him, inwardly rejoiced.

'Very well,' he said, without letting anything appear of what he felt, 'they shall ferry you across with your luggage.' And, as the sham lama had insisted that the transport should be effected rapidly, he gave orders for all the boats to be used.

While the men were busy loading the bales of merchandise, Gesar asked for something to eat. Sangyais Chab took him to his home and served him with tea, beer, boiled meat, butter, and *tsampa*. He understood that Gesar knew the ferrymen to be demons and that he had come to destroy them. Yet he wondered how the Hero would achieve his purpose.

Meanwhile, the hundred and twenty-eight ferrymen had loaded their hundred and twenty-eight boats. They then paddled their craft into the stream; but, no sooner did they reach the middle of the river, than a sudden squall swept up it, overturning the frail boats and throwing the men into the water. The strong current quickly caught them and all the demons were drowned.

157

At that moment a white rainbow appeared over the Ling camp.

Sangyais Chab, who had gone out with Gesar after the latter had finished his meal, saw the disaster and said to his guest:

'I believe you are a god and Gesar in person, but why have you killed those boatmen?'

At these words Gesar reassumed his natural form and answered:

'I have as mission the conquering of Hor. I shall continue my route today and nothing shall prevent me.'

And instantaneously all the phantom animals vanished, only Gesar and his horse remained at the water's edge.

Soon after, the men of Ling rejoined their chief, and Sangyais Chab, seeing Gesar surrounded by so many brave horsemen, was filled with joy.

'Warriors of Ling,' their King said to them, 'I have just destroyed the pernicious beings who dwelt on the banks of this river; the passage is now free. Nevertheless, thanks to the clearsightedness that I owe to my divine nature, I know that the Horpas are on the alert, ready to attack us. It would be imprudent for you to show yourselves. Return therefore to Ling. Take Sangyais Chab with you and see that he is treated with deference and that he does not want for anything pending my return. Alone, I must accomplish the conquest of Hor.'

In obedience to their chief's command, the horsemen turned back, and, as soon as they had disappeared from sight, Gesar, mounted on Kyang Gö Karkar, crossed the river at a bound. Continuing his way, he came to the plain that lay in front of Kurkar's palace. It was a grazing-ground reserved for the King's horses, and people were strictly forbidden to camp there.

Just before reaching this place, Gesar had created a great many magic people, animals, and things, which together formed a large and rich caravan composed of lamas, nobles, merchants with their servants, and numerous tents. The number of horses and mules amounted to two thousand five hundred.

This magnificent caravan issued from a valley and, pouring over the plain before the palace, spread far out to the foot of the mountains.

On the highest part of the ground stood the lamas' tents: white, double-roofed, and much ornamented with blue and red arabesques. A little below, rose the magnificently decorated assembly tent, capped with a gold emblem (*gyaltsen*). Then came the noblemen's tents, furnished with thick cushions over which were thrown tiger and leopard skin carpets. The servants occupied special quarters close by.

Farther down, towards the bank of the stream that crossed the plain, were the traders' great tents, full of merchandise. The servants belonging there, also, had separate quarters not far off.

Finally, on the actual bank of the stream, a few tents served as shelter for the poor pilgrims and the beggars who followed the caravan. In each section of the camp there were tents exclusively reserved for the women.

Kurkar was greatly astonished at seeing this extraordinary caravan encamp in front of his palace. Who can these people be? he asked himself. They are very bold in daring to establish themselves before my walls without asking my permission. And, calling Dikchen, he commanded him to go and make inquiries.

The minister started at once, riding a red horse. Soon after he had crossed the stream he met a servant who was descending a slope leading five beasts to water.

'Oi![1] thou turbanned servant, come here! Tell me, who are thy masters? Where do they come from? Where are they going? Who is the great lama who lives in the beautiful tent, up there?

'This ground is reserved for the King's horses, no one has the right to come here. To pull up a blade of this grass is equivalent to breaking a silver spoon, and the value of two blades of grass is estimated at that of a gold one. You must pay the price of both grass and water.[2]

'The best thing for you to do is to go away at once and camp elsewhere. If you insist on remaining here, the King will send his soldiers to enforce obedience and they will seize your merchandise.'

The servant replied:

'O thou who dost question me from the height of thy horse, know that some of the masters come from India, among them is Lönpo Pekar; others come from Jang with Yula Tongyur; and others again from the land of Sindh with Kula Tobgyal. The beautiful tent that dominates the camp is that of the Pentchen (learned Ödzer Gyaltsen).

'There exists no place on earth where, in our travels, we did not

---

[1] Oi! is an interjection used in calling a servant or anyone whom one treats as an inferior.

[2] In a great number of places in Tibet, when a caravan camps near a village or on pasture land owned by herdsmen whose encampment is near, the villagers or the herdsmen claim payment for the grass and water consumed by the travellers' animals.

live free and without restraint. No one has ever demanded of us the price of either grass or water. We shall not pay for anything. The King can send his soldiers, we do not fear them. We will kill them and destroy his town.'

As he said the last words, he gave the red horse so violent a kick that both beast and rider were sent rolling down the grass slope to the edge of the stream.

Dikchen, feeling very bruised, picked himself up and, while rubbing his sides, thought: Never have I come across a man possessed of such strength. It must be Gesar himself. His coming does not portend any good for Kurkar. What must I do? . . . This King has treated me with kindness ever since my childhood, it is my duty to warn him of the danger that threatens him. If I fail to do so, I shall have rebirth in a bad world.

Whereupon, deciding to communicate his impressions to Kurkar, Dikchen returned at once to the palace.

'Sire,' he said to the King, 'an extraordinary thing has happened to me. A man whom I took for a servant has, with a single kick, overthrown the horse that I was riding. This feat is not the act of an ordinary mortal. Without doubt this caravan has brought Gesar and, probably, with him, his friends the gods. Take my advice, escape as quickly as possible, in no matter which direction. Misfortune will befall you if you defy Gesar!'

'Bah!' replied Kurkar, 'if Gesar is really here, he is alone. I know his talents as a magician. The people and beasts who appear to be with him are only phantoms created by him.

'My brothers and I, we can together muster an army of a hundred and eighty thousand soldiers. There is nothing to fear. I shall ask Kurser and Kurnag to send their troops, and we will kill Gesar, great sorcerer though he be.'

Sechang Dugmo, who assisted at this conversation, intervened:

'Wait,' she said, 'I will go, myself, and make inquiries. Gesar bears a distinguishing mark; a white hair that stands erect between his eyebrows. If it is there, I shall recognize it.'

She had a 'blue' horse (grey must be understood) saddled and started. When she arrived near the spot where Dikchen had met the man who had so summarily routed him, she saw a servant dressed in white and wearing a turban Indian fashion coming towards her. She asked him questions regarding his masters similar to those to which Dikchen had already received answers, but added:

160

'One of you had the effrontery to cause minister Dikchen to fall off his horse. King Kurkar is very angry. He intends to assemble an army of one hundred and eighty thousand men and to destroy you utterly down to the last one.

'I am Dugmo, a follower of the Good Doctrine, and I have come to intervene in order to prevent such a disaster. You must pay the price of the grass and water, and with gifts make your apologies to the King for the insult offered to his minister.'

'Elder Sister,'[1] answered the man, 'I am only a servant. I do not understand anything about these matters, but I will tell my masters what you say.'

He went away and entered a tent, pretending to speak to someone in it; then reappeared and came back to Sechang Dugmo.

'Elder Sister Dugmo,' he said, 'my masters Lönpo Pekar, Yula Tongyur, and Kula Tobgyal invite you to come up and see them.'

The young woman followed the messenger and was ushered into the tent. Her first care was to look attentively at the men who were present, and, on not perceiving on any of them the sign about which she had spoken to Kurkar, she concluded that Gesar was not there.

She politely offered scarves to the three travellers, inquired if they had had a good journey, and exchanged the usual compliments with them.

One of the three, whose face was blue[2] and who was seated in the place of honour, asked after Kurkar's health, and added:

'So you are the beautiful Sechang Dugmo. I have heard people speak of you. Drink some tea and eat something. You will present a scarf on my behalf to Kurkar and tell him that I think of remaining here about six days.'

'What do you offer as present to the King?' inquired Dugmo.[3]

'We will show you,' answered the chief.

The attendants were sent for, and having received their masters' instructions, they had several boxes brought. These they opened,

---

[1] *Aji.* A polite term when addressing a woman who is not of high social rank. To employ it when speaking to a noblewoman, as was Dugmo, was insolence on the part of the servant.

[2] This may simply mean that the man had a dark complexion.

[3] This singular demand is quite in accordance with a Tibetan custom. When you call upon a Government official or a lama, it is usual to let his servant know beforehand what you are going to offer him; otherwise you are asked the question: 'What have you to offer?' You are then received, more or less ceremoniously, according to the value of the presents you bring.

showing Dugmo a gold saddle with a gold bridle, two iron chains with an enormous iron nail, eight copper nails, a sword made of iron fallen from the sky, and a pair of gold ear-rings.

'The ear-rings are for you, elder sister Dugmo,' continued the blue-faced man. 'I offer all the other things to Kurkar.'

After having thanked him, Dugmo took out her ear-rings, which she placed in a fold of her belt, and fastened in her ears those that she had just received. Then she went back home, followed by several men who carried the boxes containing the strangers' gifts.

'Gesar is not there,' Dugmo said to Kurkar as soon as she saw him. 'These people accompany Lama Ödzer Gyaltsen Rimpoche. Far from being enemies, they have sent you presents.'

Kurkar looked at the articles that had been placed before him, and was relieved to find there was nothing to fear from the new-comers.

'Dugmo,' he said, 'tomorrow thou wilt go back to the camp with thy servants. They shall take beer to these foreigners, and thou wilt invite them to come and take their meal here the next day.'

On hearing this, Dikchen, who was still convinced that the caravan was a magic illusion created by Gesar, said to himself: O Kurkar, thou poor fool! dost thou not see that Gesar has sent thee instruments emblematic of thy defeat, which will be used in his plans against thee. But he kept these reflections to himself.

Nevertheless, Tobchen, another minister, expressed his surprise:

'What singular presents these people have sent,' he remarked. 'I think the King would do well to give his mind to an examination of these objects. Apart from the saddle, it appears to me very unusual to offer such things as gifts.'

'What Tobchen says is wise,' agreed Kurnag, brother of the King. 'The presents are strange. I suspect them of possessing a hidden meaning. They are not tokens of friendship, but bearers of veiled threats. I am very inclined to think that they come from Gesar. He will put the saddle on your back, and will drive you with the bridle; it is a symbol of your subjection. The chains will be attached to your walls to help in the escalade. The nails will be driven into the hearts of your ministers. As to the ear-rings, with which Dugmo has adorned herself in such haste, they signify that Gesar will recapture her.'

'You ramble, my brother,' retorted Kurkar, irritably. 'Your gloomy predictions lack common sense. Leave to the lamas the task of unveiling the future, it is not your business. Tomorrow, as I have commanded, the women shall go and take beer to these chiefs.'

No one dared reply. The King and the people of the court then took their evening meal, and, soon after, everyone retired to rest.

Chapter 7

The phantom caravan disappears—Discovery of a little boy in a heap of tea leaves—He is adopted by a master-smith—The child's extraordinary behaviour—The magic dolls—Gesar destroys the patron gods of Hor—Tragic ending to a sports fête—The smith's daughter detects Gesar in the person of her father's apprentice—The Hero shows himself to her for a second under his natural form—By Kurkar's order, the young smith brings him a live tiger, which he has captured in the forest—Commotion in the royal household caused by the animal—It devours the prime minister—Kurkar commands the apprentice to take the beast back into the forest

DUGMO left the palace at dawn next day, followed by a number of women carrying pots of beer. A white fog formed an opaque curtain between the high ground of Kurkar's residence and the plain where the strangers camped. As Dugmo and her companions reached the camping ground, the mist lifted. Clouds, like fringed scarves, slowly crept up the mountains, and then, to the women's astonished gaze, the great grass valley appeared in front of them, empty and desolate.

Not a trace was left of the tents, of the many travellers, of the animals. Not a blade of grass showed signs of having been trodden underfoot the previous day. Nothing, anywhere, revealed the place where the caravan had passed. Yesterday, thought Dugmo bitterly, I allowed myself to be taken in. All that display was a product of Gesar's magic power; he made game of me.

While she, vexed and anxious, remained in deep thought, her women dispersed in every direction, trying to find traces of the caravan and of the way it had taken when leaving the ground. It was thus that a young girl named Gartza Chösden came across a huge pile of tea leaves, which had been thrown there when the men emptied their tea cauldrons. She gave the heap a kick or two, saying to one of her companions:

'These people must be really very rich to be able to use such a quantity of tea.'

The kicks she had given caused the leaves to fall away at one spot and expose to view a little boy who had been half-buried under them.

The child, indescribably filthy, was covered with vermin, which played about in his matted hair, his nose ran, and he moaned as he rubbed his eyes.

'Who art thou?' the girl asked him, 'what art thou doing here?'

'My master is a rich merchant, who is as father to me,' answered the little boy. 'Yesterday, he and his friends heard that King Kurkar was assembling his soldiers to attack them, so they decided to hasten away. While they were seeing to the merchandise, the servants sent me to gather fuel[1] for the fires during the journey. Coming back, I wandered out of my way, and when I reached the camp everyone was gone. They had forgotten me.

'What are you going to do with me? Will you kill me or give me food?'

And he came out from the tea leaves and stood upright before Gartza.

Dugmo, who had approached, looked at the boy and, drawing Gartza aside, said·to her:

'When Gesar was young, he exactly resembled this boy. We must kill him. Let us throw stones at him.'

'Oh!' answered the young girl, 'it would be a very bad action if we, who are women, should kill a male. We must take pity on this poor boy who is cold and hungry.'

She returned to the child and said:

'Do not cry any more, little one. I will ask my father, smith Chuta Gyalpo, to adopt thee.'

Whereupon she took off her under robe, which was of yellow silk, wrapped it round the little fellow, and led him to the town. When she reached her home she left the boy at the door, and, going to her father, told him of the strange discovery she had made, adding that Dugmo had wanted to kill the child. She then begged the old artisan to take the boy into his house as his apprentice.

Chuta Gyalpo, whose heart was tender, replied:

'One must succour the unfortunate. Thou didst well to bring me the child. All the same, it is a very strange thing for a big caravan and its camp to vanish as a mirage.'

Gartza went hurriedly to fetch the boy.

'My father has given me permission to keep and to feed thee,' she said to him. 'Tomorrow I will make thee a pretty dress. For the moment eat thy fill.'

[1] Dried yak dung, which is collected on the grazing grounds.

She placed before him a big pot of tea, a dish containing *tsampa* and butter, and a boiled shoulder of mutton.

The little fellow began to laugh and seemed very contented.

'I am glad to have things to eat,' he said, 'but, first, I must offer black tea, red meat, and white *tsampa* to my gods.'

Standing up, he cut off the foot from the shoulder of mutton. He contemplated it for a moment, then said:

'This is not a sheep's foot, it is the foot of a god. It will be very useful to me as a stake to which to tether my horse.'

And he passed it under his belt.

'This shoulder is not a shoulder,' he continued, 'it is a life[1] . . . Kurkar's life. May I cut it, as I now cut this meat.'

He slashed at the shoulder.

'This is not a shoulder,' he repeated again, 'it is a crowd of enemies.[2] May I conquer them and break them to pieces.'

And he broke the bone into several pieces.

'This teapot is not in copper, it is the beggar's earthenware bowl. The land of Hor will be ruined. This is also a good omen for me. Just as I can easily smash this fragile vase, so will I speedily destroy Kurkar.'

With a kick he overturned the teapot, which shattered into fragments.

Gartza, who had listened to him with amazement, was terror-stricken, and rushed upstairs to her father.

'We cannot keep this boy with us,' she said breathlessly, and she told the old man all she had seen.

The old man became very angry:

'People with low and perverted minds meet their like,' he said. 'Vile beings meet a dog, the dog finds carrion—a dead cow's head, which it drags to the village, and many of the inhabitants die of the infection.

'Virtuous and noble men meet a lion with a turquoise horn, on which nine gods are seated. Thou, miserable girl, hast brought me the worst kind of vagabond.'

Reaching the height of his fury, he seized a hammer in either hand and rushed down to belabour the little beggar.

---

[1] A play upon words in Tibetan: *sogpa men srog yin—sogpa* = shoulder and *srog* = life.

[2] Another play upon words: *dpungpa ma red dgra phung red—dpungpa* (pronounced *pungpa*) also signifies shoulder, *dgra* enemy and *phung* (pronounced *pung*) = pile, heap.

166

Great was his surprise when he found nothing was broken, the meat untouched, and the boy seated on the ground, quietly drinking a bowl of tea. The lad, when he saw the smith, timidly knelt down and bowed before him.

The old man thought: My daughter is a dreadful liar, she wanted to make me get rid of the child whom she herself had brought me. He must have displeased her in some way, but how wicked of her to malign him thus.

'Drink some tea and eat, little one,' he said to him. 'Do not be afraid, no one shall hurt thee.'

On going back to his room, he severely scolded Gartza, upbraiding her for the lies that she had told and threatening her with severe punishment if she uttered any more of the kind.

The poor girl could not find a word with which to justify herself, and she wondered if she had not been dreaming. She returned to the ground-floor, and, with her first glance, saw the smashed teapot lying on the floor and the shoulder of mutton floating in a pool of tea. The little boy, who seemed suddenly to have grown, looked at her with a mocking air, his hand resting on the sheep's foot, which was passed as a dagger under his belt.

He is either a god or a demon, she thought; but said nothing.

The strange boy passed nine months with the smith without indulging in any other extraordinary manifestation. He worked assiduously and with surprising skill. His master took several pieces of his work and offered them for sale at the palace.

'Who has made these pretty things?' asked Kurkar. 'It is not thee, Chuta Gyalpo; I know thy work, and this does not resemble it.'

The smith then related to the King the story of Gartza's discovery of his apprentice. He boasted of the boy's cleverness, saying that the articles he had brought had been made by him.

'I wish to see so clever an artisan and employ him myself,' declared the King. 'Bring him here, together with eighteen yaks loaded with charcoal. He shall immediately begin work; I will require him to make many different kinds of things.'

The smith returned home and told his apprentice of the King's command. He explained to him that, first of all, he must go and char wood in the forest and bring back eighteen yak-loads of charcoal with which to fuel the palace forge.

The young boy flatly refused to go to the forest. In vain did his master promise him all the assistance for which he liked to ask. The lad persisted in his refusal. However, in the end, he appeared willing to make a compromise.

'I will go,' he said, 'if you will give me your daughter Gartza as helper. She will be sufficient aid. I do not want anyone else.'

The smith hastened to comply with his request, happy not to have to bear the brunt of Kurkar's anger; for the latter did not tolerate the slightest infringement of his commands.

The two young people started off next day. When they reached the forest Gartza lighted a fire over which to prepare the tea. The boy, in the meantime, sharpened his wood-cutter's axe, then, strolling off, told his companion to bring him some tea when it had boiled long enough.

The tea was soon ready, and the young girl, carrying the pot, went in search of the worker. She had not gone far when an unexpected and terrifying spectacle met her sight. Instead of felling trees, the apprentice had chopped the heads off of the eighteen yaks that they had brought to transport the charcoal. He had skinned and cut up the carcasses. The huge bloodstained skins and quarters of meat were hanging on the trees to dry.[1]

'Oh!' she exclaimed to the slaughterer, 'why have you killed my father's yaks? What were you thinking about? However shall we face him . . . !'

'I don't care a rap for his yaks, or for him,' retorted the young butcher. 'I have no house of my own. This place pleases me, and I shall stay here. I have provided myself with food, also with skins to keep me warm. Thou canst go and tell this to thy father. I am not in the least troubled about what he may think.'

Although well aware, by the previous experience, of what her companion was capable, Gartza lost her head, and ran as fast as she could to inform her father of the killing of his animals. At first he refused to believe her, but, because of her insistence and her agitated expression, he ended by letting himself be persuaded, and started in haste for the scene of the disaster. At a little distance from the place indicated by his daughter, he saw his eighteen yaks, laden with charcoal, coming along the road. The apprentice walked behind them, bent under the weight of a heavy sack, which he carried on

---

[1] Yak's or sheep's meat that has been dried in the sun forms the chief food among the well-to-do Tibetans. They much prefer it to fresh meat. It keeps in good condition for several years.

his back. When he got up to his master, he smiled and politely inquired:

'Father Smith, where are you going to?'

The honest old fellow immediately told him of the tale that his daughter had brought him, adding that he was very angry at having allowed himself once again to be misled by her lies and swearing that this time she would pay dearly for them.

While listening, the boy had thrown down his burden with an angry gesture.

'What a miserable liar,' he exclaimed.

'Father, lead your beasts yourself, I shall not return to your home. I shall leave the country. I can no longer live near such a wicked girl. Who knows what she will invent next? She will end by bringing me misfortune. . . . No, I will not go back with you.'

The smith was greatly concerned at the idea of losing his clever apprentice. He strove to make him alter his mind by promising to punish Gartza so severely that he could be quite certain that she would never again venture to invent stories about him.

On hearing this, the boy became somewhat pacified and followed his master. When the old smith reached home, he took a hammer and with it dealt his daughter several blows, which nearly broke her bones. Poor Gartza thought she would die of pain. Seeing that the yaks were really alive and that the apprentice had made game of her once more, she mentally registered a vow never again to repeat what she saw him do, however startling it might be.

Now Gesar knew that she was a *tulku* of a goddess, so when she bound herself by a vow he felt reassured, certain that she would not betray him if ever she came to discover his true personality. The illusions that he had created in order to deceive her had had for only object that of inducing her to pledge herself to silence.

The next day, Chuta Gyalpo took his apprentice to the palace.

'What do you desire me to do?' the boy asked Kurkar.

The latter had not formed any plan. He consulted those around him. One of the ministers advised: Let him make swords for the soldiers. Another suggested: The best thing would be for him to fashion some trinkets for Dugmo. Others expressed different opinions. They all spoke at once, and they all disagreed. The King began to laugh.

'Let him make what he pleases,' he said. 'In this way we shall have the pleasure of a surprise.'

And turning to the young smith, he said: 'Make what thou judgest to be prettiest . . . what thou canst do best. I leave thee free to choose.'

'Very well,' the boy answered laconically. 'Let me be given some gold, silver, iron, and bronze. I will begin the work at once.'

Upon receiving the metals for which he had asked, he shut himself up, alone, in the palace forge, with all the doors bolted. No one was allowed to approach the building.

When three days had elapsed, he had the King informed that his work was finished, and that he could send his servants for the articles. Kurkar, intensely curious, ordered the things to be immediately brought to his apartment. It took the servants a whole day to complete the task.

With the gold, the apprentice had made a life-sized Lama surrounded by a thousand *trapas* (monks) of smaller size. The Lama preached and the *trapas* listened to him.

The bronze had produced a King with seven hundred officials and courtiers. The King discoursed on the laws and the officials questioned him concerning the science of jurisprudence.

The silver had served to fashion a hundred young girls, who sang melodiously.

The copper had supplied a general and ten thousand soldiers. The general delivered bellicose speeches to his men, exhorting them to heroism.

In addition, the apprentice had formed out of some conches three thousand horses to serve as mounts for the leading puppet personages.

When the King had all the magic dolls before him, they began to move as real people, and, leaving the palace, spread over the plain in front of the walls, where they manœuvred into various positions.

The King and the chiefs remained the whole day watching them from the balconies, forgetting either to eat or drink.

While they were thus lost in contemplation, Gesar, to whom nobody paid any attention, thought the moment opportune for fighting against Kurkar's four great national gods, who could effectively protect the King and prevent his defeat. He therefore summoned his divine courser, which, since his master had assumed the form of a young boy, had remained in one of the paradises. As soon as the Hero was in the saddle, he flew away, invisible to all eyes, and was joined by many deities and a great number of fairies carrying 'thunderbolts'. With lightning rapidity they arrived above the rocky mountains where lived the Hor gods and threw the 'thunderbolts' on their dwellings, which were blown to pieces. Gesar's allies harpooned the four gods—who were obliged to show themselves—and, while they struggled, the Hero killed them with his sword. The fight had lasted barely a few seconds. Then Gesar returned near to Kurkar's palace, dismissed his faithful steed, Kyang Gö Karkar, and, having reassumed the form of the little smith, went back to his master. During this time the King, the chiefs, and all the people continued to watch the parade of the marvellous dolls. Towards evening, the dolls, of themselves, re-entered the palace and established themselves there. The copper soldiers fastened the conch horses in the great royal stables, and all the magic puppets appeared to sleep as living men.

The same night, the King had a dream. He saw Ri, one of his patron gods, who said to him:

'Take care not to let the metal dolls that were made by the young smith escape; later they will become as I am.'

Kurkar regarded this vision as one of good augury, imagining that a vast number of protectors had his wellbeing at heart. He ordered Dugmo to keep careful watch over the dolls: neither to let them leave the palace nor to allow anyone to see them. In obedience to these instructions, she bolted all the palace doors.

However, the King's two brothers, Kurnag and Kurser, accompanied by their numerous chiefs, asked that another public display of the dolls might be given during the day. Dugmo explained that such a thing was not possible and gave them the reason for the refusal.

Certainly, thought the brothers, Kurkar's dream is of good omen. Let us rejoice in the fact by holding a sports fête[1] on the plain in front of the palace.

The King, on being consulted, approved of the project. Tents were pitched on the site where the phantom caravan had camped, and all the men fitted to take part in the games were called together.

The apprentice smith knew, as everybody did, what was in

[1] Tibetans are very partial to this kind of merry-making. They pitch their tents in a suitable place, eat and drink copiously for several days, and, during the time, engage in various sports such as: horse and foot racing, sack racing, jumping, target shooting, dances accompanied by singing, skipping with ropes, etc. All these activities, including the last mentioned, are performed by men; women only taking part in the dancing and singing.

preparation. He asked his master if he would be permitted to go and see the fête with him.

'Alas! no, my son,' answered the good man, 'it will be best for thee to remain at home. The Hor soldiers, who will be there in great numbers, are bad men. They would play thee all sorts of nasty tricks, would handle thee as a ball, throwing thee from one to another, and would amuse themselves by tormenting thee in many ways. It would indeed be a stroke of good fortune if thou didst leave their hands without having an arm or leg broken.'

'If you will let me accompany you,' resumed the boy, 'I will serve you all my life, but if you refuse to do so, I will leave the country.'

The smith became greatly troubled. His apprentice was very useful and the idea of losing him was exceedingly displeasing to him.

'Listen,' he said, 'thou shalt go; but I must hide thee and not let thee be seen by anyone, especially by the soldiers, otherwise harm will befall thee. I shall arrange matters.'

The day of the fête come, the worthy man made the boy get into a sack, which he placed behind him on his saddle, covering it with a fur rug.

'Thou hast a bag of *tsampa* and a piece of butter near at hand,' he said to the youngster, 'eat what thou wilt. When we shall have arrived, I will put thee on the ground; but, be content then to look through one of the holes in the sack, without showing thyself and without uttering a word.'

They started, and, as he had promised, Chuta set his apprentice on the ground, spread the rug over the sack, and himself sat down on a corner of it.

Various games were played, in which the chiefs and people of the court participated. Then one of the 'braves'[1] named Shedchen Riwo Pangkhur lifted a mountain that was on one side of the plain and carried it to the opposite side.[2] Unanimous applause greeted this amazing feat, and the spectators shouted that none other in the world was capable of such an achievement.

'I can do much better,' said the apprentice.

'Hush! Shut up!'

But the warning came too late; the King had heard.

[1] A *pawo*, hero; means here a soldier.
[2] This exploit is met with in a number of Eastern tales. In the Rāmayāna, Hanuman, the hero monkey, hesitating as to which plant to gather for medicine, takes the whole mountain to the wounded Lakshman in order that Sushena, his physician, may himself choose the healing herbs.

'Who spoke?' he said in a severe tone. 'Who boasts thus?'

'I,' answered the voice in the sack.

Surprised at hearing someone speak without seeing anybody, Kurkar added:

'Let the one who has spoken come here before me, instantly.'

Chuta trembled in all his limbs. He went up to the King and tried to excuse his pupil.

'Chief,' he said, 'he who has spoken is my apprentice, the boy who has made those metal dolls that have so pleased you. He is a scatter-brain, who, without thinking, says all sorts of foolish things. . . .'

'Never mind,' said the King, interrupting him, 'let him come here and sit among the warriors.'

There was nothing to do but to obey. The lad got out of the sack and went forward, while his master wept, thinking they would certainly kill his apprentice.

'Ah! It is thou, boaster, who darest to say thyself capable of removing mountains. How wilt thou set about it?' said the King.

'Chief,' the boy answered quietly, 'certainly I am not capable of it. This warrior is gifted with extraordinary strength, and I am only a boy.'

'Thou shouldst not have boasted,' retorted Kurkar, 'so much the worse for thee. Thou hast challenged this warrior by declaring that thou couldst do better than he, now thou must fight him.'

'How can I do that?' implored the boy. 'I have not the necessary strength. Nevertheless, since the King commands it, I must obey. I desire only that he give me his word that if I am killed, my adversary shall not have to pay blood money, and if, on the contrary, I kill him, father smith shall not owe his family anything for the price of his blood.'

'Very well,' said the King, 'it shall be as thou dost ask, I give thee my word on it before all the chiefs. And now, begin the fight at once.'

Pangkhur was a man of gigantic stature. He felt deeply humiliated at having to fight a puny urchin, who, as he stood before him, resembled an ant in front of an elephant. He made up his mind to kill him instantly.

The signal given, the boy bounded forward, and, with the first blow, overthrew the giant, on whom he then sat.

How could this have happened, thought the stunned soldier . . . how heavy the lean youngster is. Just now, when I carried that mountain, I did not feel its weight, and now this child is crushing me.

Meanwhile his victor was defying him:

'Eh! "brave", what hast thou done with thy strength, canst thou not get up, bestir thyself?'

Pangkhur tried in vain to move.

'Move thou, thyself,' he said to the apprentice, hoping thereby to take advantage of a favourable moment for regaining his feet.

The boy got up, seized his adversary by the foot before the latter could make a movement, and then threw him right in front of the King's seat, against the black rock that was 'the life'[1] of the Horpas. The soldier's skull fractured, his brains gushed forth, and he expired instantly.

The King was dismayed. He had never imagined that the fight could end in this way. He thought that the giant would inflict some kind of punishment on the presumptuous lad, which would make everyone laugh, and there the matter would end. However, as he himself had commanded the fight, and had also given his promise before all the people, he could not punish the apprentice. Therefore he contented himself with saying:

'It is a sad thing! It is to be deplored that this boy should have killed my brave soldier. . . .'

And he called Chuta.

'Thou shalt not pay blood money,' he said to him. 'I promised not to claim it, but thou shalt give me thine apprentice in place of the man he has killed.'

In vain did the smith plead that he was old, that a helper was indispensable to him, that he could never find another the equal of the present one; Kurkar was immovable. Neither the smith's words nor his tears could make the King alter his decision.

There was no further question of games. The King, his brothers and the chiefs returned to the palace and the crowd left the plain after them. Everyone commented on the extraordinary incident that had saddened and spoiled the happy fête. A vague uneasiness overshadowed their minds; the Horpas saw in the giant's death a possible precursor of coming disasters. Thus the day so pleasantly begun ended in sadness.

Kurkar was no sooner home than he hastened to tell Dugmo what had occurred. She was seized with terror.

[1] See note at the end of Chapter 2.

'There can be no longer any doubt about it,' she said, 'this boy is Gesar. At all costs he must be killed. So long as he lives, we cannot be safe.'

'That is true enough,' replied Kurkar. 'If this strange boy is really Gesar, we are in great danger, and, judging by the cleverness and extraordinary strength he has shown, it could well be that he is the King of Ling. . . . Certainly we must kill him. . . . But how?'

'I know a means that should prove successful,' answered the Queen. 'I will tell it you. Send him tomorrow to capture a tiger in the forest that lies beyond the mountains north of the palace, as you desire to chain one to your door. There is a man-eating tiger in those thickets. It will rid us of our enemy.'

Thinking the advice good, Kurkar sent for the little smith.

'Thou art artful and vigorous,' he said to him. 'Thou hast proved it. Thou wilt go into the mountains and catch a live tiger. I want one to fasten at my door. Think for thyself how to accomplish this task; that is thy business. Thou art cunning enough to pull it off. Only, do not appear before me without the tiger . . . to do so would cost thee dearly.'

'Chief, in what can a tiger be useful to you?' humbly asked the young boy. 'You have already three bears and two monkeys tied up in the courtyard. In the garden, there are caged leopards and parrots on perches.[1] By commanding me to bring you a tiger, you are sending me to my death.'

'Thou hast shown thy cleverness in more ways than one,' answered Kurkar sarcastically, 'and as to thy strength . . . a tiger is not stronger than was the brave warrior whose skull thou cracked. It is for thee to manage now as thou hast done before. Say no more, it would be useless. Go and get to work.'

'Very well, Chief,' answered the apprentice. 'I will go in search of a tiger and bring it to you.'

He left the palace and returned to his master's house, where he found Gartza alone. He told her of the interview he had had with the King, and asked her to tell him of places that were frequented by tigers.

The young girl first looked at him without replying, then going close to him, said in a low voice:

'All that has happened since you came here has not been natural.

---

[1] Many lamas and chiefs have such a miniature zoological collection in the grounds of their residences.

I think you are King Gesar of divine race. You can tell me without fear; I am entirely at your service, because I love the Doctrine that Kurkar wants to destroy and I know that it is your mission to prevent him from doing so. Tell me the truth, and I will tell you where to find a tiger.'

'Yes, I am Gesar,' smilingly answered the lad, 'but you must keep my secret. I have to destroy Kurkar during the course of this year. Now give me the information I want about the tigers.'

Gartza, having made quite sure that she was alone with him, prostrated herself before the Hero, and when she lifted her eyes, she saw him in front of her under his natural form;[1] but the vision only lasted a second, and it was again to the apprentice that she addressed herself.

'There is a red tiger,' she said, 'in the wood that stretches beyond the mountain that rises north of the palace. It knows Dikchen and comes at his call. If you can make yourself resemble him, the tiger, misled by your appearance, will come to you.'

'I could not ask for anything better,' answered the boy, and he started off.

After he had reached the mountain, he took on the appearance of Dikchen Shenpa and went into the forest. The tiger did not fail to go to him, and he killed it at once with his sword made of iron fallen from the sky. He skinned the beast and hid the skin under his robe. Then he called to his celestial brother Mitag Marpo, who had come out of one of his mother's shoulders, and transformed him into a tiger. He passed a heavy chain round the animal's neck and led it to the palace.

When it approached the villages, the sham tiger began to roar and make a pretence at struggling to get free. The apprentice on his part appeared to have great difficulty in keeping hold of the chain. The terrified villagers fled before them and took refuge in their homes. In this manner the strange hunter and his captive arrived in the courtyard of the palace. Kurkar, surrounded by his intimates, immediately came down to see them. He was more than ever astonished at the young boy's accomplishment of the task, and yet, he could not bring himself to believe that the lad was really Gesar.

'There is your tiger, Chief,' said the lad, chaining up the animal. 'I had great difficulty in getting it here. It is ravenous now. Food must be brought to it at once, otherwise it will become furious.'

[1] This kind of miracle often occurs in Tibetan and Indian tales.

176

'Quick! Quick! Bring meat,' the King shouted to the servants.

'No, Chief,' resumed the apprentice. 'It will not be satisfied with yak's or sheep's meat. I am told that this beast is a man-eater, and, as you know, when once a tiger has tasted human flesh, it will not eat any other. You must give it a living man or one that has recently died.'

'What shall we do?' said Kurkar, looking interrogatively at those around him. 'We have no one under capital punishment at this moment, nor the body of a murdered man, nor of one killed by accident.'

The tiger, seeming to resent the delay, began to roar furiously.

'Let them give it that man of Ling, who is a prisoner of war,' commanded the King.

The poor wretch was released from his cell and thrust in front of the animal. But the latter, after having sniffed at him, turned away with perfect indifference and began to snarl again savagely.

'What is the meaning of this?' asked Kurkar.

'I do not know, Chief,' answered the boy. 'It seems to me that the smell of the Ling people is displeasing to this beast. It is accustomed to eat Horpas.'

'Begone!' said the King to the prisoner. 'The tiger will have none of thee; thou art not even good to eat!'

The man did not need telling twice and, as he was no longer guarded, he rushed away as fast as he could run.

The fury of the tiger increased; it stood on its hind legs, making every effort to break its chain, straining in Kurkar's direction with open jaws.

'Be quick! Be quick! Chief . . . if it does not have something to eat it will break its chain and spring on you.' The boy shouted this warning while retreating to the gate, as if in readiness for flight.

Desperate, mad with fright, seeing the iron stake to which the tiger was attached begin to quiver and the beast bare its enormous fangs at him, Kurkar clutched frenziedly at his prime minister, who by ill-luck was at his side, and sent him rolling in front of the savage brute.

The tiger jumped on the unfortunate man, and, in a little while, nothing remained of him but a few big, bare bones.

The King had fled to his private room and all the others had made their escape. When the animal had finished its meal, the boy led it to the King's ante-chamber, chained it up near the door, and left the palace.

After he had recovered a little from his fright, Kurkar rang for some tea. To his great surprise not a servant appeared. He rang again, but still he got no answer. At last, from the distance, a voice cried:

'Chief, we cannot come, the tiger is outside your door.'

And, as if to underline the words, a muffled roar made itself heard.

Oh! thought the King, I said to this accursed sorcerer that I wished to chain the tiger at my door. He has taken me at my word, and now it is not in front of the palace door that he has put it, but before that of my room. . . . It is to be hoped he will come soon, that I may make him take the beast back to the courtyard.

But the hours passed and night came. The servants had shut themselves up in a distant part of the building and no one answered his calls. Kurkar barricaded his door by piling several chests against it, then went to bed without either eating or drinking.

The next day, exactly the same conditions persisted. He heard the tiger getting excited and rattling its chain against the door. He hailed a man whom he saw passing in the courtyard and commanded him to go in haste and fetch Chuta's apprentice The man returned and reported that the boy had gone into the mountains to gather *tumas*, and that his master did not know when he would be back. At this moment the tiger gave a great roar; the messenger fled without waiting for further orders.

Three days pass thus. The King fasted, and, as it was not possible for him to leave his room, it became indescribably filthy. The tiger, also fasting, roared despairingly, and began to wear away the door with its claws.

At last Kurkar caught sight of Dugmo at a window and called to her to have the little smith fetched.

The apprentice had just returned with his sack of *tumas*. He came at once to the palace, and the King, seeing him cross the courtyard, promised him all the money he wanted, if he would take the tiger back to the forest.

So the boy started off, dragging the animal along. When they were both out of sight, Mitag Marpo resumed his natural form and returned to the Paradise whence he had come. And Gesar, throwing over his shoulders the skin of the tiger that he had killed a few days before, went back to the King.

'Chief,' he said, 'that tiger was really a ferocious animal. I had scarcely reached the wood when it sprang at me and tried to devour me. It was only with great difficulty that I escaped. I killed it and have brought you back the skin.'

'Ah! that is very good,' exclaimed the King, completely reassured. 'Thou shalt tan the skin. Dost thou know how to do it?'

'Not very well, Chief,' replied the boy.

'See here,' said Kurkar, 'thou wilt rub it, beginning with the head.'

'Very well, Chief, I will not fail to do so.'

He carried away the skin, thinking: Come, come, this is an excellent omen; may I soon rub the heads of the Hors chiefs in the same way.

Chapter 8

SECHANG DUGMO and the King's brothers, Kurnag and Kurser, became worried at seeing Kurkar pay no attention to the warnings that they had given him and remain undisturbed by the strange doings of this boy who had come from nobody knew where. They therefore agreed that together they would take steps to try to arouse his suspicions and to persuade him to find out, through the medium of a *mopa*, the apprentice's real identity and the reasons for his stay in the country of Hor.

Having come to this understanding, they went to the King.

'Brother,' said Kurnag, 'your family and your friends are anxious concerning you and Hor. It is now about a year since Chuta's apprentice was found by Gartza on the very day that the mysterious caravan vanished without leaving any traces. Since that time the boy's conduct has differed from that of everyone else's. He has produced marvellous work and, puny as he is, has knocked down and killed a giant who was capable of carrying a mountain. He has captured a fierce tiger, which has devoured the wisest of your counsellors; he has now led this terrible beast back to the forest, as he would have a dog, and brought you its skin, pretending to have killed the animal. All these things are very extraordinary, and we beg you to consult a learned *mopa* on the subject.'

'I had bad dreams during the time the tiger was here,' said Kurser. 'Could it be that the young boy is Gesar? That seems doubtful, however, as it is nearly ten years since Gesar disappeared. If he were still alive, he would probably not have waited so long before trying to avenge Ling's defeat. Nevertheless, it would be better for us to make certain on that point.'

Dikchen supported the chiefs.

'I also think Gesar is dead,' he said, 'but as you have had bad dreams it would be as well to consult a *mopa*, and there does not exist one of greater renown than the hermit of the country of Jong, Gomchen Chujag. The King would act wisely in sending for him.'

'That would not be a bad thing to do,' answered Kurkar. 'Apart from whether the apprentice is Gesar or not, the *mopa* could enlighten us on many subjects.'

'I am glad to see you take this decision,' said Dugmo. 'I know Gesar's power. He is a mighty god, who is protected by the Precious Guru. Even dead, he is capable of troubling your mind by dreams and of creating magic emanations of himself, which would deceive you and cause your ruin.'

'Dikchen,' commanded the King, 'thou shalt go thyself and beg the Gomchen to come. Be careful to assure him that suitable presents shall recompense him for the trouble he will take in coming here.'

The next day, Dikchen mounted his red horse and accompanied by a single servant, set out for the Lama's residence. This was situated at four days' journey from Kurkar's palace. When he arrived there, he learnt that the Lama was in retreat (*tsam*), and could receive no one. After having explained the motive for his visit, Dikchen had a scarf and some presents taken to the Gomchen by the *trapa* (monk) who was in special attendance on him. Later, the hermit sent the reply that he had undertaken a retreat for a period of three years, three months, three weeks, and three days, which time had not yet half elapsed, and, as misfortune inevitably comes to him who breaks his vow of seclusion, it was very difficult for him to leave his hermitage. Still, the dignity and authority of the King of Hor did not admit of his disobeying the monarch's commands, therefore he would start the next morning for the palace.

Having passed the night at the Lama's house, which was at the foot of the mountain on which the hermitage was perched, Dikchen left with the Gomchen. The latter was accompanied by two attendants, and two mules carried his luggage, which included the many books, symbolic drawings, and instruments that are used on important occasions.

Gesar, who was able to uncover the most carefully guarded secrets, soon knew that Kurkar had sent to fetch the *mopa* in order to question him with reference to himself. He also knew that Lama Chujag was deeply versed in occult science and in the art of penetrating and counteracting the most subtle ruses, and he greatly feared that the Gomchen would end by discovering the true identity of the apprentice smith. He therefore resolved to make certain if the *mopa* would recognize him under a disguise, and if he did so, to prevent him from seeing Kurkar.

By his supernatural power, he inspired Dikchen with the thought of going on in advance of the Lama in order to apprise the King of the latter's arrival. When the diviner was alone on the road with his men, Gesar went to meet him under the form of a fair-skinned chief who wore a helmet crested by a little white flag and rode a white horse. Twenty-five phantom men, absolutely similar to him, formed his escort. On approaching the Lama, who was coming in the opposite direction, Gesar politely saluted him.

'Have you undergone hardship,[1] "Long-hair"?[2] Where do you come from, and for what reason are you going to Hor?'

The Lama told him that he came from Gyang Mugpo (misty Gyang), and that he was going to Kurkar, who wished to consult him. In his turn, he asked the mounted stranger whence he came and what was the object of his journey.

'I am Lönpo (minister) Pekar of India. Twenty valuable horses have been stolen from the King of my country, and the thieves have remained undiscovered. He sent me to Hor thinking that perhaps the *jagspas* (highwaymen) of this region had got the beasts; but I did not find them there. As I have the good fortune to meet you, will you kindly do a *mo*, so that I may know where they have been taken to. If I go to Ling, as is my intention, shall I recover them there?

'I will offer you whatever you desire; here are already thirty gold pieces.'

Gesar knotted the coins in the end of a scarf and, dismounting, gave them to the Lama.

The *mopa* smiled amiably; this munificent gift, as a beginning, was most pleasing to him. Descending from his horse, he sat down on the carpet that his attendants placed for him, and had his books,

---

[1] Prescribed form of politeness.
[2] *Ralpachen.* A Lama belonging to the sect of ascetics who let their hair grow.

dice, some grain, scented herbs, and various other things, brought to him.

After being absorbed for a long time in his calculations, he raised his head with a sorrowful air and said:

'The horses of which you speak do not exist anywhere. Misfortune comes to me. . . . You are my enemy. . . . These twenty-six horsemen before me are only one person, who is Gesar; the others are just shadows. Go your way, and I will go mine. . . .'

And when his instruments had been repacked, he slowly continued his journey to Hor.

This is annoying, thought Gesar. The Lama has recognized me in spite of my disguise. He will now go and inform Kurkar of all that concerns me. . . . He must never reach the palace.

The Hero then called his celestial brothers to his aid. They caused a severe hailstorm to break, and the Lama with his two secretaries was forced to shelter under a rock. Immediately Tungjag Karpo (the child who had come out of the nāgī's head) threw a thunderbolt at the rock, which fell in pieces, crushing the hermit and his two monks.

Gesar took possession of the diviner's luggage, created two phantoms, which resembled the two monks who had just perished, and took on, himself, the appearance of the dead Lama. Disguised thus he arrived in front of the palace. As soon as he was sighted, the King sent chiefs and horses[1] to meet him, and he was conducted in great pomp to the royal castle.

The next morning, he had all his magician's paraphernalia taken from their boxes and, presenting himself before Kurkar, asked him what *mo* he desired him to do.

The King said:

'My brothers and I have had bad dreams. A tiger was brought here in a strange way and has devoured the prime minister. The smith has an apprentice, who comes from we do not know where, and performs the most amazing feats. Is he Gesar? If enemies attack us, shall we be able to repulse and defeat them? Will the country continue to be prosperous? Shall I have a long life?'

'Very well,' answered the Lama. 'I will give you the answers in three days.'

He had a great many *tormas* (ritual cakes) prepared by his

---

[1] These horses are sent to allow travellers whom one wishes to honour, and those who accompany them, to change mounts, their own being possibly tired.

acolytes, lighted many altar lamps, burnt so many incense sticks that his room grew dark with their perfumed smoke, and, finally, shut himself in alone, leaving the two monks to guard the door.

The fourth day, at dawn, he returned to the King, who, surrounded by his brothers, Dugmo, and the principal chiefs, anxiously awaited him.

'My *mos* are truly surprising,' said the diviner at once. 'Some are favourable and others predict misfortune. Certain of them are veiled. You are encompassed, Chief, by mysteries that are difficult to fathom. For some time still, the King and the country will enjoy peace and happiness. Later, troubles will come, but their consequences are hidden from me. Neither can I clearly determine the term of the King's life. The head that hangs on the city wall is the cause of your bad dreams, it is also that which brought about the minister's death and which is disturbing the atmosphere of Hor. It must be taken down and buried.'

'In what manner must it be taken down and buried so that the dangers that threaten us may be averted?' asked Kurkar.

'I shall have to do another *mo* on the subject,' replied the sorcerer. 'You will have the answer tomorrow.'

He again shut himself up in his room, and, reappearing the next day, he brought the following revelation:

'A long iron chain must be forged, that has at one end a solid hook by which it can be attached to the palace's highest roof. The hook must catch on by itself, by a man throwing it at the roof from below. The other end of the chain must then be fixed to the ground outside the palace walls by means a strong iron stake that has been well driven into the earth. He who will be capable of climbing up this chain and in this way attaining the head on the wall is the man chosen by the gods to take it down and bury it.'

The King immediately sent for Chuta and his apprentice and commanded them to forge a chain exactly similar to the one described by the *mopa*.

'A great quantity of iron will be required for this work,' said the apprentice; 'if the King does not provide it, the chain will not be long enough to reach the palace roof.'

Kurkar answered:

'I have not much iron at the moment. This is very annoying because the head must be taken away without delay, and for that to be done, the chain is necessary. There is, however, in the palace

184

treasury a big piece of iron, but it is the "life"[1] of my ancestors. Sometimes sounds come from it, at other times it speaks. It would be a very serious thing to destroy it. . . . I must consult the Lama before deciding anything.'

After another day supposedly spent in doing *mos*, the sham hermit declared that that particular bar of iron was precisely the one that must be used. If the chain were made from another piece of iron it would break, it would be too short, or else an accident would happen, consequently the head would not be removed in the desired manner and the dangers that menaced Hor would not be averted.

From that moment Kurkar hesitated no longer, and the heavy bar of metal was taken to Chuta's forge. The latter, knowing that this sacred iron had been venerated for many centuries and that in it reposed the vital essence of the dynasty of the Kings of Hor, said to his apprentice:

'The King has given us a bad piece of work. The fire will be powerless to redden this divine iron. It is folly to think that it will let itself be forged. The chain will not be able to be made, and Kurkar will punish us severely.'

'Do not worry yourself, father smith,' replied the boy. 'Go quietly to sleep, and, above all, do not come down to the forge tonight on any pretext whatever. Leave me only Gartza as helper; we will speak again of the chain tomorrow morning.'

The old man, accustomed to his apprentice's strange ways, went up to his room and left the young people together. They shut themselves up in the forge and then, piling the coal into a heap as high as a mountain, placed the piece of iron in the middle of it. When this was done, Gesar invoked his celestial brothers, his friends the gods, and the nāgas his kinsmen. They came running in a band, armed with hammers, pincers, and other tools, and began to work on the iron, making such a tremendous noise that it shook the three worlds.

Chuta, waking with a start, realized that his apprentice was once again indulging in some magic feat. Fearful, but curious to see what was passing in the forge, he went down and put his eye to a chink in the door. His forehead had hardly touched the wood, when a big spark from the fire passed through the crack and landed in his eye, burning it terribly. Moaning with pain, the poor man returned to his bed. He had not been able to catch a glimpse of the gods at work and had lost an eye.

[1] See footnote at end of Chapter 2.

The next morning, the apprentice entered his room and said:

'Father smith, get up, we must go to the palace and deliver the chain. As it is very heavy we will ask help in the carrying of it.'

'Oh!' wailed the old man, 'there can be no question of my getting up, I cannot move. Last night, on hearing such a great noise coming from the forge, I wanted to see what thou wast doing. A spark flew through a hole in the door and burnt one of my eyes. I suffer horribly.'

'The dog bites the one who prowls at night,' answered the boy. 'Did I not warn you not to leave your room? I am grieved that such an accident should have happened to you, but it is of good augury for me. It signifies that those who would spy on my plans will be blinded.'

The enormous chain having been carried to Kurkar, he wished to have it immediately hooked on in the manner directed by the Lama. There was no lack of strong men about the King, but not one of them succeeded in throwing the chain as high as the golden roof[1] that crowned the palace. The servants tried first; after which, priding themselves upon their great strength and adroitness, ministers and chiefs made the attempt. Many injured themselves in the endeavour, but it was to no purpose. The apprentice smith then asked the King's permission to try, and, having obtained it, caught the roof with his first throw. The hook became embedded, and the chain remained firmly fixed. Some men then drove the iron stake into the ground on the other side of the wall and attached the lower end of the chain to it.

The only thing that now remained to be done was to climb up the chain as far as the head and take it down. Again many tried in vain.

'As thou art successful in all things,' said Kurkar to the young smith, 'thou canst no doubt do this climb. Go ahead.'

'It is not easy, Chief,' replied the boy. 'What will you give me if I succeed?'

'Thou shalt thyself choose thy reward,' promised Kurkar. So without further ado, the apprentice hauled himself up the chain, reached the head, detached it, and returned with it to lay it at Kurkar's feet.

---

[1] The residences of the great Lamas and of important chiefs are crowned with golden roofs.

'The Lama has told us to bury it,' said the King. 'But where? We must ask him.'

Dikchen was commanded to go to the long-haired hermit, who still remained at the palace, and consult him.

'A big hole must be dug at the foot of Zangser Ri Mugpo (the dark mountain of copper and gold),' answered the latter, 'and the head, wrapped in a cotton cloth, placed in it on a bed of thorns. The opening of the hole shall then be closed by a large flat stone.

'The head must be carried to this spot by the smith apprentice who has taken it down. Tongzö[1] Yundub and General Petur Chung will accompany him with a hundred horsemen.

'If you exactly carry out my directions, all will be well with Hor and the King will recover his peace of mind. You now know that which you desired to learn. I have no reason for remaining here any longer. You will therefore tell the King that I wish to take leave of him and to return to my hermitage this very afternoon.'

Dikchen reported the diviner's words. The King was extremely happy on hearing them. All his worries were dispelled.

He fixed the burial of the head for the morrow, and gave magnificent presents to the Lama. Some hours later, the latter left the palace, seeming to proceed in the direction of his residence in the Gyang country.

In accordance with the instructions given by the sham soothsayer, the head was carried to the foot of Mount Zangser Ri Mugpo. While the soldiers began to dig the hole, the General and Tongzö Yundub sat at a little distance drinking tea.

When they had both rested, the apprentice very respectfully asked the General to go and see for himself whether all the Lama's directions were being properly carried out.

'The matter is of such vital importance to the King and to the whole country,' he said, 'that it were better not to leave such work entirely in the hands of common people.'

The General, thinking the advice good, approached the workers.

'As to us,' continued the boy, addressing Tongzö Yundub, 'let us go and search for a stone such as the Lama described. When we have found it, we can call the men to remove it.'

---

[1] This word shows a Chinese influence and places the origin of the poem at the eastern frontier of Tibet. *Tongzö* signifies interpreter and is borrowed from the Chinese dialect of Kansu. The Tibetan word for interpreter is *skad nis*.

They had left the others but a few moments when, through the intervention of Gesar, a landslip occurred on the side of the mountain. An enormous quantity of earth intermingled with masses of rock was suddenly dislodged and the General and all the soldiers were buried under it.

'Come away, come away!' cried the apprentice to his companion, and they both rushed off. Profiting by the inattention of Tongzö Yundub, who was wholly engrossed in thoughts for his own safety, Gesar sent Gyatza's head to the Paradise where his friend now dwelt.

Out of breath and still running, the two survivors, with haggard, terrified faces, reached Kurkar's palace.

'What has happened?' asked those who saw them. 'Where are the horsemen and the General?'

They told the story of the catastrophe, adding that only a miracle had saved them from sharing the fate of their companions.

The King and his brothers were immediately informed of the disaster. They were greatly bewildered at the news. What could have brought about this fresh calamity, when the Lama had so definitely assured them that once the head was taken down and buried all danger would be averted? The idea of doubting the diviner's capacity and honesty never entered their heads, but they wondered whether General Petur Chung, or one or other of his men, had not disobeyed the Lama's orders, and as a consequence displeased either the gods or the demons.

During the night that followed this fateful day, Kurkar saw in a dream one of the patron gods of his ancestors named Namthig, who said to him:

'Kurkar, thou must consult the omens concerning the extraordinary and unfortunate events that have occurred within thy territory. Tomorrow thou shalt send several men with their bows to the place where the archers usually practise, near the red rock on which the target is designed. Thou shalt select Tongzö Yundub, Garbe Pangtsen Lhadub, Tobchen Thugö, Dikchen Shenpa, and the apprentice-smith for the expedition. If their arrows hit the rock and split it, so that the splinters fall on the plain, it will be a good omen.[1] Thou wilt then know that the *mopa* has seen correctly when predicting that all the perils would be averted. As to the death of

[1] Regarding this way of deducing omens from the result of a shooting competition, see *My Journey to Lhasa*.

the soldiers and of their General, it is the result of their own bad actions and does not concern thee.'

Kurkar awoke suddenly. It was midnight. In his impatience, he could not wait for the morrow, but had the men whom the god had chosen called at once. When they were before him he commanded them to prepare their bows and arrows and to leave immediately for the target ground in order to arrive there at dawn.

The men, greatly affected by the accident of the day before and fearing the demons, were intensely frightened at the idea of setting out in the middle of the night; however, since they could not disobey the King, they started, and reached the red rock as the sun was rising.

'We are going to shoot, because such is the King's command,' said Tongzö Yundub, 'but certainly not one of us will succeed in splintering that hard polished surface. And if we are unable to do it, Kurkar will be furious and fine us heavily.'

'I shall not shoot,' said the apprentice. 'I had a bad dream last night. I saw a red man riding a red horse, who held in his hand a red lasso; he threw the lasso and noosed one of those who was with me.'

'That is unlucky,' observed Tobchen Thugö.

'You are very bold, youngster, in daring to say you will not shoot and so disobey the King,' rejoined Garbe Pangtsen Lhadub. 'Whatever may be the meaning of your dream, we must obey orders.'

They began to shoot. Their arrows rebounded, broken, from the rock, without causing the smallest particle of the stone to become detached. All at once, a red man, mounted on a red horse and swinging a red lasso, sprang out of the rock and galloped towards them, with an expression on his face that only too clearly showed his malevolent intentions. Scared, defenceless, the marksmen ran away. The red man then threw his lasso, caught Tobchen Thugö and, dragging him along, hoisted him to the top of the rock. At this moment, four demon girls appeared carrying iron stakes. With these they nailed the ill-fated archer, upright, to the rock, disembowelling him with the centre stake.

His four companions returned in haste to the palace, and, not daring to present themselves before the King, went and related the fatal event to his brother Kurser, who was overwhelmed by the recital. He was nevertheless obliged to inform the King, who immediately told Kurnag and Dugmo of the advice he had received, in dream, from the god Namthig, and what had been the result.

Kurnag did his best to restore his brothers' flagging spirits.

'Perhaps,' he said, 'Tobchen's death should not be considered as an omen that directly concerns us, just as Namthig has declared with regard to the death of the General. We have no doubt neglected to make offerings to our ancestral gods, and they are angry with us in consequence. We must propitiate them. In a few days, we will go and adore them on the mountain and offer them sacrifices. All our troubles will then be at an end.'

The King and those around him unanimously approved of Kurnag's suggestions, and it was decided that the lamas should be requested to officiate at a great festival in honour of Namthig, Barthig, and Sathig. The matter being settled, Kurser and Kurnag left for their respective residences in order to see to the preparations for the ceremony.

The apprentice, who had gone straight back to the smith's house, not wishing to face Kurkar's anger when he heard the terrible result of the archery match, awoke that night to find his room illumined by a great light, and Padma Sambhava descending to him on a white rainbow.

'Wake up,' he said to Gesar. 'This is not the time for sleep. I wish to speak to thee.'

Gesar prostrated himself several times before the Guru, and the latter continued:

'Up to now, everything has gone well for thee. Thou hast been able to kill the General, his soldiers, the prime minister, the Lama who could have disclosed thy disguise, and many others. Terror reigns in Hor, and Kurkar, who is distraught, is incapable of sane action. But thou must have done with him quickly, for the year in which thou canst destroy him draws to a close. If thou dost not succeed in doing so promptly, the planetary influences will change and Kurkar and the demons who surround him will all recover their strength. They will, then, become invincible.

'Tomorrow, thou shalt create the magic forms of three Indians, each carrying a monkey, as do itinerant jugglers, and thou wilt show thyself before the palace. Thou must speak with Dugmo.'

Without explaining further, Padma Sambhava disappeared and returned to Zandog Palri.

In obedience to the order that he had just received, Gesar created seven magic figures. Two of them represented Indian conjurers, another assumed the appearance of the apprentice-smith and was to remain at the forge while he, himself, played the part of the third juggler. Lastly, three other figures took the form of three monkeys and the fourth that of a lean donkey, which carried the traveller's luggage.

During the time that Gesar was receiving the visit of Padma Sambhava, Sechang Dugmo was being tormented by bad dreams. She, unlike Kurkar, had lived in constant dread for many months. Every day, she expected to see Gesar; and, now that she had fallen in love with Kurkar and had had a son by him, she looked on the possible arrival of her husband as the greatest misfortune that could befall her.

Even more agitated in her mind than she was wont to be, she climbed up to the roof to see if anything abnormal was to be seen in the surroundings. It was in this way that she perceived the three Indians, clad in robes of many colours, advancing with their beasts.

She was struck by the unusual appearance of the new-comers. This time, she thought, there is no doubt about it, these conjurers are a projection of Gesar. People of this kind have never before passed through our country. She quickly left the roof to go and warn Kurkar.

On her way to his apartments she passed by Dikchen Shenpa's room, the door of which was open.

'Where are you going, Lhacham Kushog?'[1] he asked her.

'I am going to the King,' she replied. 'I have just seen three strangers, such as never come here. They must be Gesar, in disguise, come to harm us.'

She then described the people whom she had seen.

'Bah!' exclaimed Dikchen. 'Gesar is a single person, not three. And you also say that there are three monkeys and a donkey. Are they Gesar also?' He began to laugh.

'Believe me,' he continued, 'Gesar is a chief; he rides a horse, carries arms, and is followed by a train of horsemen. He does not go about with performing monkeys. These people are just beggars; ask them where they come from. You will soon be reassured.'

'It is Gesar,' Dugmo insisted. 'You do not know the extent of his magic powers as I do. I must warn the King.'

'Do you want to increase the torment of his mind by your fancies,' angrily rejoined Dikchen. 'Women are as dogs, without

[1] It is the very polite term used when addressing a married woman of high rank. It means approximately: 'The noble lady wife'.

intelligence, without shame. Do not make the King more anxious. I, who am a scholar, well versed in all that concerns the three worlds, I do not know if it be Gesar. How then could you know?'

Dugmo reflected for a moment. After all, she said to herself, Dikchen is right. If I am wrong, and the King, after listening to me, has those beggars killed, a grave sin will weigh on me. Thinking thus, she went down and out of the palace gate near to which the Indians had halted.

'From where come you, men of India?' she asked them. 'It is not wise for you to remain in this country. You are in the Kingdom of Hor, whose chief is very severe. The Religion is not respected here. If anyone so much as allows himself to utter a single word in its praise, he must hand over a horse as penalty; while, if another only kills an insect in defiance of the Doctrine's precepts, he receives a yak as proof of the King's pleasure. It is not virtue, but vice that is exalted here. The law is so inflexible and regulates so rigorously the actions of everyone, that neither the sun nor the moon have permission to shine, nor the dogs to bark, nor the horses to neigh.[1] I advise you to go away at once. If the King learns of your presence in his land, he will have you beaten.'

The eldest of the jugglers then spoke with a faulty pronunciation, punctuating his speech with phrases in a foreign language:

'All that you say is true. I am Zamba Atta, a man out of the ordinary. I have just arrived, and tomorrow I will destroy Hor.'

As Dugmo appeared not to understand his jargon, he continued a little more plainly:

'Is Kurkar really as mighty a chief as you say? And who are you, my pretty girl? By what right do you live in this palace?'

On hearing herself addressed with such familiarity by a vagabond, Dugmo became annoyed:

'It is very impudent of you to speak to me in this way,' she exclaimed. 'The King of Hor reigns over many states. No one is as powerful as he. I am the beautiful Sechang Dugmo of Ling. My husband is King Gesar. He left for the gloomy North Country nearly ten years ago and has never returned. Now I live here in sorrow.[2] Have you heard of these events?'

[1] Word painting that illustrated the restraint under which Kurkar's subjects lived.
[2] She was still uncertain as to the true identity of these three strangers, and, in case one or the other of them should be Gesar, she wished to show the feelings of a faithful wife.

'No; but why did your husband go to that far country?'

'To kill Lutzen. You who have travelled so much, have you never heard of Lutzen? Did you never meet Gesar?'

The three Indians appeared to give each other understanding looks, then the eldest spoke:

'So your husband was that chief wearing a helmet and mounted on a bay horse, who wanted to kill Lutzen. Oh! now we remember him well. He was devoured by Lutzen.'

'Where?' asked Dugmo.

'Near the Duhachan Konkar pass: we were passing that way, but on perceiving Lutzen in the distance, we hid ourselves among the stones. The horseman met the King of the North and was devoured by him in a few seconds.'

Convinced, at last, that the Indians were really foreign beggars and not Gesar, and delighted to know that the latter could never reappear, the young woman smiled, showing all her pretty white teeth.

'Stay here for a little while,' she said. 'I will send you some tea and beer.'

With a beaming countenance she returned to Dikchen.

'You were right,' she said. 'It is not Gesar who is there. Gesar is dead. Those three men saw him devoured by Lutzen.'

'It must be so,' replied the minister. 'If he had been alive, he would have come back. Go and tell the good news to the King.'

Kurkar was extremely happy on learning that he had nothing more to fear from his enemy. He commanded that meat, *tsampa*, beer and tea should be taken outside[1] to the Indians and that they be asked if they could do *mos*.

Upon receiving a reply in the affirmative, the King ordered them to do *mos* to ascertain if any danger menaced Hor and if he himself would have a long life.

The foreigners cast the dice, they showed eight spots. The answer in the book indicated: 'An accident will befall the King, he will not live long.'

This answer greatly distressed Kurkar, who immediately sent

[1] Although the caste system, as prevalent in India, does not exist in Tibet, yet certain classes of people are not usually allowed to reside in towns and villages or to enter the houses of Tibetans of good society—namely: butchers, professional beggars and carriers of the dead. Nevertheless, these laws do not seem to be very strictly enforced nowadays. Butchers are to be seen seated behind their stalls in the centre of Lhasa.

Dugmo to ask the Indians if there were no way by which this unfortunate destiny could be averted.

'There is one,' replied the eldest beggar. 'I must confer a blessing on the King and on all his subjects by placing my hat on their heads.'

Kurkar was prepared to submit to anything for the sake of prolonging his life. He therefore consented to have the juggler's greasy hat placed on his head and commanded that all his subjects should follow his example. Thus twenty thousand people received, after the King, this strange sacrament.

All those who put on the hat became instantaneously semi-conscious, with their minds dull and empty of thought. The King shared the condition of his people, except that, in him, one desire obstinately resisted the stupor: the desire for a long life.

'What must yet be done that I may assure myself many years of life,' he again inquired.

'I cannot tell you, Chief,' the Indian answered, 'but the *mos* have revealed to me that your patron god will appear to you in seven days from now. He will counsel you.'

After they had received provisions for the road, the three tramps together with their beasts went off in the direction of Ling.

Seven days later, Gesar, under the form of the god Namthig Karpo, clad in white and riding a goat, descended during the night on to the balcony of Kurkar's room. He awoke the King and said to him:

'Kurkar, I am Namthig, the god of your fathers; listen to me.'

The King most earnestly prostrated himself and adored the god. The latter continued:

'I am going to reveal to thee a secret. At the place called Tsara-pedma Togten, when the sun rises, seven white spiders will transform themselves into seven men who will dance. They are the gods of my suite. Send all thy subjects, thy ministers, Dugmo, all without exception, to see this dance. As for thee, be careful not to leave the palace; thy life depends on this. If thou remainest here, the number of thy days will increase and the dangers that threaten thee will be averted.'

Having spoken thus, Namthig flew instantly away on his goat across the sky leaving a trail of light behind him.

Without loss of time, the King had all those who were in the palace awakened. He then commanded that the drum should be beaten at the four gates and all the men, women, children, chiefs, masters, and servants, told to go at once to Tsarapedma Togten to witness at sunrise the dance of the seven gods.

Dugmo thought the advice given by Namthig very strange, and was filled with misgiving. Why had Kurkar to isolate himself in this way?

She took a white silk scarf and, weeping, went to the King. She beseeched him to reconsider the matter and to keep, at least, some of the warriors near him. Since the previous celestial warnings had been followed by unforeseen calamities, could it not be that also this time there was danger near at hand? However, all she could say did not alter her husband's determination; his mind, dulled by the charm but full of the desire for a long life, was incapable of appreciating the value of her remarks.

Very far from listening to Dugmo, he became angry with her, and savagely ordered her to leave him and go at once with the others to Tsarapedma Togten. She was forced to obey; and those around the King, seeing her thus rebuffed, dared not insist further.

They all left the palace, leaving Kurkar there by himself.

At the spot indicated, the Horpas saw the seven dancers spring into view and engage in the most graceful and original of evolutions. Neither monk nor layman had ever shown in feast-day dances such agility and suppleness or worn such magnificent costumes. The dresses of the celestial dancers changed at each new figure in the dance. The performers, appearing not to feel any fatigue, danced uninterruptedly; and the audience who watched them, amazed, lost all knowledge of time. These dancers were magic creations of Gesar, who, also by his power, lengthened the duration of the day, so that it lasted as long as two ordinary days. The Horpas, not seeing the sun set, did not think of going home, but sat lost in contemplation of the spectacle that had been vouchsafed to them, believing that through the goodwill of Namthig, they were beholding a frolic of the gods.

The day that had become so extraordinarily long at Tsarapedma Togten was, on the contrary—always through the medium of Gesar—reduced to half its length in the town of Hor. Kurkar, unaccustomed to solitude, was bored at first then felt vaguely disquieted at the silence in his palace. He wondered why Dugmo, ministers and the people did not return now that the sun was sinking below the horizon, for he was unable to realize that at the hour when twilight darkened his room, the sun had not yet reached the meridian at Tsarapedma Togten. Tired of waiting, he finally fell asleep.

A dazzling light immediately enveloped the palace, and the King, waking with a start, saw Gesar standing before him in his glittering armour and holding in his hand his sword of celestial iron. His person shone as the sun.

'Dost thou know me, Kurkar the demon?' he said. 'I am Gesar of godly race, the son of Korlo Demchog and Dorje Phagmo, the envoy of Padma Sambhava, the King of Ling and the Conqueror of the Universe. Thou didst invade my country and make thyself its ruler, thou didst carry away my wife and my possessions, thou didst kill Gyatza, my childhood's friend, and didst desire further to outrage him after death and humble the people of Ling by ignominiously hanging his head on thy palace wall. I am here now that thou mayest answer for thy heinous crimes.'

'Ah!' ejaculated the King, his eyes dilated by surprise and terror, 'how blind I have been not to understand that you were here! Everyone said that Lutzen had devoured you!'

Gesar did not give him time to say anything more. With a single stroke of his sword, he cut off his head, which rolled into the middle of the room. The Hero left it there, and, concentrating his thoughts, directed Kurkar's 'spirit' to the Western Paradise; he then flew away into the sky. Precisely at this moment, the seven dancers suddenly disappeared in Tsarapedma Togten, and all the Horpas returned home delighted with their day's pleasure, of which they never suspected the length.

On entering the King's room, Dugmo at once perceived the severed head lying on the floor. Her terrified cries brought those who were in the palace to her.

'This is Gesar's work,' the Queen said to them. 'All my presentiments were true. Gesar has returned. It is he who has caused the wonders and calamities that we have witnessed during these last months.'

They all lamented, fearing that Gesar would appear and destroy them as well.

A certain number of the chiefs wanted to mobilize the army at once and prepare for war, whilst others, among whom were Dikchen Shenpa and Tongzö Yundub, felt disposed to surrender to the mighty Hero. Dikchen spoke out boldly:

'Gesar and I,' he said, 'we are children of the same mother. Whosoever attacks him will find me in front of him. Besides, it is madness to think of resisting a power such as his. The best thing we can do is to prepare for his reception. I will go myself to meet him with a scarf in my hand.'

A section of the people, Dikchen's own vassals and those of Tongzö, sided with him, the rest ran to fetch their weapons.

Then, in the direction of Ling, Gesar appeared surrounded by many gods and followed by six hundred warriors of divine race. Those who resisted him were massacred to the last man. As to the other Horpas, he spared them, both chiefs and people.

After his victory, Gesar returned to Ling.

Chapter 9

SECHANG DUGMO had remained hidden in the palace, not daring to appear before her victorious husband, and Gesar had left without troubling himself about her. After his departure, Gartza, the smith's daughter, urged the unfaithful wife to go with her to Ling to beg for Gesar's forgiveness. Dugmo let herself be persuaded and they started, accompanied by Dikchen Shenpa and Tongzö Yundub.

Upon their arrival, the two men found lodging in a small hut that was hidden away in one of the palace yards; the two women, carrying presents, went to prostrate themselves at the King's feet. Gesar already knew of the coming of Dikchen and Yundub, and commanded that they should be brought before him, secretly, that night. They duly presented themselves with scarves and gifts, very uneasy as to what fate had in store for them.

'Do you remember your previous lives?' Gesar asked the two men.

As they remained silent, he brought back to their memory the meeting of the gods that had taken place under the presidency of Padma Sambhava in the paradise which faced Zandog Palri. He related how they, both of them his ex-companions, had been born among men in order to help him in his mission, and, having issued from the same mother, were his brothers in their present life.

'Three children were found in the sack that Todong ordered to be thrown into the river,' he reminded them. 'One of them, the dark-skinned Tobchen Thugö, completely forgot his origin and the task for which he had been incarnated as a son of the human race. Fighting on the side of Hor, he killed Gyatza, my childhood's friend, and has now died in expiation of his crimes. You two, only, remain today: thou, Dikchen of the flame-coloured face, and thou, blue-complexioned Yundub.

'Listen attentively to my orders. You both must return to Hor at once, taking Dugmo and Gartza with you. You shall give Dugmo as wife to the two chiefs Kurser and Kurnag, and you shall serve these last, making every effort to please them and to gain their confidence. Do not speak of me, do not let them suspect our kinship. Later, when my mission will have ended, we shall reunite in the Western Paradise.'

Then, by Gesar's magic power, all four instantaneously found themselves back in Hor, where their absence had not been noticed.

They immediately went to Kurser's palace. The chief was unaware of his brother's death and of the fight that had taken place near his castle. He was astonished to see these unexpected visitors and received them graciously.

As soon as they had told him of the dance of the seven gods that they had witnessed and of the murder of Kurkar, which had happened during their absence, King Kurser exclaimed in desperation:

'Doubt is no longer possible; all these things are the work of Gesar!... A messenger must be sent to Kurnag to tell him to muster his warriors in haste. I shall do the same. We must send a hundred thousand men to Ling and ascertain exactly the whereabouts of the King.'

The courier was despatched immediately, and Kurser asked Dikchen for his advice as to the best way of attacking Gesar.

Kurkar's ex-minister, having had re-awakened in him the consciousness of the task that he had accepted before the Precious Guru, had severed his ties with the house of the demon Kings of Hor. He, therefore, decided to mislead Kurser for Gesar's benefit.

'My opinion, Chief, differs from yours,' he said. 'These disasters have not been caused by Gesar, but by the gods Namthig, Barthig, and Sathig. A great festival had been promised them. Perhaps Kurkar did not show enough eagerness when summoning the lamas to make offerings to these gods. Perhaps he lacked faith, or perhaps the offerings that he purposed to present did not appear very satisfactory to our protectors. Deities are difficult to please; they get irritated at our slightest fault and promptly punish us for it. . . . If you wish for my opinion, I should counsel you, Chief, to assemble the lamas without delay in order to propitiate Namthig, Barthig, and Sathig. As for Gesar, he is no longer in Ling.'

Dikchen had spoken so persuasively, that Kurser once again began to have doubts about all that related to Gesar. Instead of calling his warriors together, he had the lamas summoned, and sent another message to his brother, asking him to assist with a few of his chiefs at the solemn adoration of the Hor gods on the mountain that was dedicated to them.

At dawn the next day, flags, banners bearing inscriptions, lances and halberds ornamented with bits of material of various colours, and beribboned bows were placed near the altar to the Hor gods[1] at the summit of the mountain. Incense sticks burned among the *tormas* and the various offerings. The lamas[2] recited conjurations in a loud voice, accompanied by a great sound of drums, bells, *gyalings*, *ragdongs*,[3] and cymbals. The clamour and noise of their instruments ran along the mountain as the rolling of thunder.

While they were thus occupied, Kurser, seated in a magnificent tent, awaited with impatience his brother's arrival. The latter's residence was far distant from the place where the worship of the national gods was being celebrated. However, the attendants who were on the watch for his coming finally informed the King that they descried Kurnag and seven horsemen crossing the plain that lay at the foot of the mountain.

Gesar knew that Dikchen had deceived Kurser and that, at this moment, the Chief, his lamas, and his principal officers were on the mountain adoring the gods. Flying into the sky on his horse Kyang Gö Karkar, he invoked his celestial friends and relations, who immediately surrounded him in vast numbers, carrying 'thunderbolts' in their hands. They came as a great cloud, darkening the sun. Arrived above the spot where Kurser and his people stood, the gods let their 'thunderbolts'[4] fall, and all those on the mountain were reduced to ashes.

---

[1] These altars to local and ancestral gods are simply built-up heaps of stones, often of great dimensions, covered with dried branches interspersed with banners bearing inscriptions, or, among the herdsmen, with sheep's wool, yak tails, etc.

[2] These lamas were *bönpos*, followers of Tibet's former religion: Shamanism.

[3] *Gyalings*, kind of hautboy: *ragdongs*, very long Tibetan trumpets.

[4] The Tibetans believe that thunder is produced by the great celestial dragon throwing down eggs. These eggs are the thunderbolts that kill all those they hit. There are a number of people who pretend to have seen these eggs fall during a storm. The bard who recited this poem to me boasted of having done so. Nevertheless these 'thunderbolts' may also be taken as resembling, in shape, the *dorjes* that are used in lamaist rites.

Dikchen, Yundub, and Sechang Dugmo, who had remained at the palace, were unhurt, as were the rest of those who had not gone to the Celebration. At the moment when Gesar was destroying the worshippers of the three gods, they saw a great light, which had the shape of a tent, descend upon the mountain. Thinking that the gods had come to bless Hor, they prostrated themselves in the direction of the miraculous apparition. It was in this position that Gesar found them, when his flying courser touched ground in front of Kurser's palace.

Its doors opened at that instant and Dugmo, Dikchen, and Yundub advanced towards the Hero, followed by all the palace attendants, who carried lighted lamps, rich scarves, and burning incense.

Gesar and the gods who accompanied him then preached the Good Doctrine to the people of Hor, explaining it to them in various ways, each of which was appropriate to a particular class of hearer and in accordance with his degree of intelligence. Thus the teaching was profitable to all. When this had been done, the Hero conferred an initiation upon the people and firmly established the Religion in the country of Hor. He afterwards remained for a month in Kurser's palace.

As for the third King of Hor, Kurnag, accompanied by seven of his chiefs, he had reached the summit of the mountain a little after the death of his brother and of the other worshippers. He could only contemplate, horror-stricken, their calcined bodies.

'This is the work of Gesar,' he exclaimed aghast. 'It would be vain for us to try to contend against him. Let us hasten away, no matter where, so long as we escape him.'

Ripatarbum, his minister, shook his head sadly:

'Whether we go to India or to China,' he said, 'there does not exist a place on earth where we could feel in perfect safety. I have read many times in the prophetic writings of demon Gara that Gesar would march over the earth, subduing nations and preaching the Law of Justice. However, let us endeavour to reach a very remote and completely uninhabited spot; perhaps, Gesar will scorn to follow us there.'

They went to a place called Achung Babu Dzong in the region of Ngari (S.W. of Tibet).

Gesar knew of their flight and reflected thus: What shall I do with Kurnag and his men? I could destroy them as I did Kurser and the worshippers of Namthig, but among them is Ripatarbum, who is the foster-father of Tongzö Yundub and who has always behaved well to him. It would be wanting in kindness to kill him with the others. Seven men cannot do much harm: let them live. And he spared them.

These seven Horpas are still alive, hidden in the mountains of Ngari. They are of such gigantic stature that taking an ordinary man in their hand, they can roll him between their fingers as we do a flea. In their retreat they have multiplied and there now exist a great number of their kind.

At the end of the present period of the earth, they will come out in a body and destroy the Buddhists.

For the time being, the Great Lama of the Sakyapa Sect, direct descendant in the spiritual line of Sakya Penchen, has control of these giants and prevents them from leaving their retreat.

Nevertheless, one of them, wishing to know if the time had not come when he and his could attack their enemies with success, did succeed in eluding his vigilance and in going out to reconnoitre. He managed to get as far as the precincts of the Sakya monastery, but the Great Lama, becoming conscious of his presence, snapped his fingers, and the giant fell dead. The Lama then ordered his disciples to decapitate the corpse and to hang the head at the top of his residence, where it remains to this day.[1]

*   *   *

Now that Gesar inhabited the Hor palace, Dugmo lived in perpetual dread; for the son whom she had had by Kurkar was with her and she feared lest her husband should discover him. Gesar, she thought, will hate him, and because, as Kurkar's son, he is of demon stock, he will want to kill him. Therefore, she earnestly beseeched Gartza not to betray her secret.

'You are under a delusion,' the latter said to her, 'if you think that Gesar does not know of this child's existence. The King is omniscient; nothing escapes him. This boy will be of no use to you, you can expect no good from him.'

'No matter,' rejoined Dugmo. 'He is flesh of my flesh. The fact that, later, he may destroy the Religion and its followers does not trouble me. I will not let Gesar kill him.'

[1] A head really hangs above the palace of the Great Lama; but, no matter what the credulous devotees may say, it is not a human head.

'How can you speak in this way?' retorted Gartza. 'Have you forgotten that you are an avatar of Dolma Karpo (the white Dolma). Still, we will see what happens. Meanwhile, I promise to keep silent.'

Having remained a month in Kurser's palace, Gesar thought of returning to Ling. Yet, the knowledge that a son of Kurkar's was living preoccupied him. He resolved to kill the child, but he hesitated to tear him from his mother's arms, because of the grief she would feel. He decided to have recourse to a ruse for getting her away from the boy.

'Tomorrow,' he said to Tongzö Yundab, 'thou shalt bring Dugmo before me. I am returning to Ling. Tell her that if she likes, she can start with me.'

Yundub delivered his message, and Dugmo answered that it would give her great pleasure to see her own country again.

She immediately began preparing for her departure, packing the precious things she wished to take with her. These formed the load of a great many beasts.

As for her son, she wrapped him in silken garments and sat him in a sandalwood box,[1] recommending him to the care of her faithful attendants.

'I am leaving you in order to go to Ling,' she said to the little fellow. 'I shall not stay there long and shall hope to find you well when I return. We will then live together without separating, and, when you will have attained the required age, you will become King of Hor.'

'Mother,' answered the child, 'I am now three years old. When I am six, I shall go to Ling to fetch you, if you still linger there. Afterwards, I will kill Gesar and destroy the Religion he upholds.'

Dugmo was delighted at hearing him express such courageous sentiments, but advised him to be prudent.

'That which you say is very good, my son, but be careful not to speak in this manner before anyone but me. Gesar is not an ordinary man, he is a powerful magician. Be on your guard against him.'

She then went to Gesar, who was on the point of leaving the palace.

His escort was composed of eight hundred soldiers, and ninety mules loaded with luggage followed them.[2]

---

[1] Probably one of those seats shaped as a case, which the Tibetans call box-seats.

[2] It must be understood that, according to the custom of the country, the soldiers carried their rations in bags hung on either side of their saddles. The ninety mules must have been laden with booty and the victor's personal luggage.

When the travellers reached the foot of Mount Kongkartisum,[1] where, formerly, Dugmo had hidden the silver vases, Gesar pretended to have suddenly remembered a valuable article that he had left behind at the palace.

'I must return to get it,' he said to his wife.

The latter, always fearing for her son, tried to dissuade him.

'Why take the trouble,' she answered. 'Dikchen, Gartza, or I can go for you.'

'No,' replied Gesar. 'It is a question of a sword made of iron fallen from the sky that I received from the gods. It is the one with which I killed Kurkar. I left it in a sandalwood box. No one but I can take it.'

Dugmo then understood that he knew of her son's existence and intended killing him.

'I see that you know I have a son,' she said crying. 'If you kill him, kill me also, it were better so.'

Gesar feigned astonishment.

'Have you a son? I did not know it. I shall not kill him. My sword will not touch him. I shall not injure him in any way.'

Dugmo thought she could trust his word, and the Hero flew away on his celestial horse. He landed on the palace balcony then, looking into the interior through a chink in the shutter, saw the little boy, who was awake.

The child stood upright, motionless, reflecting. Gesar, who could read another's mind, knew what he was thinking: 'I am not yet three years old; however, I shall grow up, but, later, when I attack my father's murderer, shall I succeed in killing him? I must try and know for certain by means of an omen.' He took his little bow in his hand and placed an arrow in it, saying aloud:

'If my arrow pierces the door that is over there at the end of the yard, this will signify that I shall be able to kill Gesar.'

He shot his arrow. It hit the door and split it.

Gesar understood that if the boy grew up, he would become a powerful enemy, as formidable for Ling as for himself and the Religion. He had a great desire to kill him, but was held back by the promise he had given to Dugmo.

[1] *Dorje Tsi Gu* (see Chapter 6). The bards did not agree regarding its name. One told me that it had two different names, which is not a rare thing in Tibet. Another said that Kongkartisum was a mountain in the *Dorje Tsi Gu* range. But, of course, none of them knew anything for certain about it.

At this moment Lha Tsangspa and Manene appeared and, seating themselves on his either shoulder, spoke into his ear.

'Do not hesitate, O Hero,' they said to him, 'this demon's son must be destroyed. We will help thee to rid thyself of him without using any weapon.'

Whereupon the gods lifted one of the pillars of the hall in which the child stood, and Gesar, seizing the little fellow by his feet, pushed him under the pillar, which the gods at once let fall into place again, crushing their victim under its weight.

Gesar immediately sent the poor boy's 'spirit' to the Paradise of the Great Beatitude, and afterwards hastened to rejoin his caravan.

Dugmo asked to see the sword that he had gone to recover, and he showed her the first that came to his hand. She then inquired after her son and whether Gesar had seen him.

'I did not see him,' he answered, 'but I saw a great number of gods round the palace. Perhaps he is dead?'

Dugmo understood that her husband had misled her by an ambiguous promise. Gesar has probably not killed my son with his own hand, she thought, but he has many friends among the gods, and these have been able to perpetrate the murder in his stead. Her sorrow was great, but she did not doubt that, according to his charitable habit, the King had secured his victim's happiness by sending his 'spirit' to be reborn in some blest abode. This thought somewhat softened the bitterness of her maternal anguish; moreover, she was helpless in the matter. She bowed her head and remained silent.

In a single day, the travellers would cover a distance equal to four ordinary stages in the journey. They soon reached the place where the territories of Ling karma chugi yada, Ling tu maggi yangrab, and Dotha Lungpai Sumdo conjoin, and they camped there.

Gesar then said to Dikchen:

'Up till now thou hast followed as a free man, but tomorrow the people of Ling will come to meet me, and, on seeing thee,[1] they will remember that thou didst command the troops that invaded their country. If I do not punish thee, my people will wonder and grumble. It is therefore necessary that thou shouldst accept the consequences of thine acts.'

---

[1] During Dikchen's last very short stay at Ling, after Kurkar's death, he had not been seen in public.

He had him fastened to a stake by an iron chain.

Sure enough the next day, the villagers of Ling, together with their chiefs and lamas, arrived, some on foot, others riding, to the number of ten thousand men.

Aku Chipön gave an address, congratulating the King on his victory, and they all offered him scarves and presents.

Todong came last and, seeing Dikchen chained up, rejoiced exceedingly. Here is that great minister who spoke to me from on high, he said to himself. Approaching the prisoner he called to him:

'Hallo! red-bearded Dikchen, thou mighty minister. Hast thou forgotten the time when thou didst invade Ling at the head of a hundred and twenty thousand soldiers, didst kill our chiefs and carry off our Queen Dugmo? . . . Thou miserable wretch! I, the *tulku* of Tamdrin and chief of Ling, am going to bind thy hands and feet and beat thee until thou succumbest.'

And, without waiting further, he hit him several times with his heavy stick, kicked him, spat on him, and shouted:

'I shall have thee given five hundred strokes of the stick, cursed demon!'

'Thou hadst best keep silent,' rejoined Dikchen. 'When I arrived at Ling, thou didst hasten to surrender, placing thyself on the side of the stronger—even before their victory was certain—betraying thy fellow-countrymen in order to gain favour with the King of Hor and obtain the resultant benefits.

'I was Kurkar's servant, his debtor since my birth, therefore in duty bound to carry out his commands; but thou didst desert Gesar's cause, that of thy King. Thou art nothing but a vile traitor. If I deserve punishment, thou deservest it ten times more.'

At hearing these just remarks, Todong became violently angry.

'Ah!' he said, 'this time, I will kill thee!'

He was drawing his sword from its scabbard, when Yundub, attracted by the noise, came up. Dikchen made him a sign and the latter intervened.

Kurkar's ex-minister explained the trouble to him and made an appeal to Gesar, maintaining that it was not right that he alone should be punished and have to support the insults and blows with which a traitor was overwhelming him.

Yundub hastened to inform the King of what was happening, but the Hero replied that he had no time to give to the matter, and merely issued orders to the effect that the two enemies were to be separated: Dikchen was to be left chained up and Todong brought near the royal tent.

'What is this that you say!' exclaimed Yundub. 'You have no time to administer justice? Is there anything in the world more urgent, more necessary? Do you know of one? Are you or are you not a son of gods who has incarnated on earth for the purpose of making equity reign?

'If you have no time to judge these men, they will settle their quarrel themselves, fighting as two brute beasts.'

'Very well then,' answered Gesar, 'let us leave the force of their past actions, which justly rewards the good as well as the bad, to operate by itself. If Dikchen succeeds in breaking his chain, I will permit him to fight Todong. If he is incapable of doing so, he shall remain chained up for life.'

Yundub repeated the King's words to Dikchen; and as Todong, seated in safety at a little distance, continued to insult and defy him, fury multiplied the ex-minister's strength, who was then able to break his chain and throw himself on his enemy.

When the cowardly Todong saw Dikchen rushing towards him, he felt his hair stand on end. He tried to escape, but his stoutness prevented him from moving quickly. Dikchen was on him in an instant, and, seizing him savagely by the beard, lifted him several times before finally flinging him violently on the ground.

Todong's yells resounded throughout the camp, and soldiers came running from all sides to see what was happening. Although Todong was not a favourite with the people of Ling, Gesar was afraid lest they might seek to defend their chief and do harm to Dikchen, in this way provoking the Horpa's anger and once more making an enemy of him. Accordingly, he sent some of his attendants to separate the two adversaries and bring them before him.

'Why dost thou permit thyself to insult Dikchen?' he said severely to Todong. 'Punishments and rewards concern me only. I desire that everyone pass in peace the few days we remain here.'

*　　*　　*

When Gesar broke camp and returned to Ling, Dikchen was led in the rear as prisoner of war. However, before the Hero's departure, Manene had reminded him that the gods had destined Kurkar's ex-minister for the kingship of Hor and for bringing him useful support in the struggles yet to come. She again exhorted him to treat Dikchen with kindness, behaviour to which Gesar was naturally inclined since Dikchen and he were sons of the same mother.

Therefore, on arriving at Ling, Gesar merely ordered him not to leave the house that he was assigning to him, and for a definite time to perform a certain number of religious acts designed to cleanse his mind from the defilement that it had suffered through his long association with the demon Kings of Hor.

When his period of penance was ended, Dikchen craved an audience with Gesar, and went to him carrying a long silk scarf and several presents. After prostrating himself before the King, he told him that he had now completely recovered his mental clarity, which had been obscured by his contact with the demons of Hor, and that he understood the full measure of his wrong actions towards him and the people of Ling.

'Kill me,' he said, 'and send my spirit to a paradise, or permit me to leave as a pilgrim for distant sacred shrines, for I live here in constant dread that the Ling warriors, who have never forgiven me for having once invaded their land, will cause me to perish miserably.'

And in speaking thus, he showed great anguish.

Knowing the will of the gods concerning Dikchen and seeing that he had become worthy to reign over the converted Horpas, Gesar replied that he should leave Ling as was his wish, but, with him; and, as their departure must be kept secret, he enjoined him not to speak of it to anyone. He then conferred upon him an initiation that gave him back full possession of the faculties that he had enjoyed as a god's son in his previous life.

Long before daybreak the next day, Gesar, mounted on Kyang Gö Karkar, and Dikchen on his red horse, left Ling and rode in the direction of Hor, without having been seen by anyone. However, before leaving, the Hero had created a phantom exactly resembling himself. This phantom, which remained at the palace in his place, was to perform all the actions customary with him and in this way deceive those who approached it. When Sechang Dugmo and the attendants entered the King's room to bring him his morning tea, they found him, as they did each morning, seated on his couch reading the Sacred Writings, so that not one of them suspected his departure.[1]

[1] The Tibetans attribute a similar wonder to the Tashi Lama. Escaping from Shigatze some years ago, he had, according to them, left behind him—to cover his flight and deceive his enemies—a phantom that perfectly resembled him. For details on this subject see *My Journey to Lhasa*.

Nevertheless, since no phantom representing either Dikchen or the King's horse had been left in their place their disappearance became known. For a long time the people searched for hoof-marks and finally found some that went in the direction of Hor. This fact, coupled with that of the disappearance of Dikchen and his horse, seemed convincing to those who knew of them: Kurkar's ex-minister was the culprit. That enemy, whom Gesar all too generously had spared and even treated with kindness, had proved traitor—a result which was only to be expected—and had stolen the divine courser Kyang Gö Karkar.

An excited crowd ran to the palace with the news of the theft, asking for directions in following the thief. They were received by Sechang Dugmo, phantom-Gesar having declared that he wished to pass some days in meditation and would see no one. However, the importance of the event appeared such that the Queen ventured to disturb her husband in order to tell him about what she had just heard. Crowded near the threshold of the royal apartment, the people's delegates strove to hear the orders that their Chief would give.

But phantom-Gesar just smiled.

'Kyang Gö Karkar is of divine race,' he said, 'and no one is capable of stealing him. Now withdraw, and go in peace to your homes.'

They were all greatly astonished, but none of them dared to expostulate, so they departed in silence. As for Dugmo, knowing the Hero's magic powers, she began to suspect that the mysterious absence of his horse and of Dikchen was his doing.

In the meantime, Gesar and Dikchen had arrived in Hor. Gesar immediately had the 'drum of the law' beaten to summon the chiefs and the people, and, when they were come together, he made known the command of the gods concerning Dikchen, whom he then established as King of Hor. A great festival took place at Kugar Yatsii Chud, at which the Hor tribes solemnly pledged themselves to be Gesar's allies and to fight under his command each time he should require their aid.

Thereupon Gesar took the road back to Ling. On his way, as a result of his clear-sightedness, he noticed a *Chide* (kind of demon), who wandered at random up and down. He recognized him as the reincarnated spirit of a Hor lama, guru Amun. The latter, a mighty sorcerer, equally well versed in both Bön and Buddhist doctrines, had by his witchcraft caused much evil to the people of Ling and, in the end, had been killed by them. Dying, animated by feelings of hatred, his 'spirit' had reincarnated as a malevolent being and, under this new form, could continue to be very harmful.

Gesar deemed it expedient to convert him. In order to do so, he took on the appearance of the *mopa* Lama Dungo of Hor, a friend of the deceased. Amun, as soon as he saw him, was very distressed, thinking that his friend had been killed by the Ling soldiers and that, owing to the rite of *powa* not having been performed for him, his 'spirit' could not find the path to rebirth in a paradise.

Prompted by feelings of friendship, and unaware that he, himself, was dead and, precisely, in the situation in which he imagined Dungo to be, he immediately came towards him with the intention of helping him by directing his 'spirit' to a happy dwelling-place.

Gesar then told Amun that he no longer belonged to this world; but the latter at first obstinately refused to believe him, saying that he did not remember his death in any way. So the Hero captured him by the 'lasso of the Void',[1] and, as he knew him to be learned, he explained to him the law of causality according to both the Bön and the Buddhist doctrines. Whereupon the Lama understood that he was really dead and, the disposition of his mind having been changed, he repented of his bad actions and no longer wished to commit others of the same kind. In response to his earnest requests, Gesar transferred his 'spirit' to an abode of the blest, and the demon, who had been animated by it, fell dead.

Back again at Ling without having been seen by anyone, Gesar reabsorbed the phantom he had emitted. The next day, his people found Kyang Gö Karkar in its usual place. They hastened to bring it food and to announce its happy return to their master.

Listening to them, Gesar smiled again.

'It is well,' he said simply.

Dugmo then, knew, that the real Gesar had returned.

[1] A mystic expression.

Chapter 10

King Satham's dream—He wishes to conquer a dependency of Ling—Misfortunes attributed to a conch statue—The favourite Queen is hurled from the roof terrace during a hurricane—Satham shuts himself up with the corpse, hoping for its resuscitation—Dikchen carries off Satham's eldest son—The magic sticks that give invisibility—Satham's brother is lifted into the air and killed by flying horses—Gesar, in the form of a bee with iron wings, enters into Satham's body and kills him—The Hero meets an adversary of his own strength and fights with him on the bank of a poison-lake—The taking of Satham's citadel, massacre of all those in it—Gesar establishes Satham's eldest son as King of Jang—Gesar goes into retreat for a period of thirteen years.

IN the land of Jang, King Satham had a dream. He saw the patron gods of his ancestors.

Namthe Karpo Rakarkya, in a tent made of multi-coloured clouds, sat astride a bay horse. He was clad in a cloud, a moon-coloured coat of mail, and wore a gleaming helmet. He flourished a sword; the hilt of which was three-pointed.

He said in a persuasive voice:

'O Satham, awake! Rise up, O Satham. Go! Seize the excellent nutriment that gives life to beings,[1] O Satham!'

On the path where creeps the dawn, in a proud citadel made of interlaced serpents, Sathe Nazgpo rode a black yak. His eyes were shaped as the crescent moon. He wore armour of iron. His lasso was a serpent, which, curled round his head, served him for turban; and the sword that cuts life was passed through it as ornament.

He said in a powerful voice:

'O Satham, awake! Rise up, O Satham. Go! Seize the excellent nutriment that gives life to beings, O Satham!'

Behind a screen of mist resembling a spread beard rose a palace made of dark storm-clouds. There, in anger, Barthe bestrode a speckled goat. His armour flashed as lightning and his sharp sword glinted red.

---

[1] It is impossible to translate exactly the terms *zas kyi bchud; bchud* signifies sap, the nutritive principle of a thing; that which in food or in the earth is the nutritive element that sustains life.

He said in a terrible voice:

'O Satham, awake! Rise up, O Satham. Go! Seize the excellent nutriment that gives life to beings, O Satham!'

'O Chief of Jang,' continued the gods, 'why dost thou remain inactive? Touching thy frontier is a land of abundance, whose ever-fertile soil assures well-being to the people who possess it. It is the country of Markham, over which Gesar already extends his influence and of which, soon, he will make himself completely master. Do not wait until this moment has come, for, if thou dost not forestall him, the King of Ling, after having established himself in Markham, will invade thy territory.'

And all three gods exhorted him, repeating in turn:

'Rise up, O Satham! Go, conquer Markham's fertile soil, O Satham! . . .'

As soon as he awoke, the King related his dream to his minister Petul and expressed his intention of obeying the injunctions of his ancestral gods by mobilizing his troops.

Petul listened to him without enthusiasm and even with disapproval. For some time past, he had noticed that a regrettable change was taking place in Satham's character. Whereas formerly he was good-tempered, thoughtful, and prudent, he now appeared to be the victim of an inordinate restlessness, which made him prone to change his mind and to decide upon unreasonable acts. The minister frankly told the King of his observations, and even communicated them publicly to the State councillors, who had assembled to discuss the project of a campaign in which, apparently, the troops of Jang would have to meet those of Ling.

'Gesar is of divine race, O Chief,' repeated Petul. 'He is invincible; to give him cause to attack you is to go to your ruin. Remain, as in the past, at peace in your flourishing state.'

Queen Asi and the King's daughter, Pemachösden, supported him and insisted on the inadvisability of provoking Gesar.

A few of the chiefs shared their views, but the majority of them sided with Satham. Yula, his eldest son, was the most eager to fight.

'Why,' he said, 'should we remain in timorous inaction? Such conduct is not fitting to warriors and, moreover, our King and our gods command us to fight. It is not for us to discuss their orders, but to obey them.'

Satham, with hard and insulting words, enjoined obedience upon those who dared question his will. When he had finished speaking, he shut his mouth, making his teeth snap together noisily; and his eyes, kindled by anger, rolled in their sockets as glowing balls of fulgent copper.

He then gave orders concerning the strength of the different brigades, their disposition on the field, and the chiefs who were to command them.

*　　*　　*

While King Satham was preparing to invade the land of Markham, Manene, riding an eagle and escorted by several gods, appeared one night to Gesar in his palace in Ling.

'Awake, noble Hero!' she said to him, 'do not think of resting. Satham Gyalpo, King of the West, whom it is thy mission to destroy, is hastening himself the hour of his destruction by making ready to attack thee. He is a redoubtable enemy. Under his command there are clever generals of proved valour. Thou must begin the campaign at once, but beware of advancing incautiously against the troops of this powerful chief. Beware, above all, of provoking his son, Yula. He is of divine race, his strength is equal to thine, and none can overcome him. You both have been linked in friendship during a previous life. He forgot this tie when, on account of certain of his faults, he was begotten of a father of demon race. Thou, remember it. Later he will prove a precious ally, therefore treat him with consideration and, by ruse, keep him away from the fight. Likewise, by stratagem, reduce the power of Jang before giving battle, and, tomorrow, send for Dikchen. He must come with his warriors. His assistance is indispensable to thee.'

On hearing the voice of the goddess, Gesar had hastened to do her homage by burning incense and lighting the altar lamps. With joined palms, he assured her of his readiness to fulfil his task concerning Satham as he had fulfilled it with regard to Lutzen and to the three Kings of Hor. He only prayed that she would make known to him the means he must employ in order to ensure victory, and that she would grant him her assistance as well as that of the gods.

'Listen to me attentively,' answered Manene, 'I will tell thee what thou must do.

'During the reign of the first King of the Satham dynasty a statue representing a horse was made in shell. By means of powerful charms, learned magicians caused it to become possessed of special protective virtues for the guarding of the princes of that line. This statue is even capable of speaking when the necessity arises to warn the King of the presence of an enemy, but it can be heard only by him. Thou must destroy it in order to deprive Satham of its protection, and thou hadst better do so quickly, so as not to leave it time to inform him of the approach of thy troops.'

Having spoken thus, Manene disappeared.

As soon as it was day, Gesar sent for his ministers and councillors. He informed them of the order that he had received from Manene, and commanded them to mobilize the Ling warriors and to send a message to Dikchen, demanding his presence and that of his troops. This last order gave rise to violent opposition. The Ling generals and ministers vehemently refused to collaborate with their ancient enemy and showed themselves to be very offended at the idea that the King should judge them incapable of carrying off the victory without outside help. They made a great noise, protesting that Gesar was wronging them and beseeching him to abandon the idea of calling Dikchen, declaring themselves ready to march against the men of Jang and to be certain of conquering them.

The Hero was obliged to speak authoritatively to them and to impose his will. A messenger started for Hor; and Gesar, mounting his flying horse, rose in the air and was quickly out of sight.

The shell horse was in a pavilion at Yumdung Jigdzong. This pavilion stood among yellow flowers in a garden that was enclosed by doorless bronze walls. Gesar transformed himself into a *kyang* (wild ass), created two other phantom *kyangs*, and the three animals appeared in the garden, nibbling at the flowers. A palace servant, perceiving them from a window, immediately informed the King of the presence in the doorless enclosure of three wild asses, which, by miracle, had entered there.

The King then remembered an ancient prophecy. It foretold that Gesar, after having triumphed over Lutzen and Kurkar, would attack him. But Satham made a mistake with regard to the true nature of the animals that grazed round the sacred pavilion. He thought: These must be *tulkus* of the shell horse, which it has created for the purpose of protecting me in the campaign that I am about to undertake to forestall the King of Ling's attack and to prevent him from invading my territory. I shall first look at the animals, then I will ask the *mopa* lamas to enlighten me concerning them.

As it was impossible to enter the enclosure because of the doorless walls, Satham Gyalpo, accompanied by the favourite Queen and the lords of the court, went up to the roof-terrace of the palace in order to look down into the grounds of the shell horse temple. The servants hurriedly spread tiger and leopard skin carpets to serve as seats for their masters, but the latter had not time to seat themselves before a terrific hurricane swept the roof, whirling the carpets about, throwing the men down, and, in the midst of the general confusion, hurling the Queen[1] from the roof. Her body fell into the secret garden, where it lay motionless with fractured skull and broken bones. At the same moment, the three *tulkus* disappeared in a white rainbow.

The anguish of the King, who was very much in love with his younger wife, was painful to behold. All the ministers, nobles, and attendants passed the night mourning with him, and their distress was the greater because, owing to the impossibility of recovering the Queen's body, they were unable to perform the customary funeral rites.

The next morning, three pilgrim lamas presented themselves at the palace gate.

'Their arrival is opportune,' said the sorrowing *gyalpo* (king). 'Bring them before me; perhaps they will be able to do *mos* about the three mysterious *kyangs* and the means by which we can lift the Queen's body out of the sacred enclosure.'

After they had been duly informed of Satham's extraordinary dream, of the military expedition that he was on the point of undertaking, of the predictions concerning the attacking of Jang by Gesar, and the sad occurrence that had just taken place, the lamas declared themselves to be skilled in the art of *mos* and capable of enlightening the King on all matters.

Towards evening, they made known the result of their divination.

'The King and his subjects are all victims of an error,' they said. 'The shell horse is not Satham's protector, but a demon enemy who has long been preparing for Gesar's victory. It is this demon who has killed the Queen. He now proposes to kill the King, then later his ministers and the country's chiefs. If you hasten to destroy the statue, the King and the chiefs will live long and the land will be prosperous.'

The situation was serious; the pilgrim's words contradicted

---

[1] The different versions are rather confused with regard to this 'Queen'. She cannot have been the one who had wisely counselled her husband to abstain from attacking Gesar, for that one appears again at the end of the war. Perhaps she was the King's second wife. Although little practised, polygamy is legal in Tibet.

an ancient and respected tradition. The ministers hesitated to lay hands on the shell horse, but the King, overwhelmed by grief, refused to listen to reason.

'Since the shell horse has killed my beloved wife, it shall be destroyed,' he said.

And turning to the lamas, he asked them if they could undertake its destruction.

'We can,' they answered.

With heavy axes they breached the wall and smashed the shell statue; then, lifting the Queen's body, carried it to the King's room.

'Now, Chief,' they said to him, 'do not try to distract your mind from your sorrow and do not proceed with the obsequies. Keep the Queen's body on her couch and remain by it, in complete isolation. Later, she will come to life again.'

Counting on this promise, the King immediately shut himself up with the corpse in a dark room; and the lamas went away, appearing to continue their journey.

Once out of sight, their forms vanished and Gesar, of whom they were the *tulkus*, flew away on Kyang Gö Karkar, encircled with a white light. Awaiting him in his palace, he found the Ling warriors whom the Chiefs had mustered, and Dikchen, who had preceded the troops.

'The initial part of my work is accomplished,' he told them. 'We can now take the field; nevertheless I must first remove another obstacle out of our way.

'In the paradise where I dwelt was an Indian magician called Lhabtu Ödpa Dungnal, who was my friend. He was reborn as King Satham's eldest son and named Yula Tongyur. He is invincible, and communicates his strength to those who fight under his orders. So long as he remains at the head of the men of Jang, we shall not be able to conquer them. Even if Yula were to be wounded by one of us, it would be a regrettable thing, for, not only has he been my friend, but he has to become my trusted ally in future campaigns. I wish him to remain out of the fighting. I shall cause him to have a dream that will give him the wish to go to Tsamtsoka (a place near a lake); Dikchen will go there and wait for him, and, by a ruse, get hold of him.'

The next night Satham's eldest son had a dream. He saw himself at Tsamtsoka. There he met a red man near to whom grazed a red horse. The stranger and he drank tea and talked amicably together.

When he awoke in the morning, he related his dream to his mother and showed a desire to go to Tsamtsoka.

The Queen tried to dissuade him.

'Gesar of Ling,' she said, 'is an adept in magic. He has led the three Hor Kings to their destruction by means of false dreams. I have reason to believe he thinks of attacking us. Be careful, my son; do not go to Tsamtsoka, I pray thee.'

But the young man refused to listen.

'The dream is too marvellous,' he answered. 'I want to see the sequel, if there be one.'

And saddling his horse, he rode off.

Dikchen had arrived at the lake-side before dawn, so he prepared tea and got out some dried meat and *tsampa* for a meal. While waiting, he reflected upon what he was going to say and do in order to get hold of Yula and lead him back to Ling.

As the sun appeared in the horizon, the young man came galloping up.

'Wonder of wonders!' he exclaimed to himself on perceiving Dikchen and his horse. 'Here is the man and the horse I saw in my dream.' And he went towards them.

'Who are you? Where do you come from?' he cried to Dikchen, as soon as he got within shouting distance.

'I am Dikchen Shenpa of Hor,' answered the other politely. 'I go to Jang[1] to see Yula. He and I have been brothers in a previous life.'

'This is marvellous!' exclaimed the Prince. 'I am Yula, and I dreamed last night that I would meet you at this very spot. It is a good omen.'

Then Yula took off the carpet that covered his saddle and spread it on the grass near Dikchen's, and they both sat eating and drinking.

All the time, Dikchen kept asking himself how he should set about his task. He mentally invoked Gesar and the latter, hearing him, came with the rapidity of the wind and alighted, invisible, on the forehead of Yula, who went into a deep sleep.

Blessing the Hero for his help, Dikchen securely roped the young fellow's arms and legs. When the Prince awoke he found himself

---

[1] The territory over which Satham ruled must have included the towns of Likiang, Yunning, Shungtien, and Atunze, situated north of the present Chinese province of Yunnan. These are still inhabited, with the exception of Likiang, by Tibetan tribes. The Tibetans, to this day, call these places by the names mentioned in the Gesar Epic.

firmly bound, and he passionately reproached Dikchen for his treachery.

'Do not be angry with me,' answered the Horpa Chief, 'I am obeying Gesar's commands. He has ordered me to bring you to him and he only wishes you good.'

'I will not go to Gesar,' rejoined Yula; 'I do not want to see him!' And he struggled so violently that Dikchen was afraid lest he should break his bonds. He succeeded, however, in tying him on to his horse and in carrying him to Ling.

Gesar, who knew that Yula was approaching, commanded his people to go and meet him with scarves of welcome, to greet him in such a manner as to dissipate his fears, and to bring him to him.

When the young Prince was come into his presence, Gesar looked kindly at him and said:

'Yula, do you not know me?'

At these words, memories gradually awoke in the captive's mind. He remembered his previous life in a paradise and how, during it, he had become Gesar's friend. Greatly distressed at the thought that he had been born with a darkened intelligence in a land of demons, he began to weep.

Having been freed from his bonds, he was bathed in the 'milk of a white lion'.[1] Then, arrayed in a yellow silk robe and wearing an iron helmet ornamented with a little flag, he sat in front of Gesar, on a red tiger-skin.[2]

The next day, the Ling army started for Jang. Five generals, each leading a hundred thousand men, took the advance. Gesar followed, accompanied by Serwa Nibum and Yula, with an escort of eight thousand soldiers. They all camped that night at Tsamtsoka.

In the meantime, Satham was told by his brother that his son Yula, after having a strange dream, had left for Tsamtsoka and had not returned.

'It is my opinion,' he said, 'that the predictions concerning Gesar's expedition against us are beginning to materialize, Gesar must be approaching. We can immediately mobilize forty thousand

---

[1] Figurative expression, signifying a particular 'initiation'.

[2] According to this version, Yula does not participate in the war. But, according to another version, he commands one of the three army-corps that Satham sends successively against Gesar and that, one after the other, are put to rout and massacred by the Ling warriors. However, Yula is not killed, and the two versions agree in making him reign over Jang after Gesar's victory.

well-trained soldiers; let us call them out at once. Let us also send men to look for Yula and spies in different directions to watch the movements of the Ling troops.'

The King approved of his brother's advice, and the ministers unanimously agreed that it should be followed without delay.

Seven men were sent to Tsamtsoka. Gesar, by his clear-sighted-ness, became aware of this fact as well as that of the mobilization of forty thousand soldiers near the capital.

'These seven men must be made prisoners,' he declared. At this command, seven officers placed their saddles ornamented with gold on their horses' backs and, with lasso in hand, waited for the enemy scouts.

Gesar possessed *dipshings* (small sticks that have the property of rendering men and things invisible), which he had brought from his friends the gods. He thrust them in the ground round his camp, which became invisible. When Satham's seven men arrived, they found the borders of the lake deserted, so they sat down to eat, thinking they would have nothing to report to their Chief. At this moment, the seven officers threw their lassoes, and each of them secured a prisoner whom he dragged back to the camp. When they had all reached it, Gesar withdrew his *dipshings*, and Satham Gyalpo's people saw themselves surrounded by a great army.

Yula then offered a scarf to Gesar and begged him to allow the captives to live, because they were not of demon race, but real human beings from Jang.

'Tomorrow,' he added, 'my father's brother will come. He is a real demon and you can kill him.'

Gesar consented to spare the lives of the seven men, but he had them fettered and placed under guard.

At the Jang palace, Chula Pönpo Serbachen, the King's brother, went again to see the sovereign in the room where he still remained secluded.

'Beyond a doubt,' he said, 'Gesar must be prowling in the vicinity. Just as Yula does not return, your scouts do not. I will go myself to Tsamtsoka, and will search out Gesar in order to kill him.'

During the following night Manene awoke the Hero.

'Be on your guard, O Gesar,' she said to him. 'Tomorrow Chula Pönpo will come here. Chula is a powerful demon. Do not, thyself, venture to fight him; no man can prevail against him.

'Leave at liberty beyond the camp thy horse Kyang Gö Karkar and, with it, Dikchen's red horse, which is swifter than the wind, also Dema's white horse and Se Dabla's blue[1] horse, both of which fly as eagles. The four coursers, endowed as they are with supernormal faculties, will succeed in overcoming the demon.'

The goddess, having spoken, returned to her paradisal abode.

At daybreak, Gesar gave orders in accordance with the directions that had been given him, and when Chula Pönpo arrived he saw no camp, but only four horses, that wandered about the solitude. Among them he recognized the Hero's celebrated horse and inferred from its presence that its master could not be far away.

Approaching the animals, he seized Kyang Gö Karkar by the mane, passed a rope round its neck,[2] and began to ride it up and down, shouting loudly:

'Hallo! Gesar, show thyself, coward! I, Chula, am here, riding thy famous horse. Come and recapture it, if thou be not a craven!'

He made a great noise, insulting and defying the Hero.

All at once, Kyang Gö Karkar rose in the air, carrying away its dismayed rider. Higher and yet higher it mounted in the blue. The three other horses followed, as geese do while travelling,[3] and when all of them had reached a point above the middle of the lake, Kyang Gö Karkar turned on his back and rolled in the space as a playful horse rolls on pasture land. Chula Pönpo was flung off its back and, his body lashed at by the other horses, fell with the rapidity of a stone into the water below.

The horses, then, returned to the camp.

Gesar immediately sent three scouts to Jang to discover the enemy's positions, and the men upon their return confirmed that forty thousand men guarded the capital.

After hearing their report Gesar assembled his soldiers, and, having chosen those who were to participate in the first attack, exhorted them to conduct themselves bravely and not to give quarter to a single adversary.

[1] It must be remembered that, in Tibet, a 'blue' horse means a silver-grey horse.
[2] When leading a horse a little distance or riding a pack-horse Tibetans do not use a bit.
[3] The country in which the action takes place is visited by large flights of wild geese.

The troopers rode off carrying a great number of different coloured flags and blowing down long trumpets.[1]

The chiefs who had assembled at Gyang[2] knew that Gesar's troops were arriving, and General Dus Jegyal Tukar went out from the ramparts at the head of his men.

Advancing bow in hand, he defied the bravest of the Ling officers, proposing a duel in which they should shoot arrows at each other's faces. And, taking Dema for Gesar, he let fly at him three arrows in succession, which went wide of their mark.

Then Dema, undaunted, said:

'O Brave! who art mounted on a white courser, know that I am Dema, the *tulku* of god Sera Hur, and Gesar's minister. I have been predestined to slay thee. I shall do so forthwith.'

And aiming at the General's forehead, he sent an arrow through his skull. Jegyal fell dead.

By this time the Ling army had already massacred ten thousand of the enemy, while their own losses numbered but a hundred men. The Jang troops, panic-stricken, were flying in disorder to seek refuge within the town walls. Gesar's soldiers pursued them, but on coming up against the gates of the fortress, which had been hastily closed after the entrance of the fugitives, they were forced to turn back.

'We have gained a victory,' they declared to Gesar upon regaining their camp, 'but we could not continue the battle because the men of Jang shut themselves up in their fort.'

'That suffices for the day,' answered the Hero. 'We shall receive counsel as to what will be best to do tomorrow.'

During the time that his troops were suffering defeat, King Satham remained in his room. His prime minister, disregarding the instructions that forbade anyone to pass the threshold, informed him of his army's defeat, describing the massacre of his soldiers and of his best generals. He begged the King to come out of his retreat, to put himself at the head of his warriors, and endeavour to repulse the Ling forces.

'I will do so tomorrow,' answered Satham, 'but in order to ensure

[1] As is done to this day by Tibetan and Chinese soldiers, especially in the frontier region.

[2] According to the version that I follow, Gyang must have been a town situated within the Jang territory. There exists at the present time a place of the same name. Perhaps it is only a question of difference of pronunciation and the town was called Jang as was the surrounding country. Nevertheless there also exists, in the region where the action passes, a place called Jang.

myself the aid of the gods, I wish first to go and wash my hands in the "Lake of milk", where a nāgī[1] is in the habit of bringing me the elixir of life.

'Tell my people to take heart; when I shall have assumed command of my army, I will annihilate Ling's to the last man.'

On having the King's words repeated to them the people of Jang rejoiced and no longer doubted their ability to carry off the victory.

The next night Manene warned Gesar of Satham's intentions and counselled him to enter the King's body by magic means, for there was no other way of killing him.

'I must go alone to meet Satham Gyalpo in order to rid the world of him,' the Hero said to his officers, whom he had called at daybreak. 'No one is capable of helping me in that which I have to do, therefore remain all of you in camp.'

The officers were very distressed. They could not make up their minds to let the King face, alone, the redoubtable chief of Jang.

'Alas!' they said, 'Satham is a demon, crafty and strong. He may devour you if you go within his reach!'

But Gesar assured them that, because of his kinship with the gods, no harm could come to him; and, mounting Kyang Gö Karkar, he rode rapidly away.

As for Satham Gyalpo, according to his decision of the day before, he had gone very early in the morning to the border of the lake. He began by burning incense and chanting the incantations that usually made the nāgī appear, then he devoutly dipped his hands in the milky water and waited; but the nāgī did not show herself.

Time was passing. The King and his suite remained silent. The last thin threads of smoke from the incense sticks rose among the pebbles of the shore, and beneath the rays of the sun, which was rising in the sky, the lake glittered, empty as far as the eye could reach.

It is of bad omen for the King, thought the attendants. Satham, too, was becoming uneasy.

At this moment, Gesar reached the outskirts of the lake. In order not to betray his presence, he immediately transformed his horse into a tree, his saddle into a small pond, his armour, helmet, and garments into flowers growing round the water, and he, himself, into a little iron bee with sharp-pointed wings.

[1] A feminine deity belonging to the class of serpent-gods. The mother of Gesar was herself a nāgī.

Under this form he gained the spot where Satham, becoming more and more anxious, continued to wait.

The nāgī, who knew of the Hero's plans, had expressly delayed in showing herself in order to assist him. As soon as he approached the lake, she emerged from the water. Resembling a beautiful girl, she carried with both hands the vase destined to contain the elixir of immortality, but which had, this time, been filled with non-consecrated water, devoid of any virtue.

On seeing her advance gracefully towards him, Satham experienced great relief. He thought he had worried himself unnecessarily and, quickly stretching out his hands[1] to the goddess, with avidity drank two mouthfuls of water. Bee-Gesar availed himself of this opportunity, and, flying into the liquid, passed with it into the King's stomach.

The nāgī at once disappeared under the water, and the sharp wings of the sham bee came instantly into action, causing deep wounds in the Chief's stomach. Mad with pain, Satham rolled on the ground screaming. His affrighted attendants hastened round him, powerless to relieve him, and unable to guess the nature of the sudden illness that had stricken their master. Not knowing what to do, one of them hurried to inform the minister Petul of what was happening, and the latter arrived galloping on his swiftest horse.

'Alas! Alas!' he said at seeing the King's terrible state and on hearing that he was being wounded inside his body. 'Alas! Gesar knows all the magic secrets; it is possible that he has succeeded in entering into you. However, as we cannot be certain of the fact, it will be best to consult a *mopa*, who will settle the point for us and indicate the remedies necessary for your cure.'

'How could Gesar have entered me?' answered the King. 'That is a ridiculous supposition.'

The minister sent a servant to fetch the physicians. While they were waiting for them, Satham's sufferings continued to increase in intensity until the latter came to believe that Gesar really was inside him. Whereupon, beside himself with rage, he seized his sword and slashed at himself wherever he felt the bee's wings cut into his flesh.

'Where art thou, Gesar?' he shrieked. 'Where art thou? I will

[1] In order to receive consecrated water, the lamaists place the right hand open on the palm of the left hand and the officiating lama pours the holy liquid in the hollow of the right hand. Usually they pour only a few drops, but the nāgī increased the quantity and, according to the text of my manuscript, 'the King drank *hup hup*', namely: two big gulps.

pierce thee with my sword, thou shalt not escape!' And he continued to hack at his body. His blood flowed from him in streams, and, when the doctors arrived, he was already dead.

Petul did not doubt but that Gesar was the murderer. Not having been able to save the King, he wished to save his country by destroying the powerful enemy who threatened it. Gesar, he thought to himself, is in Satham's body; he must be prevented from leaving it. I must have it burnt at once; in this way the murderer will be consumed by the flames at the same time as his victim. He therefore had the mouth of the corpse sewn up and all the other orifices of the body carefully plugged, so that no opening was left through which Gesar could escape.

All these precautions were in vain. While the funeral pyre was being prepared the Hero, abandoning the form of a bee, transformed himself into a tiny red fly, and created a little black fly, into which he caused the 'spirit' of the deceased to pass. Then, the red fly guiding the black fly, both ascended the canal of the *uma* vein as far as the summit of the skull and, there, on red-fly Gesar uttering the ritual cries *Hik! Phat!* in the required manner, a tiny aperture appeared in the cranium through which both flies escaped. Satham's 'spirit' turned in the direction of the paradise where Gesar was sending it, and the latter, resuming his human appearance, restored his horse and the other things that he had metamorphosed to their original forms and rode towards his camp.

As he skirted the Peritug lake he saw Petul coming his way. The minister, who had gone to the palace to see about the royal obsequies, was now returning to where Satham's body lay. On drawing near, Petul recognized the Hero, and, in a frenzy of rage, barred his passage.

'It is thee, miserable wretch,' he shouted, 'who hast killed my King by thy magic artifices and dost also plan the destruction of the Jang tribes. Thou shalt go no farther. On this very spot, I will stretch thee dead upon the ground. So far thou hast faced only the infirm, that is the reason of thy victories. Today, thou shalt know the power of Petul Kalön (Petul, the minister), the strongest being existing on the earth.'

Gesar placed an arrow in his bow and replied:

'Petul Kalön, thou dost not know me. Know that, in the paradise facing Zandog Palri, I was the god Thubpa Gawa, chief of ten thousand magician sages. My present name is Gesar, the one who sends the "Black-haired" people by thousands to better worlds.[1] I am the protector of my followers, Padma Sambhava's envoy, and god of the whole earth. I despise demons of thy kind!'

He shot his arrow, but Petul avoided it. In his turn, the General discharged one, which grazed Gesar. They continued thus without either being able to touch the other, until both of them had emptied their quivers. And as they fought, they never ceased to insult each other and to recount their respective exploits.

Throwing away the now useless bows, they attacked with swords. Their steeds, with foam-whitened coats, reared, and mingled their angry neighs with the vociferous cries of their masters.

In avoiding a thrust from Gesar, Petul made a sudden movement that jerked him out of the saddle. The Hero at once leapt from his, thinking to stab his adversary, but the latter had already risen, and the two men began a hand-to-hand fight on the edge of the lake.

Petul was endowed with extraordinary strength. For the first time, Gesar felt himself weakening. The effect of the magic words he uttered was at once neutralized by the equally powerful words that were shouted by the demon minister, who was himself deeply versed in magic. By a violent effort, the latter managed to push the Ling Hero nearer the poison-lake. Gesar's foot sunk into it, and the water's corrosive action had already made itself felt on his skin, when, with all his strength, he called Manene and Padma Sambhava to his aid. These two were, by the force of his thought-concentration, as irresistibly drawn to him as the paper kite is to the one who pulls its string, and they hastened to him with the speed of a stone falling from the sky. Both of them immediately seized Petul and hurled him into the lake, where, by the effect of the poison, his skin separated from his bones and was soon consumed.

Gesar then returned to his camp and, without further delay, led his men back to the attack of Gyang. Dema, his general, pierced the head of the enemy General Chimed Chagrdo with an arrow, and Dikchen Shenpa dealt General Mignag such a terrible blow with his battle-axe that his ribs were cloven asunder and he fell dead upon the ground.

The three mighty demons, Petul, Chimed Chagrdo, and

---

[1] That is to say he kills them, then sends their 'spirits' to the various paradises. The 'black-haired people' is an expression used by the Chinese to designate themselves. Does the declaration here attributed to the Hero indicate that the historical Gesar was one of the Tibetan chiefs who victoriously waged war in China towards the seventh or eighth century? See Introduction.

Mignag, who were the supports of the Jang army, having been killed, the soldiers, deprived of their leaders, lost their heads and scattered in confusion. The Ling troops entered the fortress and made a great slaughter of those in it.

Whereupon Queen Asi came out from the palace with her two youngest sons, Yutikong and Datimindug, who walked on either side of her. They offered Gesar, with the customary scarves, seven gold pieces of money, a very valuable turquoise, and seven perfectly round agates, then, prostrating themselves before the conqueror, begged for mercy.

Gesar reassured them, and told them that Yula was safe. He gave orders that they were to be treated with the greatest deference, for Asi was an incarnated goddess. Whereupon the Queen beseeched him to spare the remaining soldiers as well as the villagers from the surrounding country.

The Hero established himself on the upper floor of the palace, while his men were billeted in the fortress and in the town. Gesar remained for three months at Gyang, during which time he preached the Good Doctrine to all.

Before his departure he installed Yula Tongyur, the deceased King's eldest son, as Chief of Gyang.

'You are now King of Jang,' he said to him on leaving, 'and you are surrounded by wise ministers, therefore reign in peace and according to justice.

'Of the four enemies whom I was given the mission to destroy, three are dead. There remains one. When I go to attack him, if I ask you for soldiers, you must supply them.'

At a thirteen days' march from Jang there is a place called Mayul Shokya Ringmo. Gesar and his men camped there for three days, after which the army disbanded, everyone returning to his own country. Some went back to Jang; Dikchen, two other chiefs, and their people left for Hor; and Gesar, escorted by a hundred horsemen, continued his way to Ling. At the palace door stood Sechang Dugmo with four daughters of chiefs; they presented him with beer and meat. For five days there were great rejoicings and all ate and drank abundantly; then the Ling soldiers rejoined their families in their tents.

When they had all dispersed, Gesar said to his ministers and those of his household:

'In the course of the wars that have just ended, I have killed many beings, and a far greater number still have been killed, at my command, by my warriors. I must guide the "spirits" of those unfortunate dead to happy dwelling-places. I am therefore going to retire to a secluded part in the palace and live there as a recluse for thirteen years that I may accomplish this duty.'

Whereupon he had rooms prepared in the manner required for a strict retreat, and, having shut himself in, he was not seen again.

Chapter 11

Gesar enters upon a campaign against King Shingti—Minister Kula is flayed alive—Gesar's soldiers set fire to Shingti's citadel—Shingti tries to scale the heavens by means of a magic ladder—Gesar breaks it with an arrow—Shingti falls into the flames—His daughter miraculously escapes by flying over the burning fortress—Gesar takes possession of Shingti's treasures—He gives the young princess in marriage to Todong's son.

ON the 15th day of the fifth month of the year of the Iron Horse,[1] Manene appeared to Gesar, who had been in seclusion for ten years.

'Gesar,' she said, 'hast thou forgotten that one of the demons whom it is thy mission to destroy is still alive? Shingti, King of the South, continues to prosper; his position is becoming firmly established. If thou dost not conquer him during the course of this year, it will be impossible for thee to do so later.'

'How can I go on a campaign now?' replied the Hero. 'I decided to remain in *tsams*[2] (seclusion) for thirteen years, and only ten have elapsed. To break a vow of *tsams* brings misfortune on him who does so. I do not refuse to accomplish my task; as soon as the period of my retreat will have come to an end, I will march against Shingti.'

'No,' answered the goddess, 'it will then be too late.'

'What is to be done,' asked Gesar. 'I have promised the numerous beings who have perished in the wars I brought about to direct their "spirits" towards happy dwelling-places; I cannot fail in this duty.'

Manene was perplexed. She therefore went to consult the god Tsangspa (Brahmā) in his paradise. The latter thought the case a grave one, and, mounting a white lion, returned with Manene to Gesar in order to persuade him to come out of his retreat. The Hero was difficult to convince; he feared that the breaking of his pledge

---

[1] The 15th of a lunar month is the day of the full moon, and this day of the fifth month, is that of the great annual Buddhist festival. The year of the 'Iron Horse' is the designation according to the Tibetan calendar.

[2] Concerning the different kind of *tsams*, see *With Mystics and Magicians in Tibet*.

228

would entail his reincarnating as an inferior being in a world of pain. Tsangspa assured him that this misfortune could not befall him, because of his divine nature. Gesar then acceded to his request and promised to enter immediately upon a campaign against the King of the South.

As soon as the deities had disappeared, the Hero called his wife to him. The Queen was extremely astonished; she had not seen him for ten years,[1] and she knew that he had not yet completed the period of his retreat.

'What is the matter, Chief?' she anxiously asked him. 'Are you ill or is your food insufficient? Are you hungry?

'If you are ill, I will have the physicians called; if you desire food I will bring you tea and a supply of dried meat; only do not interrupt your *tsams* before the fixed time, otherwise evil will surely come to you.'

Gesar told her of the command that he had received from both Manene and Tsangspa, and said that he could not disobey it.

Weeping, Sechang Dugmo again insisted that to come prematurely out of *tsams* was a bad and dangerous act. The Hero, however, relying on the authority of his divine counsellors and trustful of their wisdom, ordered her not to importune him further but to have delivered, without delay, the letters of convocation that he was sending to the Ling chiefs.

A few days later, about a hundred of them were assembled in the great hall of the palace, each seated, according to his rank, on tiger-, leopard-, or fox-skin carpets. They asked the King why he had come out of his retreat before the date that he had fixed, and what was his reason for wishing to attack King Shingti of the South.

Gesar informed them of the orders he had received; and they all agreed that the ordinary rules respecting *tsams* could not prevail against the will of the gods.

It was decided to ask Dikchen to co-operate in the expedition at the head of three hundred thousand of his Hor subjects and to inform Yula Tongyur of Jang that Gesar expected from him as great a number of soldiers as it would be possible for him to mobilize.

---

[1] A strict seclusion resembles the rule of the Carthusians, in that the meals of the recluse and the things that he may need are passed to him through a wicket. The duration of the Hero's retreat may appear exaggerated, but such a period would not be considered as extraordinary in Tibet, where still at the present day, lamas shut themselves up for as long and, sometimes, even, for their whole lives.

While awaiting the arrival of their allies, the Ling warriors saw to their weapons and their horses, and the women packed the provisions.

Dikchen came with his three hundred thousand Horpas and Yula Tongyur brought with him sixty chiefs and five hundred thousand men. The number of Ling troops amounted to three hundred thousand.

The immense army, manœuvring round the palace with thousands of red and yellow flags, resembled a sea of dancing flames.

Five days later, all the horsemen set out under Gesar's command, and, the same evening, they reached the banks of the southern Kham River (*Kham lho chu*).

The river was spanned by a bridge made of planks resting on iron chains and overlooked by a fortress that guarded the frontier. Those who inhabited the fort were very surprised at seeing this host of armed men spread themselves over the *thang* (flat place) in front of them and pitch their tents there.

'Are they friends or foes?' they wondered. The two governors,[1] Tamotongdup and Yumdug Poye Lobe, decided to go themselves to inform King Shingti of this strange occurrence and receive his instructions. They found him seated on a bloodstained human skin, and, after having offered him some furs as a present, they told him of the matter that had brought them.

'I do not understand any more than you do who these men can be,' the King answered. 'I will send for the sixty state ministers and consult them.'

The Council assembled, but not one of its members was able to discern the intentions of the foreign army. Unanimously they agreed that only the hermit lama Thebsrang[2] of the Tagkar Oma Jig dzong was capable of enlightening them. The King at once sent messengers to the cave that served the lama as a dwelling to ask him for his help.

'Return to your Master,' the hermit said to the envoys, after having read the letter that they had handed him. 'I have no answer

---

[1] Each *dzong* has two governors: the *tunkor* (written *drung hkhor*), a layman, and the *tsedung* (written *rtse drung*), a member of the clergy. The mention in the poem of these two governors marks an addition of relatively recent date, in any case later than the seventeenth century, the epoch when the temporal power of the Dalai Lama was established.

[2] According to the term *Thebsrang*, this lama must have been of demon race. The *thebsrang* form one of the innumerable categories of demons catalogued by the Tibetans.

to give you and I do not need the horse that you have brought to take me to the palace. Begone!'

The King's messengers were very troubled: they did not know if the lama refused to accede to Shingti's request, or whether he intended to do the journey on foot. However, hermit Thebsrang was not one of those of whom it was possible to ask questions. He had sent them away, and the King's attendants went.

As soon as they had disappeared, the lama re-entered his cave, seated himself cross-legged on the bearskin rug that he used as meditation seat, and remained motionless. After a while, a nebulous form emerged from his body and, separating from it, solidified. Now, there were two lamas Thebsrang exactly similar: one seated without movement, the other upright in front of him. Then the lama who was standing went to the entrance of the cave, and, passing outside, walked off at a giddy speed in the direction of Shingti's residence. On his bearskin rug, cross-legged, with spine erect, impassive of face, the other lama Thebsrang remained sunk in deep meditation.

On being told of the arrival of the foreign army, lama Thebsrang pensively shook his head.

'This does not presage any good for you, Chief,' he said to Shingti. 'There is no doubt about it, these people are enemies.'

'It will be best to make certain,' said the King. 'Thou Tamotong-dup, and thou, Menchen Kula, go and speak with these people and inquire of them their intentions.'

Upon which the governor and the minister who had been chosen to accompany him, mounting respectively a red and a yellow horse, rode down to the river. When they arrived in view of the camp, they called loudly to the strangers.

At this moment the chiefs were deliberating in Gesar's tent. On hearing the shouts, two of them went out and, walking to the river, shouted back to Shingti's men.

'If you wish to speak to us, come here.'

Shingti's emissaries had not dared cross the bridge before first making certain of the strangers' feelings towards them. Having been invited to do so, they went over to the other side and stopped at a little distance from the camp. The two men who had spoken then came forward. One of them had a blue complexion and rode a blue horse; the other had a red complexion and rode a red horse. Both of them wore iron helmets ornamented with a little flag.

'What have you to say to us, O Braves!' they asked.

And the envoys of the Southern Kingdom replied:

'Who are you, O Braves, who have arrived in such great numbers, and who is your Chief?

'Why have you not asked permission to camp here and paid the price of the grass. Go up or down the river, retrace your steps, go where best pleases you, but do not stop here. King Shingti does not permit it. Beware of offending him, O Braves; his anger is terrible, it would reduce you to dust.'

The man with the blue complexion answered:

'O warriors of the South, know that I am Yula Tongyur of the royal line of Jang. This is Gesar's camp. If our stay is long, it will last a year; if it is short, it will last three months. We shall neither pay the price of the grass nor of the water. We came to speak to King Shingti.'

'Ling beggars!' shouted the officer Menchen Kula, 'what can you have to say to the mighty Sovereign of the South. Tell me and I shall report it.'

Then Dikchen, the man of red complexion who was mounted on a red horse, pulled from his *ambag*[1] his huge gold pipe, which weighed nineteen *sangs*[2] and held as much as a *bau*[3] of tobacco. He filled it, lighted it, and said:

'If you wish to know why we have come here, O Warriors, I will tell you.

'Chief Todong of Ling has for son a brave aged twenty years. Every year, since his childhood, a *mopa* does a *mo* to know who the girl is that must be given to him in marriage, and each year comes the same answer: He must marry King Shingti's daughter. If her father gives her to us in a friendly spirit, we shall offer him gold and silver[4] in return. If he refuses to give her, things will turn out badly for him; we will ravage his estates and carry off his daughter as slave.'

'Impudent fellow!' exclaimed Governor Tamatongdup. 'Know that the King's daughter, now fifteen years old, is his only child. She will inherit his territory and will succeed him on the throne.

[1] The kind of pocket that the voluminous Tibetan robe, which is drawn in at the waist by a belt, forms over the chest.
[2] About two lb.
[3] A large measure for measuring grain.
[4] In Tibet, it is usual to pay the bride's parents a sum that is estimated as equivalent to the amount that they have spent on her.

Dost thou think that Shingti will send her to a land of beggars, such as Ling is?

'If I repeat thy words to him, he will massacre you all to the last man. But since thou dost wish it, very well. It shall be done according to thy desire. We shall see what will be the result.'

And, wheeling round, Shingti's messengers rode back to the fortress.

They reported to the King the result of their interview with Gesar's lieutenants. However, they now abandoned the attitude of scornful assurance that they had affected before them, and counselled the King not to rouse the Hero's anger, but to consent willingly to his daughter's marriage with Todong's son.

'Gesar,' they said, 'was only thirteen years old when he killed the giant Lutzen; since then, he has conquered Hor and Jang. It is dangerous to make an enemy of him.'

This advice was exceedingly displeasing to the King, who became furious and swore at the two officers.

'I certainly will not give up my daughter to a member of that beggarly horde. You both are despicable cowards. Let my army be assembled. It will not take me long to punish Gesar for his arrogance.'

The next night, Shingti's daughter Metog Lhadze (beautiful goddess flower) had a terrible dream and, as soon as it was day, she described it to her father.

'I saw our country plunged in gloom,' she said to him, 'and blood flowing in streams through the citadel. Inside the palace, the precious turquoise pillar was broken. Minister Kula had been flayed alive and his four limbs nailed to the ground. I, myself, was going away towards the east, holding the end of a white rainbow in my hand.

'Believe me, Chief,[1] it were better to send me to Ling than to endanger your precious life and that of your subjects on my account.'

The King refused to listen further. He brutally ordered her to hold her tongue, telling her that she was incapable of understanding anything regarding a question of this kind and that she was speaking as a fool.

War was decided upon at the ministerial council. The chiefs immediately mustered troops round the citadel-palace and despatched

[1] Tibetan etiquette does not permit the children of a man of high social condition to call him father. They must give him his title.

scouts to discover what forces Gesar had at his disposal. A thousand men guarded the bridge across the river. The next day, two generals, each commanding ten thousand men, took up positions that barred the road to the enemy. They were to be reinforced the day after by two other generals, each at the head of thirty thousand men. King Shingti, who did not suspect the number of Gesar's soldiers, deemed his own troops more than sufficient to overpower the people of Ling.

While the King of the South was making his preparations, Gesar had a dream. He beheld a white horseman, who wore a silver helmet with a little white flag and rode a white steed. The rider advised him to cross the river at once.

Without delay, the Ling Army moved forward. Arrived at the bridge, they saw the soldiers who were guarding it and the reinforcements behind them. Tamotongdup, who was standing ahead of his men, killed twenty Ling warriors in an instant, then turned back to hasten the advance. Dikchen, followed by his troops, crossed the bridge and pursued the governor, shouting in a terrible voice:

'If thou dost not know me, understand that I am Dikchen of Hor, son of gods and the most mighty of warriors. Thou shalt experience the effect of my strength.'

So saying, he cut off Tamotongdup's head with one stroke of his sword made of iron fallen from the sky.

Yula Tongyur with the men of Jang crossed the river, lying flat along the backs of their swimming horses. Joining the Ling 'braves', they together made a great slaughter of the Southern soldiers. Those of the enemy who succeeded in escaping rushed inside the citadel.

On hearing of the disaster, Shingti became mad with rage. He commanded that other troops under the leadership of Generals Kula and Tongchung should immediately attack the invaders.

The mêlée was terrible. Each chief loudly proclaimed his titles and exploits. The warriors fought with arrows, swords, and spears; while the shepherds of the black tents, skilled in throwing the lasso, caught their adversaries from a distance, jerked them from their saddles, and dragged them along the ground under the horses' hoofs.

In this way the two generals Menchen Kula and Tongchung were captured; for their victors wished to show them alive to Gesar. They stretched Kula out upon the ground and, driving spears into his four limbs, nailed him to the earth. Tongchung was fettered. When Gesar saw them, he said, pointing to Kula:

'He is a veritable son and chief of demons. His skin possesses magic properties, which I have discerned by my clear-sightedness. The day will come when it will be useful to me. I wish to have it. As for Tongchung, he has some divine ancestors. Later on, I shall give him an important position in my kingdom. Do not kill him, but keep him as prisoner and in chains until the end of the war.'

The soldiers led Tongchung away and gave him into Todong's keeping. They flayed Menchen Kula alive and, when he was dead, threw his body into a deep hole. A big white *chorten* was afterwards raised over the spot.

While his troops were suffering a second defeat the King became anxious at receiving no report. Fearing they had not been strong enough to repulse the enemy, he decided to send further reinforcements the very next day.

During the night, the god Tsangspa informed Gesar of what was in preparation, and urged him to surprise Shingti before fresh troops could occupy a strategically favourable position on the heights above the narrow passage that had to be climbed in order to reach the royal residence.

Following this advice, Gesar and his soldiers marched through the night. Before daybreak they were in front of the citadel, which they invested and set on fire at the four cardinal points.

The fire spread rapidly. Shingti, awakened by unusual sounds, found himself surrounded by flames. On seeing that all the exits were closed by blazing barriers, he tried to escape his fate by a magic device. A demon's son and very versed in occult science, he had made a ladder by means of which he could climb into the sky, should the necessity for doing so occur. Hastily unrolling the ladder, he ran up its rungs and was about to get away when Gesar perceived him. With a well-directed arrow the Hero broke it, and Shingti was flung into the flames.

As for Metog Lhadze, she ran madly hither and thither, vainly searching for an outlet that was not cut off by the fire. Gesar caught sight of her as she leant out of a window of the burning palace and, from afar, called to her, saying:

'If thou art of divine race, come to me through the air. If thou art of demon race, fall into the flames.'

The young girl then threw herself into the void and, passing high above the blazing city, dropped, light as a leaf, on the Hero's knees.

The war was ended. Gesar took possession of Shingti's treasures, which were kept in a subterranean building in the mountains. Among the precious articles stored there was a jewel that had the form of a new moon three days old. It changed colour according to the nature and feelings of the one towards whom it was turned, or following the friendly or hostile forces that were at work around its owner; thus providing its possessor with valuable information.

On his return to Ling, Gesar gave the young princess in marriage to Todong's son. Then, having celebrated the victory by many great banquets, the troops of the allies returned respectively to Hor and Jang, the Ling warriors went back to their tents, and the Hero withdrew into his palace.

The mission that he had undertaken was accomplished, the demon kings existed no more. The force incarnated in them formerly malevolent but, now, transmuted by him into beneficent energy, would remain for a time at rest, attached to their 'spirits' in the Western Paradise of the Great Beatitude, then it would manifest itself afresh under the form of new beings.

And those beings, uniting by their acts with other forces, becoming, with them, more powerful in goodness or losing, with them, beneficent virtues, would give rise to happiness or suffering. Thus turns and turns the 'round'. Happy the one who frees himself from it.

AUṀ MANI PADME HŪṀ!

The Gesar Epic does not end with the death of the three demon Kings. Later, the Hero engages in a series of wars that does not directly relate to his mission, which, as has been explained in the Prologue, consisted in destroying the Religion's enemies. As King of Ling, he will provide this country of poor and uneducated herdsmen with certain elements of civilization and well-being. Already, at the beginning of his career, he has supplied it with medicines. He will now improve the strain of his herds by seizing King Tazig's cows, and the horses of a Mongol chief. As booty, he will bring back gold from Torgöts and then silks and tea from China.

To follow him in these various expeditions, in which incidents frequently repeat themselves, would furnish enough matter for another volume. I shall limit myself to relating the first among them, which is, in some details, a sequel to Gesar's victory over the King of the South.

Chapter 12

Notwithstanding his ninety-three years Todong desires a young wife—In order to obtain her, he gets King Tazig's blue horses stolen for him—This King's spies come to Todong's house during the nuptial banquet—Todong, who is drunk, boasts of the theft—Tazig sends soldiers to punish him—The coward hides himself under an overturned cauldron—He is discovered, beaten, and sentenced to be cut in pieces—He obtains his pardon by offering to betray Gesar for Tazig's benefit—The Ling warriors refuse to fight for an unjust cause—The support promised by the gods and the lust of gain make them change their minds—A hermit is transformed into an incandescent mass —The fire escapes from his cave and surrounds Tazig's fortress with a lake of flames—Gesar extinguishes it by the magic skin of Kula, whom he had had flayed alive—Gesar's victory and massacre of Tazig's troops—Gesar goes to the mountain palace where Tazig's treasures are kept—On the way there, Todong pursues some maidens who are female demons—Seized by their parents, he is imprisoned in a salt-box preparatory to being devoured—Gesar rescues him—The Hero establishes Tazig's widow as Queen—He brings Tazig's treasures to Ling and divides them among all those who have participated in the campaign.

HIS son's marriage with the fifteen-year-old princess had left Todong dreaming. As he watched his new daughter-in-law trip light-footedly about his house and gracefully serve her husband, he became gradually filled with the desire to acquire a similar butterfly for himself. After all, he thought, I am only ninety-three years old. It is the prime of life. My old wife is before me as a worn-out vessel. Why should I not marry a young girl of fresh, fair complexion, whose little supple body bends as the grass of our Chang Thang. . . . Why not? . . . I am much better fitted to make a woman happy than is that youngster, my son. . . .

Having made up his mind, Todong passed in review the various virgins living in the neighbourhood, and the result of this critical examination was that only one among them pleased him. She little resembled the imaginary portrait that he had drawn. The chosen one was twenty-five years old. Of majestic stature and ample proportions, she portrayed in nothing the graceful slenderness of a blade of grass; and she had a dark complexion. Nevertheless, it was she whom Todong wanted.

Todong, in spite of the confidence that he drew from the

238

knowledge of his position as chief and of his great riches, was very perplexed as to how to obtain this girl in marriage. Her father, Tsajong, one of Gesar's ministers, was the possessor of a fortune at least as great as his, and the hoary lover rather feared to have his proposal rejected by him. After much thought he came to the conclusion that it would be well to have the eloquent Dabla, Gesar's adoptive son, proffer his suit for him. Dabla, a power in Ling, was the son of Gesar's friend Gyatza, who had been killed by the Horpas, and the grandson of Singlen. He, Todong, was Singlen's brother, therefore great-uncle to the young man, which fact would justify Dabla's interference in the matter.

The choice of negotiator settled, there remained another point to decide. It was necessary, according to custom, to begin by offering the intermediary a present. Now, it was not possible to offer Dabla a shabby litle gift, and Todong never could without great suffering give away the least of his belongings.

He remembered that Dabla's favourite horse was getting old and becoming rather slow for racing. A fine horse could hardly fail to please the young fellow. Then, in the inventive mind of the old chief rose a marvellous idea. He knew where to find, not only one, but three horses. Beasts the like of which were not to be found anywhere else in the world: King Tazig's famous blue horses! He would keep one for himself, would give another to Dabla, and the third he would offer to the father of the bride as the price of his daughter.

It was a perfect combination, nothing was now lacking except the horses.

He confided the business of skilfully securing them to three individuals, his serfs, named respectively Gyai Pepui Thugsgös, Thong Thungthung Mergo Khyeno, and Gyab Kespe Pipe Lebled, who had the reputation of being artful robbers.

They each received thirty ounces of gold, and Todong entrusted the three accomplices with his precious *dipshing* (a magic stick that causes invisibility), which might prove useful during the expedition. In addition he promised them a generous reward should their efforts meet with success.

Thirteen days later, the three men reached the borders of King Tazig's territory.[1]

[1] Tazig appears to signify Persia. It is impossible that horsemen leaving the region where today we find Ling, could in thirteen days have reached Persia, or even the western extremity of Tibet—as far as to where a chief of Persian origin might have advanced. It would have taken them about three months to do that

239

It happened that not far from the frontier, at a place called Memoyu Thang, the King and his court had come camping for the purpose of adoring the country's gods and of afterwards amusing themselves in the open air. Todong's emissaries soon perceived that the attention of both the nobility and the people was held by the horse-races, archery competitions, and different games that were in progress. Down to the humblest servant, each one thought only of eating and drinking copiously and of amusing himself. The sun had not yet reached mid-heaven when already everybody was agreeably drunk.

Nothing could have turned out better for us, thought the three rascals.

The King had commanded that thirteen watchmen should guard the camp each night and that they should on no account lose sight of the tent that sheltered the three precious horses. However, when night came, the watchers, who had feasted with the others, were apt to see double or not to see at all.

Taking with them the stick that causes invisibility, Gyai Pepui Thugsgös and his two helpers penetrated into the camp during the fourth watch of the night, when the King and his subjects were fast asleep. They did not easily discover the horses among the many tents pitched on the plain; however, in the end, they discerned a pretty red tent standing a little apart from the rest, and, on carefully lifting its flap, saw the three blue horses. Taking them gently by the halter, they led the animals out of the camp.

Then, having rejoined their own mounts, they placed their saddles on Tazig's horses, jumped astride them and, followed by the other three beasts, that were happy to be going home, galloped away towards the east.

The King and the 'persons of quality', filled to repletion, slept late. When the servants awoke, they heard the other horses neighing, but not the three blue ones. Feeling uneasy, some of them went to the red tent, and, alas! found it empty.

The Master of the Horse, as soon as he was told, was overcome with rage and sorrow. What would the King say, and what

---

journey. Of course we must not expect too much verisimilitude in fantastic legends. However, as the Tibetans often pronounce and write the name of this King, Tags Zigs, which means leopard, it may be that the tradition refers to 'King Leopard' and not to the 'Persian King'. This Tazigs or Tags Zigs, *nor gyi dagpo*, 'Possessor of riches,' is a character often mentioned in Tibetan legends and tales. Who the chief of this name was, and if he really existed historically, we do not know.

punishment would he inflict on him? . . . He had all the grooms and stablemen called, and ordered them to scour the country in search of the beasts. In the hope that the horses would be retaken, he put off reporting the matter to Tazig.

The men returned in the evening, crestfallen. They had found neither the horses nor any trace of their going. The King had to be informed. He, however, appeared less angry than the Master of the Horse had feared.

'There are no thieves in my Kingdom,' he said. 'The horses have escaped and will come back of themselves.' Three days passed; the horses did not come back. Tazig then sent three chiefs and six hundred men to search for the thieves.

When they arrived at a place called Memanachen Kongma, some of the men discovered the hoof-marks of the most beautiful of the three horses, and all the troop followed these traces as far as another place called Siling Mamtu Kongma. There, they spent the night at the foot of a pass. The next day, having climbed it, they saw that the valley at their feet branched in three directions and that not far away was a caravan composed of thirty chiefs, ninety assistants, and a number of servants leading a thousand loaded mules.

Chakardenpa, one of the chiefs sent by Tazig, hailed the people of the caravan, making unmistakable signs with his arms, but the travellers continued their way without answering. Soon after, however, Tazig's people came across a man dressed in white, who had remained behind, and they asked him who the merchants were, where they had come from and where they were going to.

Chakardenpa gave his name:

'I am one of King Tazig's ministers,' he said. 'My master is camped at a little distance from here, and three superb horses of his have been stolen. They each have a distinguishing mark. One of them has the design of a shell and an eight-petalled lotus engraved under its hoofs. We saw the imprints of it on the other side of the pass; but, here, because of the numerous animals that have trampled the ground, we cannot discern anything more.

'If you can give any information concerning these beasts I shall reward you liberally, but if you lie, my King will know how to catch and punish you.'

The horseman replied:

'I am Pagyar Yundub; and the Chief of all these merchants is the well-known Tsang-Gartag *tsongpa*.[1] We are carrying merchandise from Siling,[2] which we will exchange in Tsang for gold and silver. I have seen neither your horses nor any traces of them, I swear it.

'The Prince of Gartag and King Tazig are linked by a friendship of long standing, but it is a long while since they have seen each other. Tell me, I pray, is your King in good health? And his son, Prince Tangös Dawa, who was still a child when I paid my last visit to his father, has he now become a strong young fellow? The people and the country are they prosperous? My Chief will be happy if I take him good news of his friend.

'I am somewhat versed in the art of *mos*; if you like I will do a *mo* on the subject of your horses.'

Chakardenpa eagerly accepted the merchant's offer and the latter, on finishing the *mo*, declared:

'If you continue in the direction in which you are moving, you will never find your beasts. Therefore return to your country and, there, take the advice of a lama-diviner. To the extent that my limited knowledge allows me to prognosticate, you will find the horses if you go east from King Tazig's territory.'

The merchant then pulled out from a saddle-bag several scarves —some blue, others white—placed nine gold pieces in the corner of one and, knotting it, begged Chakardenpa to present it to his King with the message that, on their next journey near his land, the merchants would pay him a visit.

Following the advice that had been given them, Tazig's men returned to their King and gave him an account of the various incidents that had occured on the journey.

'Indeed,' said the Monarch, 'the best thing we can do will be to consult some learned *mopas*. Therefore let *tulku* Albe, who is a lama, *tulku* Mipam, who is a *Bönpo*, and also the great *mopa* diviner Tisser Dong Nag be summoned.'

Before the King and the members of the State Council, the

---

[1] This is not a name, but simply means: 'The merchant whose caravans go from the country of Tsang to Gartag'. Tsang is a vast province in Southern Tibet, of which Shigatze is the capital, and Gartag is a place situated at the west of Tachienlu. Perhaps, here, it is a question of Gartok, a much more important town in the Khan country. It is equally possible to suppose that the merchant was from another town, also called Gartok, situated at the extremity of the province of Tsang in south-west Tibet.

[2] Siling is a town situated near the frontier of the province of Kansu (China). The Chinese call it Sining.

three *mopas* worked their *mos*, each one according to his particular method, which he kept very secret.

First, Lama Albe declared: 'I do not see the horses at Ling, the country that is situated in the east, but I discover them in a dark place where the sun does not penetrate.'

While he was speaking, Mipam the Bönpo shook his head.

'The horses are to be found in the east,' he said positively, 'in a fortress that has the shape of a horn.'

'The horses are dead,' briefly uttered Tisser Dong Nag.

'Which of them is to be believed!' irritably exclaimed the King. 'Perhaps they are all three equally ignorant.'

Then, having more confidence in the Bönpo than in the other two, for the Böns are the greatest magicians in the world, he turned to Mipam:

'Begin again,' he demanded of him. 'See if the beasts are, or are not, in Ling.'

Mipam did a fresh *mo*, and, after being absorbed for a long while in ritualistic calculations, he delivered this finding:

'The horses are at Ling in the house of Dabla.'

His tone did not permit of any doubt. The King felt none, but he became violently angry.

'This Gesar,' he said, 'formerly Chori, a beggar, has made himself King of Ling. He has killed Lutzen, the Kings of Hor and of Jang, and Shingti of the South. He is now attacking me, and, like a vulgar robber, has stolen my horses. What base effrontery! I shall assemble my warriors, then, in a short time, I will carry off his wife, Sechang Dugmo, and all the rich booty that he has accumulated. The Ling territory shall pass under my rule.'

The ministers and councillors remained silent, understanding that the King was extremely distressed at the loss of his horses, which had not their equal in the world. Presently, a member of the Council named Shesarabno rose and, offering a scarf to Tazig, said:

'The *mos* are contradictory. Therefore we are not justified in immediately sending an army against Gesar. He has many chiefs, many tents, and many villages under his dominion. Even if the beasts have been taken to his territory, we do not know who the thief is, and, perhaps, Gesar, too, is unaware of the crime committed by one of his subjects.

'Let us send to Ling two intelligent men disguised as beggars.

They will look for the horses, and when they have discovered in whose custody they are, we shall then see how best to act.'

All those who were present acknowledged the wisdom of Shesarabno's words, and the King followed his advice. Minister Shakar Dema and Tongti Lalen, the Master of the Horse, having disguised themselves as *arjopas* (mendicant pilgrims), started for Ling. Each of them held a long stick in his hand and carried his luggage on his back.

The stolen horses had in the meantime been taken, by Todong's instructions, to their new owners: one to Dabla, another to Tsajong, and the third to Todong himself, who had claimed the best of the three.

Dabla really deserved his present. His task had been a difficult one. Tsajong and the members of his family had at first resolutely refused to give the young girl to the old chief; while she had clearly shown disgust at the thought of becoming the wife of a man who was approaching his hundredth year. But Dabla, who was a power in the land as well as eloquent and cunning, had insisted in such a way that Tsajong and his people had finally been forced to give in. As for the unhappy fiancée, once her parents' consent had been obtained, a few cuffs and two or three good beatings had forcibly shown her that silence and obedience were the methods best suited to young maidens. It was up to them to get their own back, later, in their new home.

So she had been escorted to Todong's house, and he was giving a great feast in honour of his new nuptials.

The same day some shepherds belonging to Chalogsang, a relation of Sechang Dugmo, led three thousand sheep to pasture at Mayul Tiratmo, a spot not far from Todong's residence, and pitched their tents there. They had arrived only a short time when the two shepherds who had remained at the camp saw two *arjopas* coming towards them. The younger of them by name Tsöndup immediately thought: Who knows but these strangers may be King Tazig's spies looking for the horses stolen by Todong. And, as the pilgrims approached the tent, he told his companion to give them a bowl of curds.

'Where do you come from?' he demanded. 'Which is your country?'

'We are from Jang,' answered one of them.

'How fortunate,' said the shepherd. 'I, too, am from Jang. Is King Yula Tongyur in good health?'

244

And he asked them different questions about the people and things of Jang.

'It is now twenty-six years since we left our country,' said the *arjopas*, 'consequently we are ignorant of what has happened there since then.'

'You seem to me to be strange *arjopas*,' retorted Tsöndup, scrutinizing the travellers. 'I have never seen any of your kind before. You must eat well on the journey and not undertake very long stages; the fat looks ready to burst through your skins and your complexions are as white as those of princes. The sun does not seem to have burnt you very much during your pilgrimages.

'Put down your packs; they do not resemble those of beggars. They must be full of money. Undo them and show their contents, we shall perhaps buy something of you. Where are you going?'

The two spies were on the rack.

Chakardenpa answered humbly:

'Honourable shepherds, the luggage of *arjopas* must not be opened. What would the Ling people think if they saw you do so? They would think that you wished to rob pilgrims. . . . I can tell you where we are going. We are going to see King Gesar of Ling. Do you know where he is at present?'

The low opinion that the young shepherd had formed of the sham pilgrims was becoming more pronounced:

'It is not permitted to the wind,' he said, 'to lift a hair of the fleece of the sheep belonging to our master Chalogsang. It is not permitted to the birds while flying to cast their shadows on the herds, nor to men to look at them. You have the appearance of rascals come to rob the flocks. I will not let you go. You shall come and explain yourselves to Chalogsang.'

The elder shepherd, good-natured but rather stupid, intervened:

'You speak offensively, my son,' he said to his young companion. 'Let these poor people continue their way.'

Then, addressing the *arjopas*, he continued:

'Cross the pass that you see over there. Beyond it lies the residence of Chief Todong, who is just now giving a great feast in celebration of his marriage. He is ninety-three years old; yet, in spite of his age, has desired a young wife. He is marrying a girl of twenty-five. In order to get her, he has had King Tazig's blue horses stolen. Go to the wedding and you will be given food.'

245

In vain did Tsöndup make signs to the old gossip to stop his indiscreet talk; the prattler paid no attention to them.

The sham *arjopas* were now triumphant. They had received the required information and felt certain that soon they would see the stolen horses. They took their leave and, still affecting the miserable bearing of travelling mendicants, made for the pass.

The next day they arrived in front of Todong's house, the door of which was shut; but over the courtyard wall, they perceived the chiefs and their wives feasting in the upper part of the dwelling.

'If we could only open this door and get into the yard,' said Chakardenpa to Tugti, 'we would very probably see the horses. But how are we to get in?'

'As we are mendicant pilgrims,' answered Tugti, 'we can cry noisily for alms, as they do; no doubt someone will then come to bring us food and, when the door is opened, we can at least glance round the yard.'

Whereupon, they began their racket, according to the custom of beggars when asking for charity.

Todong, who heard them, thought to himself: These *arjopas* travel through many countries. If I let them come in, they will see my sumptuous home and my young wife. Afterwards they will speak of what they have seen in many places and my reputation will thus be greatly increased.

So he called to a servant and ordered him to bring the pilgrims upstairs. As soon as the spies had passed through the gateway, they saw, in the stables under the house, the blue horse that Todong had kept for himself. They then mounted to the floor above, where the old chief had had a piece of carpet spread in the corner of the room for them to sit on. He asked them from where they had come.

'We have come from Tayul Tö,' they answered.

'Then pass the day here,' said Todong; 'you shall eat and enjoy yourselves.'

And he told the servants to give them beer and various dishes of cooked meat.

The two spies, pretending ignorance, asked:

'Whose marriage is being fêted? Who is the husband of that pretty girl?'

Very proud, Todong bridled up.

'It is my own wedding,' he declared.

Tazig's men appeared astonished.

246

'You are the bridegroom!' exclaimed Chakardenpa. 'But you must be at least ninety years old! Do not make fun of us, I beg you. How did it come about? How did you manage to obtain such a beautiful girl? It is marvellous; indeed, I hesitate to believe you!'

Todong had already drunk a great number of glasses of strong beer and corn-brandy. His notions of what it was good to say and of what it was best to keep secret about had become rather vague. He related at great length the history of the theft of the horses, naming Dabla, Tsajong, and himself as their present owners.

The sham *arjopas* now knew all that they wished to know.

'We are on our way to distant sacred places in China and in India,' they said. 'We cannot linger here. We wish you a long life. Perhaps we will come back one day to repay you for your kindness.'

Upon which, they took themselves off and returned to inform Tazig of the success of their investigations.

The King became very angry.

'As this is the case,' he said, 'we will assemble some troops tomorrow. The day after you will leave for Ling and bring me back the old scoundrel securely chained.'

The command was carried out. A little troop of eight hundred men, marching far into the night, hastened to Todong's house.

The old chief did not suspect the true identity of the pilgrims who had eaten and drunken so heartily in his home and did not remember to have related to them, while half intoxicated, all about the stealing of the horses.

In order that he might end his marriage feast in a devout manner, he had decided to go and venerate the local deities at Magyalpumra.

The very morning of the day on which he was to leave for there, one of his servants, going out early to fetch water, saw the house surrounded by a number of soldiers. Throwing down the vessel that he was carrying, he ran back and, rushing headlong into his master's room, shouted:

'Kushog! Kushog! Tazig's soldiers are at your door. They have come for the stolen horses. Oh! oh! What will become of us! . . .'

But, because he was brave, he was not satisfied with just screaming. He seized the sword of iron fallen from the skies that hung near his master's bed, and, having jumped on a good horse, rode towards the door of the yard.

Terrified at the thought of the punishment that would probably be his, Todong ran hither and thither, seeking a place in which to hide. At last, catching sight of a large bronze cauldron, he crouched down and pulled it over him.

During this time, the bellicose servant had struck down some fifty of the enemy while cutting a passage through them, and was galloping away. The young bride, her servants, and Todong's people, seeing that the soldiers' attention was concentrated on the fight with the wielder of the marvellous sword, were flying quickly in different directions. Therefore Todong, whose son had left home the previous day to inspect his herds, now remained alone and without protection in the house.

Tazig's men looked everywhere without being able to discover him and, perhaps, he would have altogether escaped their notice, had the coward only been able to dominate his terror and check the trembling which shook him. Because of it, a ring that was attached to his belt began knocking against the cauldron and the sound guided the searchers to him.

The thief was first beaten and then secured with chains. The single blue horse found in the stables, the other horses, and all the valuable things in the house were carried off as booty, and, eight days later, the soldiers with their prisoners reached Nemoyuthang.

Two of Tazig's ministers had the accused brought before them.

'To begin with,' they told him, 'thou wilt receive five hundred blows with a stick, then, tomorrow, thou wilt be cut in pieces. To thy cost thou shalt learn the power of the King from whom thou hast dared to steal the precious horses.'

Todong received the five hundred strokes, but the rascal, making use of his skill in magic, caused his body to become as hard as bronze and in this way felt no pain. All the same, search his memory as he might, he could not discover the faintest trace of a magic formula that would permit him to remain whole when his jailers should cut him to pieces. He had sorrowfully to recognize that his knowledge of occult science did not extend that far.

Whereupon, being seized with dismay, he humbly solicited his judges for a hearing, having, he said, important disclosures to make. They granted his request.

'I beg you to spare me,' entreated Todong. 'I did not steal the horses. Some years ago three pilgrims stayed with me, they afterwards went to India. On their return, they brought these horses with them. I did not know from where they had come. My son bought them. I gave them to no one, but Dabla and my father-in-law are powerful in Ling and they, by force, each took one. Do not kill me, I implore you. I can tell you something more.

'Ling belongs to me. The former little Chori, the Gesar of today, dispossessed me, but I remain the legitimate owner of the land. I can sell it if I wish. I will sell it to you; you will then kill Gesar, carry away the beautiful Sechang Dugmo, and your King will reign over Ling.'

One of the ministers thought: This man is a vile rogue. He has already betrayed his country and delivered it over to the King of Hor; he also helped the latter to circumvent the tricks that Dugmo invented so as not to have to give herself to the invader. It is quite possible that he wishes to begin the same game again. However, the wretch may serve us; for the moment let us spare him.

The other minister, whom he consulted, agreed that it might be well to let the thief live. So they promised him his life, if he kept his word and helped them to acquire Ling.

'I will make you its masters,' Todong declared, 'but you must have confidence in me and permit me to return there in order to make ready for your arrival. I must speak with several chiefs whom Gesar has treated badly and who desire to overthrow his authority. When I have prepared the way, I will come back and tell you.

'As for blue horses, Dugmo and a few of the Ling chiefs have got some. You will be able to take them.'

Thinking that the traitor would prove useful, they let him go. And the latter went off blessing the gods who had rendered his judges so credulous as to allow him to dupe them.

He never had had the intention either of betraying Gesar or of selling Ling. Not that such a course would have been morally repugnant to him, but because he had come to recognize that Gesar was invincible and that no one could with impunity attack either him or that which concerned him.

Therefore, as soon as he was back in Ling, he hastened to the palace to see the Hero. On his way there he encountered Sechang Dugmo, to whom he related the manner in which he had been attacked and plundered by Tazig's people—but he carefully refrained from mentioning the theft of which he was the culprit—and he declared that he was going to ask Gesar to send one hundred thousand soldiers against Tazig in order to recapture the property of which he had been robbed and to punish the offenders.

'The King is in his room, where he is meditating on the "Absolute

Oneness",' answered Dugmo. 'But tomorrow, when I take him his tea, I will repeat to him all that you have just told me.'

The following day happened to be one on which the State Council was held. The ministers and other officials assembled in a room adjoining Gesar's. An opening that was in the wall, closed by a shutter and a curtain gave them the possibility of speaking to the King and of hearing him, when he opened the shutter, while the curtain screened him from view. Dugmo alone was allowed to enter his room for the purpose of bringing him his meals, or of filling with pure water the bowls on the altar in the morning and of lighting the lamps there in the evening.

On serving him his morning tea, the Queen informed her husband of what had befallen Todong and of the request he wished to make. Gesar made no reply, but when the members of the Council were gathered in the adjacent apartment, he opened the shutter, and from behind the curtain commanded:

'Mobilize a hundred thousand warriors. Tomorrow I shall come out of my retreat to enter upon a campaign against Tazig.'

He then closed the shutter, which snapped to with a sharp clack. The councillors remained dumbfounded, looking at one another, doubting whether they had heard aright.

Notwithstanding the deference that they extended to the Hero, whose wisdom and power they recognized, the ministers decided to wait, before calling out the men, until Gesar had made known to them the motives for the war he was planning.

Summoned by him on the morrow, the chiefs came holding long silk scarves, which they offered to the King, politely enquiring after his health, as it is the custom to do when anyone comes out of *tsam* (retreat). They then begged him to explain the reasons that prompted him to attack Tazig; for they, themselves, could see none.

Gesar, by his clearsightedness, knew of Todong's doings and of the theft of the blue horses. He therefore recounted the circumstances to them, and in conclusion said:

'Todong is a dishonest man, mischievous and meddlesome, nevertheless he furnishes us with the pretext for a profitable war. I have consulted the omens, they are all in our favour. It is with good reason that Tazig is surnamed Tazig *nor gyi dagpo* ('Tazig possessor of treasures'); our victory will provide us with some valuable booty.'

'Whereupon the Master of the Horse replied:

'Todong is indeed a malicious being; he does not cease to commit bad actions. He has now stolen the horses of a King with whom we lived at peace. I do not see why we should support him and bear the consequence of his reprehensible deeds. In attacking Tazig in order to defend a malefactor, we should become the defenders of an unjust cause. Many chiefs and warriors would be killed through the fault of a despicable thief. Should we not then be sorely grieved? . . . No, King, we will not fight.'

All the members of the Council highly approved of the Master of the Horse's words. Gesar, whom usually no one dared oppose, was disconcerted, yet he could not deny the justice of the arguments brought forward by the speaker.

'It is true,' he answered, 'that we have here a personal matter between Tazig and Todong and that the latter is culpable. We are not obliged to support him. Up to now we have not received any command from the gods on the subject. Therefore let us wait. Pass the night at the palace; counsel may come to us.'

During that night, when all were sound asleep, Manene, riding a white lion, appeared on the balcony of the room where Gesar rested and awoke him:

'O Jewel of Generals who subduest thine enemies,[1] listen to me,' she said.

The King was filled with joy on hearing her. Now, he thought, comes the good advice for which I have been waiting.

'Do not trouble thyself concerning Todong's misdeeds,' continued the goddess. 'Tazig has invaded thy territory, he has pillaged the home of one of thy subjects and has had him forcibly carried away by his soldiers. The offence is serious enough to permit the people of Ling and their allies to take up arms. Tazig possesses rare treasures and enormous herds. Ling is a poor country; to stock its pastures with Tazig's cows, this is what is important. Make thy warriors understand this. As in the past, the Precious Guru, myself, and our friends the gods will accompany and help thee.'

Manene disappeared.

At daybreak Gesar sent for the chiefs and repeated to them the words of his divine adviser.

The councillors, now certain of the approbation and support of the gods, looked upon the idea of appropriating King Tazig's treasures and herds with no small favour and satisfaction. They decided upon war. Ling, Hor, Jang, and the ex-kingdom of Lutzen,

[1] *Magpön norbu dadul*, written *dmag dpon norbu dgrah hdul*.

should each supply a hundred thousand soldiers, in all four hundred thousand men.

Messengers, carrying the mobilization orders, travelled over Ling and the countries of the allied chiefs. The entire army assembled in Mayul Tiratamo, in Ling territory, where it remained camped for thirty days while the soldiers were being apportioned to the different chiefs and the weapons and provisions prepared. Then Gesar, accompanied by Dikchen and Sajong Dema and followed by the troops, started for the West country. On arriving at Kemo Yuchang they camped there.

When Todong had left the judges who had imprudently given him his liberty, he had promised them that he would return in a month. The month had elapsed, and Todong had not yet appeared. Tazig, who knew of the proposals made by the prisoner, began to be anxious.

'I fear you have been duped by this rascal,' he said to his councillors. 'Gesar is crafty, and Todong resembles him. Let us be on our guard. Who knows what these two scoundrels are plotting against us. We must send spies to Ling to see what is happening there.'

Three spies set out and, when they had reached the summit of the pass leading to Nemo Yuthang, they saw the enemy's tents far down in the valley below. From the distance they looked like a multitude of little white cairns[1] that had been placed there as offerings to the gods. Frightened at the sight, the men turned round and ran back to the palace.

Some of Tazig's familiars, descrying them in the distance, told the King of their coming.

'They have not the bearing of carriers of good news,' they said. And one of them added:

'I am afraid that the people of Ling have already invaded our territory.'

'I do not fear Gesar,' said Tazig proudly. 'Let the warriors be mustered at once.'

Seven hundred thousand men answered the call. The fortress and its surroundings resembled a gigantic ant-hill in activity.

Not far from the fort was an eerie spot, which only certain Bönpo magicians dared approach. Nothing peculiar was visible there,

[1] These heaps of stones, which are found everywhere in Tibet, are called *rdo mchod*, 'stone offerings'.

except an enormous rock which blocked the opening of a cave that overlooked the valley.

In very remote times, a disciple of Guru Togyal Yekien[1] had assiduously practised the 'fire meditation' in this cave. After many years his body had transformed itself into a flaming mass. Then, by the power of a god or by that of the hermit himself, a rock had detached itself from the summit of the mountain and, rolling down the slope, had stopped in front of the cave, blocking it completely and henceforward hiding from human sight the secret of that which was in operation within.

What had become of the hermit, no one ventured to ask, and, doubtless, no one knew.

At night a dark red glow encircled the rock, and, it was whispered that, held back by it, there existed an inexhaustible reservoir of fire from which a flaming flood could descend into the valley as does the water of a torrent.

Through the instrumentality of learned Bönpos, an ancestor of the then King had been linked by an occult tie with the mysterious inhabitant of the blazing cave, and, at the end of long propitiatory rites, had been promised by him that in the event of pressing danger, he would come down from his hermitage in his fiery form and surround him with an impassable barrier. An initiatory ceremony of adoption, celebrated at the birth of each of Tazig's subjects, rendered them immune from the effects of this fire and assured them the goodwill of the genius of the cave.

Tazig worshipped him and counted on his protection just as his forefathers had done. But he was unaware of the circumstances that had attended his own previous lives, of the beings connected with them, and of the intricate entanglement of cause and effect that was to counteract this protection.

At an era, the antiquity of which is beyond calculation, two demons had expressed powerful wishes, which two deities had answered by others that neutralized the previous ones.

One of the demons desired to destroy the human race and the other to be reborn as the possessor of immense riches protected by a barrier of flames. Tazig was the latter and Menchen Kula, King Shingti's minister, the former.

[1] The religious Master, now deified, who, according to the Böns, preached before Guru Shenrabs, who is considered as the founder of their religion in the present period of the world.

253

One of the gods had wished: 'May I suppress the malevolent being who dreams of destroying mankind,' and, as the two demons were linked in friendship, the other god had added: 'May I extinguish the flaming rampart of the rich egoist with his friend's skin.' The gods were Gönpo Pernag and the goddess Palden, both friends of Gesar.

But these things remained veiled to all save Gesar, who was endowed with divine clear-sightedness. It was because he knew of them that he had had Menchen Kula flayed alive during the war with Shingti, King of the South.

While Gesar was camping at Nemo Yuthang, Padma Sambhava appeared to him.

'Do not delay here any longer, O Hero beloved of the gods,' said the Precious Guru. 'Hasten to cross the pass that separates thee from Tazig's fortress. If thou allowest his troops to cross before thee and to descend into the vast valley where thou art now, thy defeat is certain. It is on the other side of the mountain that victory awaits thee. Take Kula's skin and go in advance of thy soldiers, for from the top of the mountain a terrible scene will present itself to thy view, and if thy diamond heart is capable of contemplating it without trembling, thy men would die of horror at the sight.'

In obedience to this advice, Gesar summoned his generals and commanded them to prepare for crossing the pass and for attacking the troops that guarded Tazig's fortress.

'Make haste,' he added. 'As for me, I will precede you in order to facilitate your approach to the citadel.'

Then mounted on Kyang Gö Karkar and holding in his hand Menchen Kula's skin, which floated as a flag in the breeze, he cut through the air and alighted on the top of the pass as a great vulture.

From there, Gesar watched. He saw below him Tazig's immense army manœuvring in the plain,[1] and his tall fortress decorated with multi-coloured banners. On the terraces of the citadel, the perfumed smoke of cypress leaves rose in offering to the gods and the *ragdongs* bellowed mightily.

At the top of the edifice, which bristled with tridents and gold *gyaltsens*,[2] Tazig appeared, dark and proud. He turned towards the mountain where formerly the hermit had immured himself, made a

---

[1] The *thang*. The *thangs* are grassy flats. Not, always, precisely plains in our meaning of the word, but bottoms of valleys that, especially in the regions depicted in the Epic, can be immense.

[2] 'Emblems of victory', ornaments placed on the roofs of temples and palaces of great lamas or chiefs having the title of King.

gesture, said a word; then, suddenly, the rock that blocked the cave rolled to the bottom of the valley. The fire burst forth and, descending in cascades, surrounded the fortress with a lake of flames, barring the road to the mountain palace where the King kept his treasures.

Tazig's soldiers moved within the flaming flood, insensible to its bite. On the high roof of his fortress, encircled with gold tridents, Tazig dreamed. And, perched like a great vulture on the summit of the pass, Gesar watched.

Meanwhile, at Nemo Yuthang, Gesar's troops were completing their preparations. At dusk, they began their march, making a great noise. Each chief advanced, preceded and followed by many different coloured banners, the men wore helmets decorated with little flags, and the horses carried saddles inlaid with gold and silver.

From afar in the distance, Gesar heard his soldiers mounting towards him.

Tazig, relying on the flaming rampart that protected his citadel, had ordered his men to retire, and he, himself, slept peacefully. All was still, and the immense sea of billowy flames, stretching as far as the eye could reach, sinisterly illumined the night.

Gesar came out of his contemplation and, remembering that the Guru Padma had commanded him to spare his people this terrifying spectacle, descended the pass on his flying horse.

Hovering over the brazier, invoking his gods and guardian lamas, the Hero spread out Kula's skin in the space and abandoned it to itself. But it did not fall as should have inert matter. Animated by a will that gave it the power to resist, it trembled and writhed in its effort to escape the fire, which, by contact, it had to extinguish.

The friendship that in long distant ages had bound the demon become Kula to the demon become Tazig remained an active force. Kula's dried skin would not destroy the barrier that protected Tazig from his enemy. But vain were its pitiful efforts; it gradually sank, drew nearer and nearer the brazier, and finally fell into it. Flames leaped to the sky, consuming the skin in an instant. Thunder rolled in the night, and a waterspout submerged the magic lake of fire.

At this moment Gesar's army came down from the pass, and, under cover of darkness, encircled the fortress.

On waking, Tazig and his people were astonished at no longer seeing the fiery glow. Looking out of the windows, they beheld a green prairie in place of the flaming lake and, on this prairie, Gesar's army, which surrounded them.

'How is this possible!' exclaimed Tazig, for he still doubted that the extinction of the fire could be Gesar's work. But the chiefs standing round him bowed their heads, saddened by the bad omen, and thought of their approaching end.

Gesar's soldiers were already attacking the fortress in the four directions. Tazig's men valiantly resisted them, but without success.

At the eastern gate, Dikchen cut off Kunkyen Mitag Shabu's head with a stroke of his sword. At the western gate, Yula of Jang pierced Je Tobden's head with an arrow. At the southern gate Chief Tamde Gykye was cloven in two, and at the northern gate Chief Shisarabno was run through the heart. Then Gesar's troops, having entered the citadel, massacred all the occupants including Tazig and his son.

The two last, leaving their bodies lying in the fortress, were escaping as disincarnated phantoms, when Gesar, perceiving them, took pity on the poor 'doubles', that would wander ceaselessly through the world. Seizing them with his lasso, he separated the 'spirit' from each and directed it to the Paradise of the Great Beatitude.

When night came the victorious army camped about the fortress. The next day, the soldiers collected all the weapons that lay about, took the armour off the dead, and baled the spoil ready for transport to Ling.

Gesar then left with six hundred men for the mountain palace, to take possession of the treasure that was enclosed in it.

As they were passing Yulong Tagmar Sum dzong, they saw on a grassy slope three pretty young girls, richly clad, who were gathering medicinal plants.

The chiefs who accompanied the Hero were surprised, and wondered who these three pretty girls could be.

Gesar already understood that they were *Sinmos*,[1] but wishing to make fun of his companions, said:

'You are three, they are three. If they please you, there is one for each of you.'

'We are too old,' answered Dikchen laughing; 'we have lost the taste for women. But among the young officers who follow us, perhaps there are some who will feel tempted.'

'Girls who wander about alone and seem to have neither father nor husband do not appeal to us,' replied one of the young officers.

---

[1] Female cannibal demons, who can change form at will.

256

But Todong, who had not ceased to gaze at the lovely maidens, said to Gesar:

'I am of another opinion. If you permit it, I would very much like to take one of them back to Ling.'

One of Gesar's attendants named Michung Kapde, who inwardly ridiculed the old rake and wanted to get a laugh at his expense came forward.

'If Chief Todong wishes for one,' he said very seriously, 'I too ask for one.'

Todong immediately became angry.

'Thou art bold to dare ask for the same thing as I,' he said severely to the speaker. 'Since when do attendants join in their masters' games? I shall take the most beautiful of the three.'

'No indeed, it is I who will have her,' retorted the boy.

Todong was on the point of throwing himself at him, when the other showed his great fists.

Gesar interposed.

'Let me reconcile you both,' he said. 'The choice shall be the prize of a horse-race. The rider who first reaches the three pretty girls can choose the one whom he most desires.'

This idea pleased Todong. I am Tamdrin's *tulku* and very versed in magic formulas, he thought. I can make a wind rise that will worry my rival, then I shall easily win. He therefore accepted Gesar's proposal with alacrity. Michung Kapde lined up with him and, when the signal was given, both started off at full speed. Todong, reciting his magic formulas, by much outstripped his rival and reached the young girls first.

He got off his horse, smiled in a manner that he thought captivating and immediately began to play the gallant after his own fashion.

'Who are you, young girls with faces round and white as the moon, who wear such beautiful jewels? What are you doing alone on this desolate mountain, tiring yourselves in the search for medicinal plants? It makes me sad to see you take this trouble. You are made for remaining peacefully at home, seated on thick cushions.

'I am no longer quite young, but I possess immense riches, precious jewels, coral, turquoises. . . . Look at my lovely necklace, I will give it to you.

'The one who desires to be pious must recite *mani*, and the one who wishes to live comfortably must marry an old husband. Do not make a mistake, young maids, do not let yourselves be duped; the world is full of deceptive illusions.'

He continued to cite proverbs, but the girls stopped listening. Nimble as wild goats they sped away, carrying their bunches of herbs.

Fat Todong, though still a good horseman, was quite incapable of rivalling them on foot; not one of his magic formulas would have been potent enough to produce this miracle. He remounted his horse and caught his quarry up just in time to see them disappear into the opening of a cave at the top of a high red rock.

I have them, thought the old fellow, highly excited at the venture. They did not dare to welcome me in the middle of the grazing-ground, and they have chosen this way of leading me to a retreat known to them. How artful women are! . . . and how lovable! he concluded.

He got off his horse once more, fastened it near to the foot of the rock, and began a difficult climb.

During this time, the *sinmos* had already related to their father, who inhabited the cavity in the red rock, how they had been followed by an old man from Ling.

'How does it happen that people from Ling are passing through these parts!' said the demon. 'Never mind, we will devour them all.'

He immediately called a hundred demon warriors and told them of the windfall that was theirs. They rushed from the cavern with the sound of thunder.

Todong heard them coming and quickly hid between two rocky spikes. The demons, whirling down the sides of the rock, failed to see him. After having vainly sought him at its base, they returned and said to their chief:

'We only found a horse tied to a tree; we have devoured it. Its master must be hidden somewhere, but we could not discover him.'

'Use the sack,'[1] commanded the demon chief.

Todong, hearing that the sack was going to be thrown, concentrated his thoughts and transformed himself into an enormous rock. The demons threw their appliance, but it could not catch hold of anything so bulky. They hurled it again. This time Todong had

[1] A leather sack, which resembles in form the drag-net. This device really exists in small. It is used by certain sorcerers, who pretend to capture demons in it by trailing it in the air behind them. The opening of the sack closes by the action of cords that pass through it, just as in the fishing net. The sack used, here, by the *sinpos* (masculine demons of the same race as the female *sinmos*) is supposed to be of gigantic dimensions.

transformed himself into a very heavy bronze box, which the sack could not move. At the third trial, Todong relaxed his thought-concentration. While he was still undecided as to which form he would take, the sack was flung and he was drawn into it. Then sinpo Rakcha Dongje, who had thrown the sack, exclaimed:

'This time I have caught something!'

And having hauled it into the grotto, he opened it and found Todong.

'How fat he is,' he cried joyously. 'I shall eat him at once.'

But his chief, sinpo Khamsum Sogchien, objected.

'No, brother,' he said. 'You must wait until this one's companions come within our reach. We will seize them and fairly divide the catch into equal shares. All of us must fill our stomachs. What could we do with this one mouthful.'

They pulled Todong out of the sack, put him in a chest that served for salting-box, and shut the heavy lid on him. By way of a joke, the demon's three pretty daughters came and tapped on the chest, and mockingly made unchaste suggestions to him.

Meanwhile, Gesar had continued his way without troubling himself about Todong, until, as night approached, he halted his men and encamped. Only then, at not seeing the old chief appear to drink tea, did those about the King become aware of his absence.

'I wanted to play a joke on him,' said the Hero. 'Perhaps it has gone too far. Those lovely girls were *sinmos*. They must have led our old fool away, and he is now probably a prisoner of the demons living in these parts. However, this is not as bad as it may seem, because it gives me a good pretext for destroying that malevolent and dangerous brood. But where must we seek Todong?'

Gesar got on his horse again and was preparing to explore the surroundings with Dikchen and a few chiefs, when Manene appeared to him.

'Be quick, O Protector of Beings,' she said. 'Todong has been taken by the *sinpos*, who want to devour him. He is shut up in a salting-box and is on the point of dying of suffocation. Here is a pill of life, which will revive him. Hasten, time presses. He is detained in the cave that is at the summit of the rock that thou seest over there.'

The goddess then disappeared.

Gesar and his companions hurried to the spot that Manene had pointed out. Leaping headlong from their retreat, the demons fell

259

on them uttering horrible cries. But Gesar, armed with his magic sword, destroyed a great number; and his companions slaughtered the remainder.

Todong was found unconscious in the salting-bin. Gesar put the pill in his mouth, and the old chief came back to life.

'What is it?' he said, still half-conscious. 'What has happened to me?'

Those around him burst out laughing.

'He who is toothless wishes to eat uncrushed grain. The old man desires maidens, he runs after them. Such a one can expect nothing else but to be made a fool of. If thou dost not know this already, thou shalt learn it to thy cost,' said Gesar, citing proverbs.

'Be thankful that I was near to rescue thee. Without me thou wert dead.'

After a night's rest they continued their way to the mountain palace, which was called Sagtzal Liti Kargyar.

Seeing Gesar arriving, the Queen attempted to escape by climbing along the face of a precipice. She ran a great risk of falling into the abyss when Gesar, descrying her from afar, called to her to come back as he neither wished to kill nor harm her. On looking round she saw him surrounded by a glorious company of gods and goddesses, so she thought that in truth he must be more than an ordinary man and really a protector of beings. Gaining confidence, she returned to the palace.

'Fear nothing,' Gesar again said when he received her. 'I wish you happiness in this life, and, after your death, I will send you to the Paradise of the Great Beatitude; but you must first open the doors of all the places where Tazig's treasures are kept. Owing to my care, he has gone before you to the blest paradise.'

The Queen went to fetch the four gold keys.

To the east, she opened a sandal-wood door and a thousand brown cows came forth. To the west, she opened a turquoise door and ten thousand white cows came forth. To the south, she opened a gold door and twenty thousand spotted cows came forth. To the north, she opened a coral door and forty thousand red cows came forth.

In the interior of the palace, Gesar found seven treasures: a cow in iron that could walk; a dog in agate that barked; a sheep in shell that bleated; a magic sceptre (*dorje*) in iron fallen from the sky; an azure-coloured dragon's egg; a statue of the goddess Dolma in turquoise; a statue of the Buddha of the Infinite Light (Öpagmed) in coral.

Gesar established the Queen sovereign of the deceased Tazig's kingdom. Then, taking away all the cows and the seven precious objects, he returned to the prairie where the lake of fire had been.

From there, after fifteen days' march, they reached Mayul Tiratamo on the Ling frontier, where they camped. Here, the Hero was welcomed by gods and fairies, and he lighted a thousand lamps in offering to the gods with the wish that the riches he had brought, after having been selfishly hoarded by Tazig, might become a source of well-being to the people of Ling, to those of Tibet, and to all the beings of the world.

The cows, the weapons, all the conquered booty was divided among those who had participated in the war. When this was accomplished the troops of Hor, of Jang, and of the Kingdom of the North, led by their chiefs, returned to their respective countries. The Ling chiefs then accompanied Gesar back to his palace, where they remained for a month feasting with him.

Chapter 13

THE END OF GESAR

'OUR work is accomplished,'[1] said Gesar to his followers. 'For the time being we may rest in peace, but we shall have to return to this world to preach the Good Law in the Western lands, after having destroyed those who feed on the substance of beings and spread suffering. The wars that we have undertaken were little wars, the one that will come will be a great war. Instead of a single sword, I shall hold two, so as to mow down the enemy with both hands.

'It is expedient that you should now retire into the solitude and meditate there for three years. To the East, at Margye Pongri, is a white rocky mountain so high that its summit reaches the sky. On its slopes are many grottoes and caves. These will serve us as hermitages.'

Guided by Gesar, they all proceeded to Margye Pongri. On arrival there, he conferred on each one of them the double initiation: 'For the Religion and for the world,'[2] and then indicated to each the cave that he must occupy.

The Hero established himself, alone, on the slope of the mountain that looked towards the East. Sechang Dugmo and twenty other women occupied the southern side. Twenty-five chiefs and eighteen of Gesar's relations,[3] including Singlen, dwelt respectively in the

---

[1] As it has been said, Gesar had brought to a successful issue several other expeditions after the conquest of Tazig's kingdom. According to tradition he must have been about fifty years old when he left this world.

[2] *Chos tang rjigs stan dbang skur* is an initiation that transmits the power to tread both the paths: that of activity in the life of the world and that of mystic contemplation, which leads to Nirvāna.

[3] Not blood relations, for Gesar was born miraculously; but by adoption, after the Chinese fashion, because of their relationship with Singlen, whom many considered to be Gesar's real father. However, some versions of the Epic do not mention a miraculous birth and give the Hero as the son of Singlen and his servant, who, in this case, is an ordinary woman and not a nāgī. She is then called Gogza (*hgog hzah*) instead of Gongmo.

caves of the western and northern slopes. They lived there for more than three years, constantly sunk in meditation, and obtained the fruit of the practice of the 'play of air in the arteries.'[1]

In the fifth month of their fourth year of retreat, Gesar summoned the hermits.

'We have more than kept our vow,' he said, 'for the three years that our retreat had to last expired five months ago.

'We have purified ourselves. The effects of the bad actions that we have committed have been consumed by knowledge. Both in mind and body we have destroyed the germs capable of causing sufferings to beings. We, now, are qualified to enter into a paradise. Those of you who desire to continue to live as hermits are at liberty to remain as such, and those who wish "to change world" can do so.

'Do not forget that nothing equals the Perfect Doctrine. No one can hold it as proprietor, no one can give it; but anyone who makes the necessary effort can possess it.

'Let those among you who have cut their hair and who wear the religious habit, strictly observe the five precepts.[2] Let them also abstain from all traffic, envy, and greediness. Let them reject all passions.

'Those of you who are laymen cannot practise the Doctrine in its entirety, it is too wide and too high, but cultivate goodness. Desire the welfare of all beings, work for it in an effective manner, and in this way you will advance towards salvation.'

They all greatly praised the Hero's wise discourse and lavished upon him many proofs of their profound veneration. They then declared their intention to live as hermits until their death and went back to their respective caves.

Gesar detained Sechang Dugmo and three others for an instant and directed them to return at sunrise on the morrow.

The next day, when they were before him, Gesar reminded them of the fact that they, as well as himself, were *tulkus* emanated from

---

[1] *Tsa lung gom* (written *rtsa rlung sgom*) a tantric practice. According to the masters who teach it, this practice can lead to a state of consciousness that differs from our usual one. It also allows the one who becomes an adept in it to bring about his own death in a state of ecstasy, as a few of the heroes in the Epic are going to do.

[2] The five precepts that are compulsory to all Buddhists are: (1) Not to kill any living being; (2) Not to take anything that morally belongs to others or that has not been given voluntarily or freely; (3) To commit no adultery and to refrain from all sexual excesses; (4) Not to lie, not to deceive, not to calumny, not to speak harshly or maliciously; (5) To abstain from all fermented drinks and from all exciting and intoxicating drugs.

deities for the purpose of accomplishing a work, which was now completed. He then urged them to dissolve their fictitious personalities and return to the paradise whence they had come.

'Let us make,' he said to them, 'a fervent *mönlam* (religious wish) for the happiness of all beings; in three days we shall leave our present form.'

All five of them remained for three days without eating or drinking, absorbed in perfect concentration of thought, wishing, with not another idea intermingled, happiness to all beings, from the highest down to the most fragile insect. Then, as they came out of their meditation, Gesar uttered in a loud voice the following wishes:

'That among the mountains, some be not high and others low;

'That among men, some be not mighty and others deprived of power;

'That some abound not in riches whilst others lack them;

'That the highlands be not undulating (literally: to have neither valleys nor heights);

'That the plains be not uniformly flat.

'That all beings be happy!'

Dugmo replied:

'If in the highlands there were no mountains and valleys, the herds would find no shelter;

'If the plains were not entirely flat, it would be bad for cultivation;

'If men were equal, all as chiefs, things would go wrong (literally: "that would not do");

'May happiness prevail in Tibet!'

'You have not understood me,' Gesar said gravely. 'My words have been uttered too soon. I shall come back to repeat them.'

Dugmo and her companions, clad in silk robes and standing side by side, chanted the hymn of prosperity (*tashi*, written *krashi*):

'May Chenrezigs watch over Tibet,

'May Chanag Dorje protect China,

'May Dorje Sempa defend Ling,

'May the Religion flourish,

'May many monasteries be built,

'May prosperity reign,

'May the rain fall and the sun shine in due season that food for beings may grow abundantly!'

Gesar looked at them pensively:

'It is not possible for us to enter in a paradise with our bodies of flesh,' he said. 'Tomorrow we will detach the "spirit" from them by the rite of *pho lang*.'[1]

Once more the five became motionless in perfect concentration of thought. The next morning, before dawn, many deities, playing different instruments and throwing a rain of flowers, appeared on a white rainbow.

The first sunbeam shot an arrow of light above the distant mountains. Without a movement, without lifting their lowered eyelids, Gesar and his companions uttered the piercing *hik*, then the grave *phat*; and, on the rocky terrace of the white mountain, there remained only five empty robes, aureoled in light.

---

[1] The rite that effects the liberation of the 'spirit' by separating it from the body and its 'double'. See the explanation given on this subject in *With Mystics and Magicians in Tibet*. But, here, Gesar and his companions intend to produce instantaneous dissolution, with no remains of their corporeal form. The performing of this marvel is attributed to a few mystics, one of whom is Reschungpa, a disciple of the celebrated Milarespa.

Chapter 14

'A MAN!'
'Get your rifles!'
'Bring in the beasts!'

These three exclamations following one after the other drew me out of my tent. I was in the wild and fascinating country of the great lakes, in the Chang Tang desert. My four Tibetan servants had just pitched our camp on a grassy spot where mountains bordering an immense tableland bent inward and formed a crescent-shaped recess. We intended to pass the night there, sheltered from the wind.

We were not following the caravan tracks, and if along these, travellers are few, they are completely missing in the regions through which we were passing. The sudden appearing of this man was very strange. For many days we had not seen anything in the way of living creatures, except wild asses and bears. Moreover, everywhere in these solitudes, man suspects man. The instinctive gesture of anyone upon seeing another of his kind is to seize a rifle, and, if he is under canvas, to bring in nearer to the camp the animals that are grazing round so as to protect them from the 'thief!' However, these little details take nothing from the charm of the Chang Tang: life is delicious there.

Motionless, on the top of a mound, a horseman gazed at us from the distance. I examined him through my glasses.

He was seated upon a superb horse, white as snow. The animal's trappings, doubtless ornamented with silver, glittered in the sun. The rider wore a yellow robe, and his hat, also yellow, was bordered with fur. He carried no visible weapon.

'Put your rifles away,' I said, 'there is nothing to fear. He is a Mongol lama.'

'Or he is a brigand who has robbed a lama and put on his robe so as to be able to approach merchants without rousing their suspicions.

266

Perhaps he is the scout of a robber band,' queried one of my servants.

'Caravans do not pass this way, what would brigands do here?'

While we were speaking, the traveller rode down from his grassy pedestal and came towards us through the meadows.

He was young and had a grand air. He probably overawed the servants, for they went forward to hold his horse's bridle. Then, yielding to force of habit and forgetting at the sight of his rich ecclesiastical costume the doubts concerning his honesty to which they had given voice, they prostrated themselves at his feet and begged for his blessing. He, with the detached manner of a dignitary accustomed to receive such marks of respect, lightly touched their heads with the tips of his fingers and said in a sharp tone:

'My *trapas* (monks) follow with the luggage. One of you go and meet them in the direction from which I have come and lead them here.'

Then moving towards me, he smilingly offered me a silk scarf, saying:

'You are Jetsun Kuchog (reverend lady), who has lived many years in Kum Bum and has stayed a long time in Kham and in Kyirku.' His tone affirmed rather than questioned.

'Oh!' I remarked, 'you appear to be well informed concerning me. How is that? And who are you, Kushog?'

'I come from Kham, my country. Some merchants from Hor Kanze and others from Kyirku whom I met, the lama of Lob, Dzogschen Pema Rigdzin, and several more have spoken to me of you. It seemed to me so strange that there should exist a foreign *naljorma*,[1] that, having learned from the Gologs[2] you had passed this way and were travelling in these parts, I came in search of you.'

Tea was boiling on the camp fire, so I invited the Lama to drink a cup with me in my tent while he waited for his luggage to arrive.

We began a friendly conversation.

Born in Eastern Tibet my guest had been recognized when a child as the reincarnation (*tulku*) of a Mongol lama, of no great renown, it seemed, but the possessor of ample means—as there exist thousands in that country. His ecclesiastical seat was a little monastery situated near the Turkestan frontier, which he called the

---

[1] *Naljorpa*, feminine *naljorma* (rnal byor ma) is the name, in Tibet for a particular kind of mystic.

[2] Tribes inhabiting N.E. Tibet.

'Monastery of the Secret Liberation', but he lived, he said, nearly always under canvas. He liked travelling, a taste he had in common with a great number of Tibetan monks. After studying at the Depung monastery in Lhasa, he had travelled over a part of India and Nepal, visiting the various places of pilgrimage. Later, he had been in China as far as Pekin and in Siberia as far as Irkuts.

He was curious regarding the object of my travels. Why, as he had been told, did I go from monastery to monastery, propounding to the lamas difficult questions concerning 'very deep points of the Doctrine'. While explaining my reasons I took the opportunity of also questioning him, and I came to the conclusion that he was a passable scholar.

His luggage arrived with his servant *trapas*. They pitched some fine tents. A beautiful carpet and thick cushions that served for couch furnished the one occupied by the *tulku*. In comparison with his camp, my very humble one took on a rather mean appearance.

It was my turn to be invited. I had supper with the lama: tea, *tsampa*, cold boiled mutton, dried meat, dried apricots; a grand menu in the Chang Thangs.

My host would have liked me to give him details of the war that had convulsed Europe, but, living in regions where the post does not visit, I was not much better informed on that subject than he.

'Do you believe,' he asked me, 'that from this war among the foreigners some good may come?'

'None; on the contrary, much evil,' I answered with conviction.

'It must be so,' he acquiesced, 'because these people fight for selfish motives and not for religion.'

It is necessary to realize that the Tibetan term *chös* admits of a number of interpretations. It signifies religion, philosophy, meta-physics; also the universal law not imposed but inherent in things, justice, rectitude, equity, and all that is excellent; and, further, the word 'thing', which in itself is capable of many applications.

'There is no more religion anywhere,' he declared.

'How can you say that,' I protested. 'Did you not tell me that you had been a student in the Depung monastery? Are there not about ten thousand monks there? Are there not thousands also in Sera, Gahlden, Tachilhumpo, and in many other monasteries? It is strange that a Tibetan should say that there is no more religion.'

'It is true that monks are not lacking,' he replied, 'but the clergy, they are not the Religion. The Brahmins of India, the popes of the

268

Orossos (Russians), the padres of the Philings (foreign priests and ministers), the lamas, they are all one. They are Mara's[1] army, who dupe the feeble-minded,[2] crush them, and make them more foolish still.

'The Chinese monks are perhaps the least harmful. The majority of them are very ignorant, but they are often kind-hearted.

'However, all of them spread false doctrines that are injurious to men and are the cause of suffering.

'Religion is the search after truth. It is illumination of the mind, right judgment, and the right action that springs therefrom.

'What is to be gained by putting one's foot on another's neck? He who does so is but preparing for the crushing of his own neck under the foot of another who is stronger than he.

'Those who are ground down by the mighty have no more religion in their hearts than have their oppressors; they are wicked, malicious, and cowardly. If they become powerful they behave in the same way as those whom they now curse.

'Nevertheless, we people of Tibet, of Mongolia, of China, we are capable of leaving the false path, because we know the power of thought and respect it. We still know how to meditate, how to pass consciously out of this world and look at it from above.

'The Whites do not know how to do this. They only know how to invent strange machines, of which they are very proud, and their machines will destroy them. The destruction has already begun and will continue. The Tökuo (Germans), the Fakuo (French), the Yinkuo (English), and all the rest will exterminate one another.'

'Unless Gesar takes the matter in hand,' I said, having at the time my mind full of the Epic, which I had just noted down.

The Lama looked at me curiously.

'Oh! you know the story of Gesar. . . .'

'Yes. I have been told that he is coming back to lead a great army to the West.'

'Do you believe it? . . .'

'All is possible.'

'He will be reborn among us. The power of our united thoughts will "construct" him. He will be the *tulku* of the minds of all of us whom the *philings* (foreigners) wish to make their slaves.'

---

[1] *Mara* = demon.

[2] The Tibetan term *lkugspa*, pronounced *kukpa*, signifies stupid, foolish, feeble-minded.

'He will hold a sword in each hand with which to mow down the enemy on either side,' I continued, quoting some words of the poem chanted by the bards.

'Do not jest. The sword can be symbolic. Its blade can emit invisible sparks, which will penetrate people's minds and transform them. Among those who will have been given arms to use against us, some will throw them away, whilst others will turn them against the demon enemies of justice and the happiness of beings.

'The true Religion will be preached, and those who refuse to act justly: the masters who insist on remaining masters, the slaves who persist in remaining slaves and in keeping others in slavery. . . .'

He ended with a significant gesture.

'I understand,' I said, 'Gesar's sword . . .'

'But, Kushog, what is religion, according to you?'

'*Nyi su med pa. Nyi su char med to*[1] (It is not two. It is not to be made two),' he answered. 'The hand must not injure the foot; they are the same body.'

'But then, by destroying the masters and those who will persist in playing the part of slaves, Gesar will cut into this one body.'

'Do not your surgeons cut away decayed pieces of flesh from the sick in order to cure them? But, these surgeons throw away the decayed pieces without troubling themselves as to what becomes of them; such a procedure only displaces the cause of evil. Gesar, on the contrary, sent to paradises the demons whom he killed in this world.

'This *chi powa*[2] (change of world) is the transmutation of the essence of the mind: that is to say, the diverging of a current of energy into another channel in order to bring about another kind of activity. You ought to know this, you who have questioned so many lamas. The demon mind must become divine mind. Dispassionately, we will kill to heal.'

He said *we*. Indeed, his words had already sufficiently revealed his feelings, but he now showed the intention of an active participation.

'And, will *you* be a great many?' I asked.

'Millions and millions,' he replied. 'The hatred of the Whites grows and spreads as a flame in dry straw.'

---

[1] Words taken from a famous philosophic work: *Sherab kyi pharol tu byinpa* (pronounced *chinpa*), the Tibetan translation of the Sanskrit work: the *Prajñā Pāramitā*. These words are often quoted in Tibet.

[2] Written *phowa*.

'If I am still in this world when these things happen I will ask Gesar's permission to accompany his army as war correspondent.'

The latter term naturally not existing in Tibetan, I had said it in English.

'Whatever is that?' asked the *tulku*.

'It is the one who follows the troops in order to give information to the newspapers of the events that are taking place.'

'There will be no more newspapers,' declared the Lama, in a superior and disdainful tone towards an institution that he evidently regarded as obsolete. 'Gesar will send his messages "on the wind".'

Doubtless he meant a wireless telegraphy brought to greater perfection than ours. Whatever may have been the Lama's ideas concerning a reconstructed civilization, I could see that they did not tend towards barbarism.

Night had long since fallen. The luminous night of Central Asia, with its thousands of stars glittering intensely in a mistless sky.

I took leave, and retired to my tent.

Before dawn next day the *trapas* folded the tents and corded their luggage. The *tulku* and his attendants were ready to start as a faint pink showed in the east.

We wished one another a good journey, and the men rode away. Soon after their departure the sun rose, encircling with a nimbus of gold light the little party that advanced with it towards the still shadowy west.

The conversation of the previous evening, still fresh in my memory, these horsemen moving across the desert, conjured up in my mind the image of Gengis Khan and his hordes. Would a Gesar really rise in the Yellow country to muster other troops less primitive than were their predecessors, better informed and more terrible than they? Following the path of the sun, even as these travellers that were disappearing over the horizon, encircled as they with a golden light, would the future army progress to 'renew the face of the earth' by a purifying destruction? . . .

I thought of the children of the Whites, sleeping at this hour in their cots. Of those who, during the course of this very day, would gambol joyously in the gardens of our great cities, without a thought of what the future might have in store for them in the depths of the little known Eastern solitudes, where men are waking. . . .

271